THE ETHICS OF HOMELESSNESS

Philosophical Perspectives

THE ETHICS OF HOMELESSNESS

Philosophical Perspectives

Edited by

G. John M. Abbarno

Rodopi

Amsterdam - Atlanta, GA 1999

Cover design based on a drawing by Janice Agati-Abbarno

♾ The paper on which this book is printed meets the requirements of "ISO 9706:1994, Information and documentation - Paper for documents - Requirements for permanence".

ISBN: 90-420-0787-7 (bound)
ISBN: 90-420-0777-X (paper)
©Editions Rodopi B.V., Amsterdam - Atlanta, GA 1999
Printed in The Netherlands

To the memory of my parents,
Peter Joseph Abbarno and Lucy Elizabeth Abbarno,
whose own shaping of "home" provided me a framework to
view this condition of homelessness as profound depravation.

CONTENTS

Foreword by Anthony J. Steinbock   1

Acknowledgments   5

Introduction by G. John M. Abbarno   7

PART ONE
VERSE AND CONVERSATIONS: HOMELESS PEOPLE

ONE   The Guardian of the Birds   15

           NOAH S. BERGER

TWO   Poetic Sounds of Homeless Verse   21

           DENNIS ROHATYN

THREE   Meditations on Homelessness and Being
           at Home: In the Form of a Dialogue   29

           ROBERT GINSBERG

PART TWO
THE MIRROR OF HOMELESSNESS: IS IT ESSENTIAL
TO HUMANITY?

FOUR   Homelessness as *Heimatlosigkeit*?   41

           PIO COLONNELLO

FIVE   The Rights of the Homeless:
           An Examination of the Phenomenology of Place   55

           PATRICIA ANNE MURPHY

SIX   Home Is Where the Heart Is:
           Homelessness and the Denial of Moral Personality   63

           DAVID E. SCHRADER

SEVEN   Homelessness, Virtue Theory,
and the Creation of Community   79

KEITH BURKUM

PART THREE
INTERNAL AND EXTERNAL HOMELESSNESS IN CHILDREN

EIGHT   Community, Ethics, and Homelessness   93

MICHAEL PARKER

NINE   Psychic Homelessness   105

RENÉ A. C. HOKSBERGEN

PHOTOGRAPHS by JANICE AGATI-ABBARNO   123

PART FOUR
NO HOME, NO CITIZENSHIP: MORAL AND
POLITICAL DIMENSIONS

TEN   The Homeless and the Right to "Public Dwelling"   141

ANITA M. SUPERSON

ELEVEN   No Shelter Even in the Constitution?
Free Speech, Equal Protection, and the Homeless   153

UMA NARAYAN

TWELVE   Social Policies, Principles, and Homelessness   171

NATALIE DANDEKAR

THIRTEEN   Failed Rights: The Moral Plight of
the Mentally Ill Homeless   187

G. JOHN M. ABBARNO

FOURTEEN   Homelessness, the Right to Privacy,
                    and the Obligation to Provide a Home   199

                    SHYLI KARIN-FRANK

                    PART FIVE
            TO HAVE A HOME: WHAT DIFFERENCE DOES IT
                        MAKE TO BE HOME?

FIFTEEN   The Homeless Hannah Arendt   217

                    JOSEPH BETZ

SIXTEEN   Talking About Those Home Improvement Blues   233

                    RON SCAPP

About the Contributors   241

Index   247

FOREWORD

Anthony J. Steinbock

These superb essays written for this volume focus our attention on a pernicious and epidemic problem: homelessness. The collection rallies a host of contributions that treat the personal, social, political, and economic dimensions of homelessness. But unlike most assessments of the problem of homelessness today, this edition also takes the bold position of regarding homelessness as a *moral* plight that needs to be redressed through concrete deeds which are tempered by philosophical reflection.

The plethora of social ills confronting us today, ranging from environmental disaster and racism to the pervasive tragedy of battering, urges us to pose the following questions: (1) Why of all issues should we treat homelessness, and why today? (2) Among all the other viewpoints, why do we need to regard the moral dimensions of homelessness through philosophical perspectives?

It may seem that the problem of homelessness is not new in the least, that it has been with us for centuries, that it is our legacy as much as it is our burden. We might point out that there have always been beggars, outcasts, transients, and that there have always been, at least in the West, punitive edicts that classify and regulate the movement of the poor, strangers, or wanderers. Punitive regulations are exemplified in laws dating from 368 A.C.E., and they extend from King Richard II's prohibitions against alms-giving in 1388 through Queen Elizabeth's Act of 1572 which promulgated and now merely chronicles the gruesome punishment of those convicted of being rogues, vagabonds, or beggars: They are "to bee grevouslye whipped, and burnte through the gristle of the right Eare with a hot Iron of the compasse of an Inch about."[1] Michel Foucault's analyses of madness in the classical age[2] and of the birth of prisons[3] would have much to say to those of us who think our contemporary practices are more "humane." In some cases these practices confine the homeless to vermin-ridden shelters having only one operable shower for five hundred men. They sometimes separate the sexes without regard to relation, impose curfews, require psychiatric assessments, and institute compulsory prayer and presence at sermons.[4] Is homelessness really that different from imprisonment? Do our reactions to it essentially differ from those in the past?

While it may appear that the problem of homelessness has been with us for ages, another extremely important characteristic of contemporary homelessness distinguishes it and concerns us in ways unique to our age. "Homelessness" expresses a fundamentally new way of looking at our world and at ourselves. For implicit in homelessness lies the question of a *home*. Reflecting our existential situation, we experientially formulate the question of the "other" in terms of a structural dyad: home and homelessness. The people who are now called the homeless are no longer depicted with a positive identity; we do not use the language of rogue, vagabonds, beggar, bums, drifters; we no longer speak of tramps, skidrowers, bag ladies, panhandlers, derelicts, hobos. Instead, groups of people are defined in terms of a lack—they are the home-less—and they are implicitly circumscribed by a solution to this lack of a home. The concept of homelessness accordingly affects our attitudes and our political and social policies.

The discourse of homelessness, then, presupposes the possibility of a home. By a "discourse" of homelessness, I do not mean mere verbiage, just another expression of a term, but a powerful set of axiological assumptions and concrete practices that directly bears on our lives and how we interact with others. Because the discourse of homelessness sketches the way we view our world and prefigures our relations with strangers; because it revalues those who may culturally or ethically diverge from an assumed stratum of normality; because the notion of home also extends to our Earth as our "primordial home," as Edmund Husserl would say,[5] and thus how we interact with our environment, the problem of homelessness and the home that we confront today is essentially of an ethical nature. In fact, since the relation between home and homelessness permeates all dimensions of our lives on many different levels, the issues surrounding homelessness and home are leading issues of our day.

The contemporary discourse of homelessness carries for us both a danger and an opportunity. Those who are labeled homeless are implicated in current social, political, economic, and moral practices that presuppose the meaning of "home." For example, when a battered woman and her children leave an abusive situation and are labeled "homeless," and when the remedy for this "homeless-ness" is assumed to be a home, then not only is misogyny concealed (and thereby perpetuated) under the general rubric of homelessness, but the so-called remedy, under our current socio-political presumptions of a homelife, would involve an execrable return to a potentially abusive situation.

This does not mean that we should or even could simply give up the discourse of homelessness and thereby change our practices regarding the mentally ill, the poor, the alcoholics, the destitute elderly, and the unwanted children. Instead, we require a deeper reflection on what home and homeless can mean as a guide to our personal and political engagement with the homeless. In other words, practices concerning our involvement with homelessness demand a critical or philosophical stance so that we will not remain in unsuspected collusion with the present context of economic, social, and political policies and ripostes which both create and ineffectually challenge "homelessness." *The Ethics of Homelessness: Philosophical Perspectives* braves such a crucial step.

We could conceive of many possible ways to engage the problem of homelessness philosophically. For example, one could view homelessness as a kind of ontological characteristic of being human, a way that is suggested by an anthropological reading of Martin Heidegger's *Being and Time*. For Heidegger,

Unheimlichkeit or uncanniness is a primordial indeterminacy that is disclosed through the fundamental mood of anxiety.[6] Existentially-ontologically, the "not-at-home" is conceived as the more primordial phenomenon in relation to which the "being-at-home" is an inauthentic way of fearfully fleeing toward determinate objects within the world.[7] Here, the notion of home is regarded merely negatively as grounded in a kind of ontological homelessness, leaving us with the insidious possibility of romanticizing the homeless.

Equally unsatisfactory would be a metapsychological perspective intimated by Sigmund Freud's analysis of the *Unheimliche* or the uncanny.[8] Here the experience of the uncanny is neither completely distinctive nor totally foreign, but is at root something homey, familiar (*heimlich*), which should have remained hidden but has recurred. This return of the repressed is a sign of alienation that manifests itself through the processes of abreaction and reproduction. In this case, the homeless would be understood as a projection of our own alienation from being home.

If, instead, our experiential formulation of the problem of intersubjectivity today as homelessness and home is any clue, then we cannot begin critical reflection on homelessness either with homelessness as a foundation for an inauthentic experience of home or with the experience of the home as the basis for abreacted homelessness. Instead, the non-hierarchical yet structural relation of home and homelessness has to be our point of departure for critical reflection and critical intervention. This is the opportunity afforded us today by the present discourse of homelessness.[9]

To transform the dangers inherent in the discourse of homelessness into an opportunity to reconstitute our socio-historical and interpersonal situation, we would have to arrive at a new understanding not only of what it means to be homeless but also of what it means in relation to "having a home" or "being home"—as the final chapter of this volume suggests. The contemporary discourse of homelessness and home points to an irreducible structure of inter-subjectivity conceived as the relation of home to alien. A careful reflection on this intersubjective structure of human being would challenge a tradition of though which has been helpless in countering the horrors of ethnic purification.

Since home and homelessness expresses an irreducible structure of inter-subjectivity, co-participating with the homeless does not mean reducing the homeless to the home by, for example, summarily dismissing their lifestyles, mannerisms, or habits, making the movement of the homeless predictable, and keeping them out of sight in shelters. The home is not something "we" possess; a home cannot be given to others from an objective third-person perspective because home is something that is co-generated with others and is experienced as such from the perspective of participation.

Participation, however, cannot mean attempting to experience homelessness by staying on the streets or in a shelter for a few days, or by keeping the homeless at a patronizing distance with a handout. Instead, as Paulo Freire would say, meaningful transformation can occur only by committing ourselves, by co-creating a home, to the plight of the homeless *as* homeless; through this, interpersonal dramas of homelessness would ultimately become our economic, socio-historical, and ethical lot.[10]

The Ethics of Homelessness does not sacrifice the urgency of action to high-altitude reflection; still less does it provide simplistic solutions to one of the leading issues of our time. Instead, the philosophical perspectives set down by these authors sketch the rich contours of a line of thought with historical exigencies. For those of us grappling with the problem of homelessness today, this invaluable fund of essays will inform both our commitments and our practice.

Notes

1. C. J. Ribton-Turner, *A History of Vagrants and Beggars and Begging* (London: Chapman and Hall, 1887), p. 106.

2. Michel Foucault, *Madness and Civilization: A History of Insanity in the Age of Reason*, trans. Richard Howard (New York: Vintage Books, 1965).

3. See Michel Foucault, *Discipline and Punish: The Birth of the Prison*, trans. Alan Sheridan (New York: Vintage Books, 1979).

4. See Anita Superson, "The Homeless and the Right to 'Public Dwelling,'" in this volume, p. 146.

5. See Edmund Husserl, "Grundlegende Untersuchungen zum phänomenologischen Ursprung der Räumlichkeit der Natur" (1934), in *Philosophical Essays in Memory of Edmund Husserl*, ed. M. Garber (Cambridge, Mass.: Harvard University Press, 1940), pp. 307-325.

6. See Martin Heidegger, *Being and Time* (Tübingen: Niemeyer, 1979), pp. 188-189, 276-277, 289. See also Pio Colonnello, "Homelessness as *Heimatlosigkeit*?" in this volume, pp. 41-42.

7. Heidegger, *Being and Time*, pp. 189; *cf.* pp. 342-344.

8. Sigmund Freud, "Das Unheimliche," in *Gesammelte Werke*, vol. 12 (Hamburg: Fischer, 1972), pp. 229-268.

9. See Anthony J. Steinbock, "Homelessness and the Homeless Movement: A Clue to the Problem of Intersubjectivity," *Human Studies*, 17 (1994), pp. 203-223.

10. Paulo Freire, *Pedagogy of the Oppressed* (New York: Continuum, 1993).

ACKNOWLEDGMENTS

This book is a coordinated effort of many people whose common dedication and beliefs about social justice are reflected in the contents of *The Ethics of Homelessness*. A few people and institutions made this otherwise onerous task a meaningful project. Of course, this work would not be possible without the many homeless people with whom I talked on the streets, in shelters, and in soup kitchens; although they wished to remain nameless, they have a long-standing role in the conscience of society. Their world-views vary in form from cohesive wholes that are nonetheless hobbled by their condition to chaotic fragment; some find themselves merely trying to regain a world-view. They provided the motivation to complete this book so that their identity can be constructed in the larger audience of concerned readers.

I am grateful to Robert Ginsberg, Series Editor for Value Inquiry Books, whose encouragement convinced me that this topic was important to the series of academic volumes that precede it. Unlike some philosophical issues, homelessness and the policies affecting it change continually, so I relied on major sources that track changing laws. The National Commission on Homelessness was always willing to provide results of their latest demographic studies as well as changes in the McKinney Act for Homelessness, which provide facts essential to gaining a sense of the larger conditions being worked on. The shelters I visited were helpful, particularly in Chicago, Illinois, and Alexandria, Virginia, and especially in Buffalo, New York, namely the City Mission and the Cornerstone Manor for Women. The stories that speak through the faces in the photos in the book are possible because of the trust these people had in the use of this book; I thank them and the photographer, my wife, Janice Agati-Abbarno. As an artist she was able to capture the spirit of these homeless men and women in a way that lets them speak. Her expert processing and printing of these pictures assured that they also stand alone as works of art.

I want to thank my son, Aaron Abbarno, for both the editorial support and his patience with my absences weeks at a time while I engaged people in this work. I appreciate the support that D'Youville College provided by awarding a sabbatical leave when I began the research and allowing me the scheduling flexibility to complete it. I offer a special note of gratitude to Jeannette Lesinski for her tireless motivation in the earlier states of preparing this work. She provided the needed transition for the final editing of this book under the skillful direction of Gwen Burda. I am most appreciative of Gwen Burda's careful preparation of this book. I want to note the generosity of the Henry Holt & Co., Inc., for the use of the excerpts from *The Poetry of Robert Frost*, first edited by Edward Connery Lathem. Last, but not least, the contributing authors of this work bring a commitment and a vigor to this topic which will encourage philosophers to write more extensively on the homeless. I am proud to be associated with these authors, and I thank them for their patience over the last stages of the process. Together we have given a voice to the moral concerns that emerge out of being without a home; this book also belongs to them.

G. John M. Abbarno

INTRODUCTION

G. John M. Abbarno

1. Introduction

The word "home" is familiar yet means different things. It most often evokes warmth, safety, rest, nourishment, and direction. Some commonplace lyrics and colloquialisms suggest the richness of its meaning: "home is where the heart is"; "home is a person's castle"; "homeward bound"; "there's no place like home . . ."; and computer keyboards are equipped with a "home" key. Contrasted with these secure images is a poignant scene in the Italian film *Cinema Paradiso*. We hear the cries of a person who appears disheveled and who sleeps in the town square; he shouts with authority, "Get out of my square!" For him—as for those who are homeless around us on our streets, in abandoned buildings, in train stations, in bus depots, and cars—this city is defined in terms of ownership. They own the sights, sounds, and pain of these places that lie hidden from us in our homes. Most of these persons dream of having, one day, a place apart from those sights and sounds of the street. One homeless person I spoke to in Washington, D.C., put his wish in these words: "All I want is a place that opens with a key."

Who are the "homeless"? And do the homeless represent a new phenomenon produced by our society? A brief history of homelessness puts our social condition in perspective. As early as Colonial days there were the very poor and homeless who sought assistance. Town leaders would consider their applications for aid and make a decision based on whether they lived locally in the town or whether they came from elsewhere. If a person showed promise of becoming self-supporting in a short period of time and was a local resident, the chances of receiving assistance were very good. Those people who were "new comers" did not have "settlement rights" and did not receive support. They were required to leave and seek support in another town, most likely the one they originally came from. These groups of people became "transient homeless" as they continued to search for a place that would give them the help necessary to settle down.

We find this same type of transiency among people in the Post–Civil War period. The added factor is the railroad extending westward that attracted young unattached men with low-level skills. Many found work on farms during harvesting season. Temporary employment forced them to sleep where they could, without hope of permanent residency. The actual number affected during this time was difficult to determine since no one actually kept records of unemployment and homelessness until the late nineteenth century.

The homeless population increased during the Great Depression of the 1930s. In cities like Buffalo, New York, Transient Centers were provided for many homeless families. Most of them had traveled from nearby states (Pennsylvania and Ohio) in search of work and a place to stay. The Center offered beds and enough food for a few days. But after that time they were sent back on their journey. In order to have an extended stay, they needed to comply with a residency requirement of one year or more. Only families with extreme needs and with young children were permitted to remain a longer time.

During the late 1930s and 1940s, especially during World War II, much of the homeless population was absorbed into the relief effort. Low-income work was widely available, putting within reach the cheap housing known as "skid row." These low-tier housing units could be found in most major cities throughout the country. The best-known was the Bowery in New York City. The Bowery population in skid row began to decrease, from 14,000 in 1949 to 8,000 in 1964, and by the early 1970s skid-row housing units had all but disappeared. Housing units for the needy were found in single-room-occupancy units (SROs), converted rooms in low-quality hotels in downtown areas of the cities. They were made to serve as residences for people with very low incomes. As urban development projects got underway in the 1970s and 1980s, many of the SROs were either destroyed or upgraded into condominiums or professional office space in a process of displacement often referred to as "gentrification." The resulting shortage forced the very poor into shelters while others were cast into the streets to make a life for themselves.

This "gentrification" is one cause of our homeless today. Several other factors also make our society's homeless different from those in the past. In response to the question, "Who are the homeless?", we recognize a mixed group, affected by economics, education, and health-care factors. The baby boomers represent the greatest percentage of our population. They compete fiercely amongst themselves for even lower-level employment. The standards of higher-income positions require a specialized education to keep pace with an economy quickly changing from production of goods to professional services; this change leads to increased unemployment and a growing inability to make rent payments or, for some, mortgage payments. As the standard of living increased sharply and the numbers of people unable to find employment grew, there grew a new composite of homeless on the streets and in shelters. Among them are older educated males and single-parent families, those addicted to drugs and alcohol, and the mentally ill persons who have been struggling in the street life for decades. As one shelter director remarked, "homelessness is not a problem; it is a condition," one that presents people with high risk of illness and psychological frailty with marginal hope. The following case is a typical profile.

Edward (name is changed), a twenty-year-old from Illinois, was in the care of foster parents for the first fifteen years of his life. He was a victim of abuse by his foster parents throughout his time with them. Shortly after the abuse was learned, he was sent out of that household to an institution that was funded by Department of Human Resources until he was eighteen. Without parents and employable skills, Edward, left to fend for himself, remained homeless on and off for two years. While in shelters he was beaten by people he called "mean spirited." They were either crack addicts or alcoholics. To escape the noise and domination of the others he would visit the nearby library. There, Edward found peace of mind on Queens Street. He said that now the folks at the library are becoming annoyed with the increased number of homeless using the library as a respite. He feels humiliated by the verbal abuse and glaring of both library staff and patrons. The city has decided to destroy the building. In a reflective pause, Edward turned his eyes away and said "Why am I homeless? I didn't want to be here and I didn't do anything to get like this! I just want to have it stop. . . . It must change. I don't want to die this way!"

2. Overview

A delicate and complicated condition, homelessness requires collaborative perspectives from individuals, institutions, and communities so that we can develop an appreciation and a deeper understanding of its impact. The sight of homeless people has always made the greatest impression on communities, but this book compensates for their silence. *The Ethics of Homelessness* is a volume of original essays that give voice to the underlying ethical components of the homeless condition. The opening chapters of Part One are perspectives arranged so as to invite the reader, as though on the streets, to encounter a homeless person. The three works provide the external climate a passerby might experience when encountering the homeless. Poems by Dennis Rohatyn and the story by Noah Berger culturally situate the reader. Verse and story both craft an image of people living in a void, where life's meaning is deliberated on a day-to-day basis. In a reflective dialogue, Robert Ginsberg muses over painful questions about one's moral, social, or personal obligations to these people. The casual style of Ginsberg's meditation raises key questions that are addressed in the three middle parts of the book, beginning with Part Two. These chapters use formal philosophical investigations of homelessness, beginning with Pio Colonnello's chapter on homelessness as *Heimatlosigkeit*. Colonnello's work provides the presuppositions of later essays as he presents the estrangement of humankind through history as unique on an ontic level. The wandering nature of being human, according to Colonnello, is part of an unstable origin that existentially propels the individual to find a place.

Whatever it means to have a "place" either ontologically or politically, moral and legal obligation become a central theme in the remaining chapters of Part Two. Patricia Anne Murphy argues that having a place is integrally a part of personhood. Without a place a person is existentially diminished. Rights, then, ought to be acknowledged for the exercise of a person's freedom which is necessary for one's sense of self. David E. Schrader's chapter on "Home Is Where the Heart Is" extends Murphy's argument, claiming that without a home, people are denied a personality. Furthermore, the United States Constitution justifies this provision for good citizenship and membership in the moral community. Keith Burkum closes this section by implementing virtue ethics in order to assess the moral practice of communities toward the homeless. A community's goal of a common good suffers incoherence if members remain indifferent to the homeless. Children, the most vulnerable among the homeless, feel most crushingly the gravity of this indifference.

In Part Three, Michael Parker and René A. C. Hoksbergen examine the "runaway" children who abandon homes to avoid mistreatment. Ethical negotiations are invoked between individuals and community to recognize rights of children as members of society. This will be a start to provide a safe recourse for support. Hoksbergen's chapter, "Psychic Homelessness," focuses on adopted children in the Netherlands. All, whether born in Holland or abroad, lack a bond with a family which results in a family's being rootless. This phenomenon persists among well-adjusted foster children as well, so that Hoksbergen recommends a way for children to learn acceptance of an "in-between" existence.

The moral and political arguments presented by the scholars in Part Four respond in large part to a lack of policies protecting the homeless. Some also expose policies designed to make their presence and way of life illegal. Seeking refuge is a common human instinct. When the homeless take shelter in public dwellings they are asked to leave. The two chapters that open this part—Anita M. Superson's "The Homeless and the Right to 'Public Dwelling'" and Uma Narayan's "No Shelter Even in the Constitution? Free Speech, Equal Protection, and the Homeless"—argue that ordinances to remove the homeless from public dwelling and bans on begging are denials of rights. Narayan shows these bans to be forms of legislative harassment. In the chapter that follows, Natalie Dandekar writes in "Social Policies, Principles, and Homelessness," that models proposed for solutions such as social engineering are incompatible with participatory democracy. Because engineered policy, like technological systems, are prone to catastrophic accidents with no identifiable loci of responsibility, policy involving homelessness requires a different approach.

In the last two chapters of Part Four, both Shyli Karin-Frank and I argue that the moral rights of the homeless have been denied. I focus on the mentally ill homeless who, I argue, illustrate failed libertarian policies. After presenting the background of the libertarian's role in deinstitutionalizing the mentally ill, I develop a "conventional" autonomy that empowers the mentally ill homeless as recognized members of the same community. Since the homeless deserve this regard as moral agents, we are morally obligated to provide them the necessities to live as autonomous moral agents: a home. Karin-Frank extends this claim in her chapter by underscoring the value of privacy to being human. Autonomy and individuality are basic moral concepts of liberalism which, she maintains, enhance moral activity. Since homelessness involves placing moral activity at risk for other human beings, we are morally obligated to provide privacy for them to flourish; we are obligated to provide a home and to eradicate the risk.

Part Five, the closing part of the book, offers a timeless example of a philosopher who, for a part of her life, was homeless. The book moves to closure, as it opened, with a story about a homeless person. Joseph Betz's account of Hannah Arendt's homelessness philosophically animates the social/political life of homelessness. Betz explains how, for Arendt, "to secure a home is the precondition of political action." The government ought to provide what is necessary for full citizenship, namely, privacy. Ron Scapp's chapter, "Talking About Those Home Improvement Blues," leads the reader to consider the type of government that plays with words and images constructed for momentary reactions, that plans homes but denies them simultaneously. The cultural critique provided by Scapp leaves us with a paradox of contemporary values, building homes for improvement but not for need.

Part One

VERSE AND CONVERSATIONS

Homeless People

One

THE GUARDIAN OF THE BIRDS

Noah S. Berger

The following is a narrative examination of homelessness through the conversations and stories of two homeless men, George Waters and John "Pops" Moore, whom I came to know through my work at a Boston homeless shelter. I use a narrative style rather than a more academic analysis because my interest in the homeless was born not out of an interest in homelessness as abstract institution, but out of many conversations I came to have with actual homeless people living on the streets, in abandoned buildings, dumpsters, and subway stations. I hope, through this approach, to move past the institution of homelessness and focus instead on individual homeless people.

1.

"You like potato pie?" George asked before hanging up the phone.

"Potato pie?"

"It's *good*, Noah. Just made it the other night. Yeah, it's not bad. I give you a slice when you come over."

2.

I wasn't sure what potato pie was and was not at all optimistic that it would taste very good. But George could cook, I reminded myself. Cooking is an art he learned down in his native North Carolina and took with him when he moved up North to Boston, where he cooked in a restaurant before becoming homeless. He had been a pro.

I first came to know George several years earlier while working at the Parker Shelter in Boston's Government Center, where he was living at the time. George and I stayed in touch even after I left the shelter; in fact, he was the only one of its former residents with whom I was still in contact. So while in Boston for a philosophy conference, I called him on the phone and we arranged to meet at his new, subsidized apartment.

I walked through quaint Beacon Hill, up the stairs of his three-story brownstone building, and knocked on the thick metal door to his apartment. Without inquiring who was there, he opened the door, smiling; I was smiling too. "No-ah!" he exclaimed, laughing.

"George!" I countered. "How you doing?"

"Oh, pretty good, pretty good. Got my own place now. It's not bad. Want some coffee?"

It was an efficiency apartment, with a separate little space cut out in the corner for a stove, refrigerator and kitchen sink. It was good he had space to cook. The apartment was dark and bare. Both of its windows looked out onto another brownstone. All he had for furniture were two folding chairs, a square metal table, a twin mattress, and an old television set, the type that still has knobs and an antenna. George kept the apartment neat. I noticed that the sheets on his mattress, just as they had always been on his bed at the shelter, were meticulously folded over the pillow.

To my delight, "potato pie" meant sweet potato pie, which sounded much more appetizing. George was right; it wasn't bad at all. The coffee was weak, but coffee is coffee. George sat opposite me at the table, his long, slender upper body hunched over the small, off-white ceramic mug cradled in his large, bony hands. A tropism of his right eye caused a walleyed stare that gave him a slightly unfocused look. He wore his hair and beard closely formed to his oblong head. His skin was strikingly dark, almost black in color. He had been to the dentist since I'd last seen him. His few teeth had been removed and replaced with a full set of shiny white dentures. He wore a bright red plaid shirt, which he said his teacher (an adult literacy volunteer) had given him. He looked good and I told him so.

George's age was anybody's guess. If you were to ask him, he'd tell you he was fifty-seven, but his medical records listed him as forty-nine. George and the world of official records were further apart than even this eight-year discrepancy reveals. He was officially listed as having been born on 31 December, but George would tell you that his birthday was in fact Christmas Day. There was even some question about what his last name was: according to George, his real name is Walters, yet the official files list his name as George *Waters*, which is the name he now goes by.

"Are you doing a lot of cooking now that you've got your own place?" I asked between sips of coffee.

"Yeah—only I can't fry nothing here; can't do my Southern Fried food like I used to."

"Why not, George?"

"Oh, I can be baking stuff, and broiling stuff—I just can't be doing no frying."

"But *why* can't you?"

"It's that damn smoke alarm! Every time I fry something, it goes off: beep, beep, beep! I can bake and broil stuff all right, I just can't be frying!" He took another sip of coffee and I put another forkful of pie into my mouth.

"You remember Pops Moore, don't you?" he asked.

"Of course I remember John Moore! How's he doing?"

"He died."

I shouldn't have been surprised. George didn't know the cause of John's death, but I remembered that while working at the shelter, I would often have to drive him out to the Shattuck Hospital in Forest Hills for treatment of numerous chronic medical conditions, including kidney failure and high blood pressure.

John "Pops" Moore was one of the nicest gentlemen—and he was a gentleman in the literal sense of the word—that I have ever known. News of his death saddened me and, to a large extent, it is in tribute to him that I write this piece now.

3.

Every morning after breakfast, John would walk slowly out into the gray pavement of the plaza outside the shelter and lower himself onto a concrete bench. As pigeons would begin gathering around him, he would open a plastic bag and pull out scavenged remains of the morning's breakfast. He would methodically tear off small pieces of pancakes, waffles, hash browns or french toast and toss them to the eager birds, making sure to feed each bird an equal amount. "There you go," he would tell them softly with each toss. "There you go."

Whenever the breakfast at the shelter's soup kitchen was unsuitable to the diet of a pigeon, John would go across the street to the Li'l Peach, the local convenience store, and purchase a whole loaf of bread for the birds. For whatever reason, he felt a genuine compassion and concern for the well-being of Boston's pigeons. I remember one morning seeing a pigeon frantically twirling in spastic circles outside the shelter. It had probably eaten something poisonous which was slowly killing it. John caught sight of the ailing bird and made his way over to it. I watched him as he witnessed the thrashings of the doomed bird, his face pursed in vivid anguish over the pigeon's plight. The pain of the bird seemed to pain him as well. Lovingly, he touched the outstretched wing of the contorted, dying bird. Each time it fell over, he righted it again. This continued for over an hour, until the animal finally died. John stroked it one last time, stood up, and walked away.

He was only in his early sixties, but looked considerably older. Although he was by no means fat, the flesh on his face hung loosely in rounded ripples which softened his features. Wet, teary eyes, beneath permanently raised eyebrows, and short, pursed lips gave him a look of sadness and concern. And his distinguished head of gray and white hair, which contrasted his milk chocolate complexion, made it a look of wise, experienced concern.

John's mumbled speech and willingness to distance himself from a confused outside world caused him to be easily dismissed and often ignored. Such treatment, however, was fine with John, who would just as soon not be troubled with the chaotic events of the world around him. And, in turn, he did not trouble it. His aloofness, however, was never an indication of a lack of concern. Within the shelter community, he was well known for giving away more cigarettes than he kept for himself. What was more, he had the respect of the other residents, and it was out of respect that they called him "Pops."

One spring morning, after monitoring breakfast, I wandered outside the shelter into the plaza. George was sitting on the bench with John, smoking a cigarette. As ashes fell over George's shirt and lap, John distributed waffles to the pigeons. The two of them sat together in silence.

"You like those birds, don't you John," I called out as I walked towards the two men.

"Oh yes," John said, "I've taken it upon myself to be the guardian of the birds."

"Why are you the guardian of the birds?" I asked him.

"The little birds need to be protected from the Goosebill. Yes that Goosebill, he hates all the other pigeons. If I don't look out for them, the Goosebill'd hurt them for sure."

"The Goosebill is another pigeon?"

"That's right. He's an ugly something-or-other with a disposition to match."

"So why're *you* the one responsible for protecting the other pigeons?" I asked.

"I've got to be," he said. "One of them took a bullet for me."

He then proceeded to tell me the detailed story of a time in which he was alone on an outdoor basketball court in Roxbury. He happened to glance up at an adjacent abandoned building. He caught sight of a figure in one of the partially boarded-up windows. To his horror, he realized that the figure was holding a rifle, and the rifle was pointed right at him. John turned to run, but before he could get away, the sound of a rifleshot echoed across the empty court, shaking the backboards and netless rims.

John checked himself over and was relieved to discover that the bullet had not hit him. He then looked down at the cement ground and saw a pigeon sitting in a pool of blood. As John tells the story, the pigeon had alertly anticipated the shooting and flew down from its perch to intercept the bullet that had been meant for John. Gratefully, he bandaged up the wounded bird and slowly nursed it back to health. He watched over it for several weeks until its strength was fully regained.

"So you see," John explained, "I've got to take care of the birds, for they've taken care of me."

"Pops, you sure got a lotta those crazy stories," George said shaking his head. He took one last puff from his cigarette and dropped the butt on the ground. Several pigeons darted over to inspect it, as George turned his head to face John. "You got another cigarette on you?" he asked.

John reached into the side pocket of his overcoat, pulled out a pack of generic Best Buys, removed a cigarette and handed it to George. "There you go," he said.

4.

Whether or not John's account of having been stalked from that abandoned building is an accurate description of an actual event, the gun-wielding figure is at least symbolic. The shot from the gun of the anonymous sniper above the basketball court was a single act of pure meaninglessness, completely random and without purpose. It is symbolic of what John saw as an explosive, callous and cruel world: the world of the streets, an environment in which he had lived his entire life. But against this backdrop of dark streets, back alleys, dumpsters, and gutted buildings, John was still able to construct meaning for himself: he was the guardian of the birds.

Pigeons are the bums of the animal world. They scavenge through trash cans for their food and sleep in doorways and on abandoned rooftops. And like the homeless, they too are vulnerable. The Goosebill, that ornithological bully, is but another incarnation of the same random brutality symbolized by the sniper. Together with these classless creatures, John "Pops" Moore formed a union of the low, the vulnerable, the untouchable, and the ignored.

5.

Michel Foucault writes of a deviant population of madmen, debtors, adulterers, ne'er-do-wells, and bums that has been characterized by silence since the seventeenth century. Normal society denies them the very possibility of saying anything meaningful. As a result, their words are stripped of sense before they are uttered: no matter how loudly they scream, their cries go unheard. In what Foucault terms "The Great Internment," they were (and still are) neatly packed into prisons, asylums, and shelters where they were (and still are) safely ignored, but always monitored. Today's homeless seem a paradigm case of Foucault's class of silence.

A similar idea comes through in Charles Lane's recent film *Sidewalk Stories*. Up until the final two minutes, the film depicts the life of a homeless man in silence, following the tradition of the silent movies of the teens and twenties. Then, two minutes before the end, the silence is broken and the homeless are allowed to speak. But Lane makes what I consider to be a critical mistake which deprives the ending of its intended punch. What the audience finally hears the homeless saying is unfortunately what we hear daily from them anyway: "Can you spare some change?" "Would you buy me a cup of coffee?" "Help me out, I'm homeless." What they really think and how they view the surrounding world remains shrouded in silence.

I am not operating here in my own text under the naive belief that in writing about John Moore, I am breaking the silence that has historically been imposed on the homeless. I cannot give voice to John's silence. In fact, in using the very clinical word "homeless," I am not even speaking the language of the street—after all, when homeless people talk amongst themselves they call themselves "bums." All I can do is provide a snapshot, a framed and focused glimpse into one small moment in John's world.

6.

I said goodbye to the two men and turned to leave. George tapped John on the shoulder. "Hey Pops," he said, "I didn't get no breakfast today. I'm kinda hungry. Can I get me one of those waffles?"

John handed him the last waffle. "There you go," he said.

Two

POETIC SOUNDS OF HOMELESS VERSE

Dennis Rohatyn

1. Clichés r Us

thanks for sparing me
those one-night stands
those furtive trysts
those sly messages
those hushed voices
those broken dates
those messy excuses
those lipstick lies
and all the
best of it
that i want(ed) so bad
sure it was a dead end
You killed it
the minute i got there
the moment i was born
hearticide's no crime
just a shame

You did it so well
with just one word
i never heard
i never will
i was dumb
now i'm deaf
shut up
i can't sleep

hey
it's not the end of the world
i can't thank you
enough
for leaving me
no place to go
but home
like they say on TV

happily never after
i can't believe
i'm still alive
can't stop running
gotta stop tilting
where's the motel?
under the cliff
nice view of god
finite regress
wait for me
ok, don't wait
hurry up
too late
too soon
to die

unrequited
lover leaps
before looking
unrequited
lover acts
without thinking
unrequited
lover lives
without loving
and vice versa
unrequited
fly united
i'm grounded
but not
unfinished

You idiot
don't cry
i can't
i'm dead
remember?
r i p
the p
stands for pain
as for the rest
forget it
i owe You

i'm saved
sorry
don't lie
be honest
tell me why
that's easy
if You
can't love me
join me
No
ifs

2. The Unbearable Brightness of Seeing

at ease
feelin fine
on the couch

not lonely
not lovesick
safe n saved
round soul
face glows
hope less

cant stay
why not?
gettin late
gotta go
later
yeah sure
call soon
never home
never at home
ha ha   true

slong
ciao
why waste words
don't look back

too our drive
don't think
can't rest
can't think
don't rest
Sisy slumped
at the wheel
bad brakes
turnoff
kill headlights
wait for dawn
open   door
closemouth
home is where?
the heart ache
home sour home
home sick mess
lost your bet
now sleep with it
all dressed down
no place to hide
wish You were . . .

wish i weren't

don't mean that
the hell i don't
ok ok
forget it
can't
lights   out.

3. Once Upon a

In the beginning was the home
And the home was
And it was OK
no one sang Homeward Bound
or hummed Goin' Home
no one had to
no one used words like *Unheimlichkeit*
or worried about infinite space

or went to Walden
to get away to it all
no one had womb envy
or chased white wails
or moaned about a golden age
or longed for paradise
or dreamed of Eden
or died for *das Vaterland*
nobody read Dante
or believed Copernicus
or trailed clouds of verse
from heavenly settees
filled with forms
nobody needed a shrink
or a confession box
or a whorehouse
to feel at home
nobody lived
on the edge
or died *en masse*
nobody tore down a wall
or put up a fence
or shot a Coke machine
just to save the world
nobody rafted the Mississippi
to make a home away from home
nobody drifted
nobody cared
nobody heard the Big Bang
or saw the solar system
evicted from a black hole
nobody gave their address
like young Daedalus
or left out the zip code
nobody froze to death
on a park bench
nobody hit home
or left it
nobody stole home
nobody touched base
nobody cried
nobody needed a home loan
or asked for $5 and dime

nobody waited for Odysseus
or found fools on bare heaths
nobody said you can't go home again
nobody dared
nobody came home from the war
nobody came home to die
nobody walked the streets
or lived in state of fear
or on welfare island
or up Donne's creek
nobody moved away
nobody stayed in touch
nobody lied
nobody had a body
or a mind to waste
nobody was schizo
or in search of self
nobody went on vacation
or sought the wholly grey
no one changed channels
or fucked a stranger
while staying remote
nobody complained
nobody stayed late
nobody quit
nobody revolted
or rebelled
or preserved
the status quo
nobody reached Ellis
nobody died en route
or sailed back to Senegal
nobody got itchy
nobody got wanderlust
nobody expatriated
nobody minded
nobody bothered gypsies
nobody persevered
nobody muddled through
nobody gave up hope
or kept on keeping on
nobody met at a motel
nobody was psycho

nobody needed a quest
or an incentive
or a goal
or a sense of purpose
or Manifest Destiny
or just for the helluvit
or carpe diem
or nihilistic despair
or effete snobbery
or Seconal
or JFK
or the Führer
or their conscience
or no reason at all
to tell them where to go
and what to do
nobody needed advice
or gave any, either
nobody begged Homey
to make 'em laugh
out loud, or even
to feel good inside
a place where
to this day
nobody lives
nobody hit the road
or strayed on it long
nobody kicked route 66
or lived in a car
or crossed the border
or died inside
nobody abandoned ship
or hailed Ishmael
nobody knew the territory
or fled from a ghost clown
no beaming brass enterpriser
went where no one went before
no one mopped the floor
or cleaned the head
or raised the kids
or walked to church
or established a beachhead
or reported to headquarters

or called in sick
or reaped rich rewards
in willies purrfumed guyrage
not to mention, on the beach
nobody had a room of her own
nobody stayed in a cell
nobody lived in solitary
nobody died alone
nobody did a Lewis and Clark
nobody had a trail of tears
nobody DPd
or ODd
or disappeared
from the face of
the mirth
nobody got gassed
or cremated
or buried alive
nobody was DOA
or bored to death
nobody died in space
or else in due time
nobody moved
nobody rested
nobody punched out
at least, never on Sunday
nobody found eternal peace
nobody was ever lost
to be honest
nobody did much of anything
hence, as it was written
everybody was happy
just being themselves
or just being, period
can you believe that, TJ?
i do, Parmenides
why?
life's so simple
in the beginning was the end
now you know
No more secrets
Yes, my child
Home at last.

Three

MEDITATIONS ON HOMELESSNESS AND BEING AT HOME: IN THE FORM OF A DIALOGUE

Robert Ginsberg

1. Robert

Homeless people who make their home on the streets make me, a tireless stroller of the city, ill-at-ease. They interrupt my passage and my vista. They are in the way. An eyesore on the cityscape, they spoil the setting in which I move. Their unwelcome presence makes something uncivilized out of the city. They don't belong here. The city is for dwellers, visitors, and even those without a home who nonetheless are provided shelter. Whether we are rich or poor, healthy or ill, the city is a mode of human organization that shares and cares.

The unsheltered homeless do not fit. Their visible existence contradicts what we have achieved: the city as home to our humanity. Either they are to be blamed, or we are to blame. Let them take the blame. The homeless are at fault. The problem with them is that they . . . are homeless. This is not my problem. I resent having their problem get in my way.

2. Ginsberg

What is my home? Where my heart is. To be at home, *chez soi*, is to feel a welcome attachment to a special place. There's no place like home. Home is where I can be who I really am. No matter how much trouble you face in the world, they will always love you back at home! You can lose your way in life, but you can usually find your way home again. You carry a return ticket to home in your heart. All roads lead home.

While a house does not make a home, a home provides the physical features that match the inner life of the person. Home grows out of, expresses, contributes to, and facilitates my humanity, my homanity. I am a better person because I have a home in which to grow. An Englishman's house is his castle, so I was told as a child. Mongolian proverb: The door shut, you are emperor in your kingdom. French saying: To each bird, its nest is bliss.

Come home with me to understand who I am. Make yourself right at home. *Mi casa es su casa.* Home is a haven for the heart. It offers security and surety. Home sweet home.

3. Robert

The homeless are threatening. They are in dire need and hence want money. Homeless people when they see me pass are likely to ask me for money. I don't want to be asked for money on the street. I don't want to think about giving money away, allocating what I have in my pocket. When I walk in the city, I may intend to pay for services or products, but I don't intend to engage in charitable donations. I prefer to consider requests for charity while sitting at my desk. Charity begins at home. There I can apportion my time to the plight of the needy in the world and budget my meager resources.

The homeless person who asks in person for money threatens the well-ordered life in which I deal from a distance with those in need. Get too close to me and I can't help you. I resent being asked on the spot when I thought I had already done my homework involving social obligations.

Even the homeless person who does not ask me for money is felt as a threat to ask. If they don't ask now, then they will ask later. If this person doesn't ask, then the next one will. If they don't ask, then what's wrong with them? I blame them even for not asking. I am afraid that the one thing they all want from me is money. I don't want be a target for handouts.

Other people have their eye on me to sell me things, but that's different. They have something to offer. I may feel flattered by their offering it to me as someone with the power to purchase. Pickpockets may also pick me out for the supposed wealth of my pockets, but I have a fighting chance not to be victimized by them.

In the case of the homeless, the victim is trying to get money for nothing from me, an unknown person. I don't want to be treated in that fashion. The existence of the homeless threatens my identity not only by the act but also by just the possibility of asking for money. I don't want to be money-bearer for victims. My life becomes impoverished by the treatment I might receive from the homeless.

Since I don't want to be asked for money on the street, I don't give it. But then I am afraid of what will happen, especially if other people have been giving money. The potential resentment of the homeless person whom I do not aid threatens my composure. I imagine that resentment in the eyes and in the heart, and I resent that.

What if words of resentment follow my refusal? Shall I answer back or hurry off? Should I stop for a dialogue, or would it degenerate into diatribe? Just as the beggar has the right to solicit money of a stranger on the street, so I have a right to refuse the request, to refrain from giving explanations, and to remain a stranger going about my business. I am not answerable to those whom I refuse to aid. I'll save my theory of charity and obligation for my writing desk.

The easiest thing to allay my fears is to give a few coins whenever asked for aid. Surely I can afford it. Will Rogers never turned down a request for a handout. How rich his life must have been, and at such small cost. I see other people giving handouts as if automatically. But I resist following the crowd. I insist on preserving my freedom. I will not give in to the fashion. If I decide not to give, then I want to stick to my decision, even though it is convenient to pay. To be shamed, cajoled, threatened, or coerced into paying is not charity. I am frightened by the hassle that may occur if the homeless ask me for money. I would feel guilty in giving in to their solicitations.

Even if I wanted to make a donation with charitable goodwill, this might not be a prudent thing to do, for I may be exposing the location of my change purse to the eyes of pickpockets, I may be encouraging others in similar straits to line up for their handouts, and I might suddenly be struck and robbed by the very person I am aiding. Whenever I am asked for money on the street I fear it is a trap.

Once in Dubrovnik, that enchanted city, before it was shelled in the recent Balkan War, I emptied my pocket of change on impulse into the hat of a stranded compatriot. It was such a good feeling, obtained at such a trivial cost, until I discovered that the key to my suitcase had been in that pocket.

4. Ginsberg

We make our homes. Not necessarily by constructing them, although some people do that. We build the intimate shell of our lives by the organization and furnishing of the space in which we live. How we function as persons is linked to how we make ourselves at home. We need time to make our dwelling into a home. Home is not built in a day. Inescapably, human beings are homemakers.

Our residence is where we live, but our home is how we live. It is the transformation of place by life meant to open our selfhood to our immediate surroundings. At home we are in our element. We domesticate ourselves by becoming attached to our *domicile* (a word derived from Latin roots for "concealment" and "home"). The homey, homelike, *haimish* (Yiddish) is not only comfortable but comforting. All the comforts of home: being welcome, being wanted, being safe, being cared for. We are irrepressible homebodies.

The womb, the cradle, the nursery, the parental home are the successive nests which protect human beings and inform our quest to make a home for ourselves somewhere on earth. Our homing instinct is this longing to return to an inner realm, a private world, which is our home away from home, our special place distinct from the rest of the world. "The home is the centre and circumference, the start and the finish, of most of our lives," says Charlotte Perkins Gilman.[1] Home is the dream that we carry with us and that guides our steps. East, West, home is best: Japanese proverb. Wherever we might be, we are homeward-bound. We take our turn with the bat at home plate and aspire to round the bases, making it back home safely. When we accomplish something good in the world, we say to ourselves, "Wait 'til they hear about this back home!"

5. Robert

The homeless threaten me with awareness of their existence. I know they exist because I can read about them. I can also write about them. All that is intellectualization. The trouble with meeting a homeless person on the street is that this is not an intellectual event. It is my encounter with another person. I don't seek or want that encounter. I may enjoy meeting some people I don't know on the street; that's part of the adventure of living in or visiting a city. But an unsought for, unexpected, and undesired encounter with the homeless person is disturbing. I then am made aware that *this* person, whom I have never seen before, and who is staring me in the eyes, may be destitute, suffering, unhappy, disadvantaged, oppressed, lonely, outcast, and gravely ill. To read about the homeless is one thing, to bump into them in the street is another thing. I am quite at home in my thoughts until I meet someone in the flesh who is without house or home.

The temptation arises of wanting to know more about them while simultaneously avoiding learning more. *Why are you homeless?* is the unasked question that resounds in my heart, often in an accusatory tone. Sometimes, fragments of an answer are evident or spoken:

> I lost my job.
> I can't get a job.
> I'm disabled.
> I'm ill.
> I've been evicted.
> I have no family.
> I have no friends.
> I have no money.
> I have no place to go.
> I have no home.

Yet we would know more: the deeper reasons and surrounding circumstances, the alternatives considered and efforts undertaken. Each case of homelessness is a complex story embedded in the life of a particular human being. If we listened to the story and verified it, we would be keen to judge the case. Inquisitive and inquisitorial, we are ready to lay blame and even to take action.

1.   If a gross injustice were inflicted on the victims, say, as refugees from war, then we would seek rectification, while we protested the injustice. So we must do something for the throngs of Tutsis made homeless by the Hutus, and for the throngs of Hutus made homeless by the Tutsis.

2.   If a systematic failure of society were to leave thousands of people no alternative but to waste away their lives on the streets, as in Calcutta, then we must call for massive social reform as we participate in massive rescue efforts.

3.   If a chain of bad luck besets the homeless, then we could encourage them to take the available steps to move up in life.

4.   If a small loan, or some work, or a meal, or a place to sleep, or counseling were needed to get down-and-out people going again, then we could refer them to the charitable organizations or social services that exist to aid in such matters.

5.   If . . . .

Cases 1 and 2 require my action. But for 3 and 4 I am not obliged to do anything. As for number 5 . . . .

I should carry with me wherever I go a chart of the types of homelessness, so that for each case I can identify what is at stake and check the authenticity of the homelessness. The spell checker of my word-processing program does not recognize the word "homelessness." It suggests this spelling for what I have been writing: "hopelessness." I don't want to be taken in by pretended homelessness or momentary homelessness. I want to distinguish from the temporary or remediable causes the hopeless situation where the person is homeless because wanting to be so. In face of such a reason, an assertion of metaphysical homelessness, I would be speechless.

We could process the appeals that are made under several headings and thereby help individuals, improve society, and feel good about our efforts, but we can do nothing about the person who refuses shelter, employment, counseling, and other social services. "I want to be homeless" is an utterance devastating to our meaning as social beings, as human beings. We dread hearing this. While involuntary homelessness is a social ill that we can understand and to which we can minister, voluntary homelessness seems a life-sickness that we cannot fathom and which renders us helpless.

We like to think that the problem of homelessness can be solved by working on the cases of homeless people. Given appropriate governmental services, supplemented by charitable organizations such as religious institutions, a truly civilized society should not be beset with homelessness. But in cities like Rome and Washington, homeless people live and sometimes die on the streets. Last night when I passed homeless people trying to keep warm on a steam grate a few blocks from the White House, I was struck with the fear that civilization had utterly failed.

I have put my heart into making civilization work for humanity. I believe we are making progress, but then I encounter a homeless person—the quintessential misfit in civilization—and I am frightened by the truth. I want to absolve civilization from causing this person to be homeless, so I incline toward blaming the person for being homeless. But I can't understand how someone would want to be homeless, nor can I see society as escaping blame. Troubling paradox.

Everything on this subject that I have read—and that I write—tells me that homelessness should not exist. Once I leave my home, I stumble over it—I should say, over them—in the big city. I want to know the answer.

I don't want to know the answer. If you look too deeply you may find what you are not looking for; so Oedipus discovered before he blinded himself. The more we ponder the problem of homelessness as the problem of others—the homeless—the more the probing strikes home until we find that it is a problem of ourselves. I just don't feel at home dealing with this problem.

6. Ginsberg

Some people spend their entire lives at home: the same house, the same neighborhood, the same metropolitan area, the same place on earth. Their home is a fixed point; all the rest of the world is outside. When away from home, they become homesick. Even if a person moves from center city to suburb, or from apartment to private house, that person may still operate from the same home base, continuing the same work and other activities, and knowing the same people. "What place do you call home?" is usually answered by naming our hometown.

Our homeland is our childhood home writ large. It is the largest identifiable realm in which we imagine that we would feel at home and which we feel obligated to protect against foreigners. "It is so good to be back home!" said the Californian stepping off the trans-Atlantic plane in New York.

Love of homeland, which signals living together at peace, somehow gets connected to willingness to kill others. Any violation of your homeland is the magnified version of violation of your childhood home. The specter of the enemy as killing babies haunts the imagination as many wars begin.

The recent Balkan War owed its beginnings to the oppression by the rulers of Serbia of the Albanian people living in the autonomous region of Kosovo, an historical homeland for Serbs. Yugoslavia split apart as a confederation of republics when several other ethnic groups asserted their identity as independent homelands. But maybe the origin of the conflict goes back to 1521, when the Turks captured Belgrade. Ever since, the Balkans have conducted a bloody struggle over homelands.

I have been one of those who moves through the world changing homes. My life so far is headed by five chapters: New York, Chicago, Paris, Philadelphia, Washington. I gave up one home in order to find my heart elsewhere. I was not content to stay at home. I felt its limitations; I felt the attractions of other places. The call of the world was stronger than the ties to home.

For some people, leaving home is a terrible experience; for me it was liberating. I could go beyond where I had been. I could make my way in the world rather than permanently adhere to the way of others. As a child I took comfort in the thought that I could always run away from home and join the circus!

I didn't run away from home. Youngsters often do, with the desire—of which they may be unaware—of being missed and then welcomed home again. The return of the prodigal. Some young people feel that they deserve better treatment at home. Others feel that they are undeserving of what is offered them at home; they punish themselves by fleeing. Still others run away because their home is really not home; it is a prison-house.

Home, then, not as where you are from, but where you are going. The world offers many places that feel just like home for people trying to get somewhere.

Oh give me a home,
Where the buffalo roam . . . .

"Where are you headed, stranger?" "I don't rightly know, but wherever it is, it will be home."

For the wanderer who might have many homes to find, each home may not be quite the right one. Some people do not feel at home wherever they make their home. They have not found their place though they may be surrounded by delightful facilities. Alienation can creep up on people while they are sitting at home doing nothing. That's why they have to get out of the house. They go dancing. They go to work. They travel. Or at home they benumb their feelings with alcohol, nicotine, cholesterol, and video. Too often, home is a hollow place. It is the commuter base on the way to our lives. Home is boring; stay-at-homes are dullards.

"Let's spend a quiet evening at home." Lovely thought. Shut out the clamor of the world, including the homeless and other victims. But then we may be missing something by staying at home: the demonstrations, the debates, the divertissements, the dying.

I confess to three modes of malaise: 1. Being at home may not feel quite right, especially when the world is filled with stupidity and viciousness. 2. Being at home may keep me from finding the next home, the place more fit for me. 3. Being at home may prevent me from feeling the rest of the world as my home. I should be at home anywhere in the world. The world as humanity on earth should have room for me and a welcome wherever I go. If I do not venture forth then I will miss knowing my real homeland. I will have mistaken some place, however agreeable it has been, for the whole world.

What in the world have I been thinking of as home, when the world itself is home to humanity? Since all human beings call earth our home planet, then we are dwellers in the same home, though luck has assigned us different rooms. As sharers of our home, we should cooperate in its maintenance, safety, and improvement. And if we see ourselves as all living together under the same roof, then we can treat one another as family and friends. The whole world is the homeland of humanity.

7. Robert

The homeless threaten me by making me encounter my shortcomings. I am not ready to help them in their concrete presence. I am not willing to probe the mystery and misery of their homelessness, for fear that it is grounded in a cause for which no answer is available. If many people live on the streets due to failure of society to provide them their due, then what is to prevent me from one day being unfairly neglected by society? If some people live on the streets due to metaphysical homelessness, then what is to prevent me from becoming infected by their ailment? I don't want to renounce being at home in the world, but . . . .

8. Ginsberg

But all this uplifting thought about being attached to everybody because we share the world as our home may be building castles in the air. For while I have been harboring such sentiments of universal homanity, I have also felt out of place. I have lived as foreigner in other countries, and as stranger in my homeland. I have felt odd. This is due to personality, physical constitution, appearance, upbringing, professional life, etc. I don't care to analyze for you all the interrelated features of my oddness, but it will suffice to confess that I am left-handed.

For more than sixty years, I have dwelled in a right-handed world. Every door, every button, every tool, every place-setting reminds me of that, though right-handed people seem totally unaware that *they* live in a right-handed world. They have missed awareness, but they profit from convenience. I suffer inconvenience yet profit from awa reness. I am so lucky to have been born and raised left-handed, for that makes me aware that I don't fit in the world. Alienation alternates with humanit arian belonging. I love the world, but I am an exile on earth.

Is this not your experience as well? You, *mon semblable*, who for some peculiarity of your own, some idiosyncrasy (from the Greek, *idios*, private), also have moments when you want the world to stop so you can get off. Everybody sooner or later is at a loss in the world. Thomas Wolfe got it right: You Can't Go Home Again.

9. Robert

Are you speaking to me?

10 . Ginsberg

Yes, Bob. I have noticed you over there in that part of our personality, thinking in your peculiar way about some things which I too have had in mind. But we may also have been overheard by others out there who find that our reflections hit home. *Is anybody home?* I wonder if they too see that even if home is expanded to mean our world-sharimg with humanity, yet we may find ourselves oddly not at home in the world.

11. Robert

Well, Mr. Ginsberg, we all ought to have that experience as crucial to being human. Because the final truth, which we—including professional thinkers like you—are afraid to face, is that our life on earth does not come with guaranteed permanent shelter. Unlike our earl y life at home, in the world we have to die. Home, in its successive forms, was meant to save us from this. But nothing can save us from death. No one gets by death homefree. Our final home, where we are said to rest in peace, is the tomb.

12 . Ginsberg

Whence arises the alienation that comes with life. We inevitably feel uncomfortable (German: *unheimlich*) in the world because we have to leave it. This is the metaphysics of being human. With a home or no home, we are not long for the world. Never long enough.

13. Robert Ginsberg

Encounter with the homeless awakens us to questions about the meaning of the world, the reality of home, and *our* place, *our* life, *our* death. The voluntary homeless seem to reject home as human necessity. They are heading toward death without the comfort of safe havens on the way. But perhaps they have accepted that life in the world provides no significant shelters, so that they live from day to day until they are dead.

Putting my mind together for this challenge, I have chosen otherwise: in the face of death, alienation, and suffering to make a home in the world and to make the world a better home for humanity. A world without homeless people, voluntary as well as involuntary, is one of the best goals. Let us make the world into a loving home for all, which we only leave at death. Since each of us must leave the common home of the world for death, then let all of us feel at home while we live together.

But even with the united sides of my thought, I am unsure, and a likely victim of circumstance, and vulnerable to a metaphysical fall. So I fear that one day I will be there on the street, homeless by causes beyond my control, or worse, by choice. You who have overheard me thinking might see me lying there. The homeless being from whom I now avert my eyes as I pass by without giving anything, is a human being, and hence myself, and yourself, in another guise. For this uneasiness, I have been blaming *them*. But now I am grateful to them for what they have given me: their existence has brought home who *we* are.

Note

1. Charlotte Perkins Gilman, *The Home*, excerpted in *Feels Like Home*, ed. Cheryl Moch (Chapel Hill, N.C.: Algonquin Books of Chapel Hill, 1995), p. 5.

Part Two

THE MIRROR OF HOMELESSNESS

Is It Essential to Humanity?

Four

HOMELESSNESS AS *HEIMATLOSIGKEIT*?

Pio Colonnello

1. Introduction

Homelessness, feeling lost and deprived of human relationships is the meta-physical condition of contemporary humanity. This condition is the focus in the existential works by Martin Heidegger and Jean-Paul Sartre. In his masterpiece, *Being and Time*, Heidegger maintained that the condition of homelessness represents the watershed between "non-authentic" being, which gives a falsely reassuring sense of living "in one's own home," and the true "authentic" being, totally estranged from the everyday world. The characteristic mood of modern human beings is anxiety. Friedrich Nietzsche went further, arguing that the return home or the place from which the individual sets out wandering coincides with the lack of a fixed abode, so that "home" and "homelessness" are seen as one and the same thing. For Sartre, the individual is alienated from a context and human society. The main goal is to strive and escape from the prison of existence since "Hell is other people."[1]

This all contrasts with the situation in Ancient Greece, when human beings felt perfectly "at home": politically the citizen was integrated with the state, and metaphysically the individual was one with the cosmos. This harmony began to break down in the Hellenistic period. It was Hegel who attempted to reconstruct the stages by which the Spirit returns home: the Idea becomes estranged from itself, passing into Nature, and then returns into itself as Spirit.

Nowadays there are a great number of "homeless" or stateless people who demand recognition. How are these masses to be answered? It may well be appropriate to reaffirm—over and above the nihilist school of thought and its late epigones the ancient idea of harmony, with emphasis on political harmony, which prevailed in the Greek world. I am thinking of the concept harmony as the representation of the idea of direct democracy, as prevailed in Periclean Athens. In the *polis* the public domain of politics pertained to political equality in spite of social differences.

2. The Existential Condition of Humanity in Our Time

If the existential condition of the contemporary person is considered in a speculative dimension which prefers the instability of de-ontology or meontology over the stability of ontology, the absence or lack is viewed as a fundamental characteristic of being. The attributes "non" and "less" stand out in a symptomatic way. Abandoning the search for a fundamental cause, whether this be Reason, Ground, or God, "the absolute and immovable foundation" of Cartesian memory undercuts the bedrock of traditional ontology. Without an ontological bedrock homelessness is realized as the human condition. The sense of the "state of expatriation," which gives a person conviction to live, has been lost. The contemporary person is aware of not being "at home" and feels that things and other people around are unfamiliar. In this sense, the aim to inhabit the earth is recognized as illusory, as this line of Rainer Maria Rilke makes explicit: "It is certainly strange not to inhabit the earth any more."[2] So the ontological-existential disposition of humankind is "utopian" not because it anticipates or pursues some far off, rose-tinted vision to substitute for the present reality, but because the human condition is to be "without a place," "without a home."

It is not difficult to see where such basic tenets lead. The problem of pain, for example, will not be resolved by a "hereafter" in the messianic sense of a conclusion or epiphany; neither is it resolved in the Hegelian sense of "being at home," which implies the return of the spirit after a period in which it had abandoned the self, or in the religious expectation of "the last coming." In both cases, we are in the presence of a final cause, *telos*, of saving grace, and an intrinsic soteriology (salvation). We must not forget this century's concern with the tragic originating from the cry of Nietzsche's madman, "God is dead."[3] If God no longer dwells among us, and the values of the Platonic-Christian ontology have lost their permanent place in the contemporary world, then the figure of "There-being humankind" in history is stripped of values and denied a stable abode.

The existentialist philosophy in the twentieth century, from Heidegger to Sartre, focuses on the theme of estrangement, the "state of expatriation," the "not true abode" or "homelessness," as the typical condition of humanity. In the beginning of time, Heidegger claims that the true nature of being of the "There-being" is never an "abstract self-projection" but is always determined by its "thrown-ness." "There-being" is always "destined to existence," that is the "facticity of existence," which is "radically different from the facticity of simple entity."[4] While "thrown-ness" is not an additional characteristic of "There-being," it tends to flee from its own condition of "thrown-ness" in order to take refuge in the presumed abstract liberty of "Oneself." This flight from the "Non-being" of the world, before which "There-being" "is seized by anxiety for its own power to be," does not place the individual in a condition of existential authenticity. In fact, the individual can feel "at home" in the tranquilizing and mundane security of living, in the banality of commerce with the entities of this world. Alternatively, there is a fundamental emotive situation, an ontological disposition which characterizes a person, the anxiety and the "There-being" which falls into a radical "state of expatriation" with regard to the everyday world. It is precisely the condition of not being or not feeling oneself "at home" which represents the divide between the inauthentic and the authentic "There-being." It must, however, be emphasized that the "state of expatriation," or, in other words, "the original and thrown being-in-the-world as feeling homeless," is a fundamental mode of being of the "There-being," even though it is "daily covered up."[5] Space does not permit a full treatment of how determination, from thrown-ness to existential authenticity, is necessarily the movement of "consciousness." The voice of this consciousness silently "calls" the "There-being" to project itself in its most appropriate being, without blaming it for any guilt it may have. It would undoubtedly be interesting to follow through the connections which link the ontological-existential foundations of consciousness and guilt, but we must get back to our main topic.

3. Heidegger and Homelessness

In his work *Brief Über den Humanismus*, Heidegger showed that it is precisely "estrangement," "the state of expatriation," and "homelessness" which characterize the historical dimension of modern humanity. From the philosophical innovations of Nietzsche, even the homecoming, the return to the place from which one set out on one's wanderings, coincides with the lack of a stable abode and the dimension of wandering itself, so that "home" and "homelessness" denote the same thing. Let us, however, look more closely at the existential analysis of the "There-being" as it is undertaken in the *Humanismusbrief*. It is common knowledge that the "There-being" is a "thrown projection," the thrown-ness is not the responsibility of humanity but of being itself, which charges individuals with the conservation of the "near-ness" and the "lighting-process" of being. Now, although people live in this nearness, one is still not "able to make deliberate use of this abode and adopt it as his own."[6] This nearness of being Heidegger calls "home" or "homeland." The use of the word "home" or "abode" in this context does not imply patriotism or nationalism. Instead, it is used in the perspective of Being-as-history, to be disclosed through the oblivious sense of being imposed by Western metaphysics. Heidegger pointed out the "confusion" between entity and being throughout the history of Western philosophy and the tendency to identify being with the "supreme being." However, when he speaks of "the essence of the homeland," he is associating it with the intention of conceiving the homelessness of modern humanity as it originates in Being-as-history. The *historical dimension of modern humanity*, implies both return to the "place" of origin and an unstable abode.

The identity of "home" and "homelessness" defines the condition of contemporary people, for only in estrangement is it possible to find oneself. A human being's only duty is to accept, without nostalgia, a personal solitude in

homelessness as a formative element of personal being. It is no coincidence that
modern poetry has exploited this theme, reelaborating it in a universal
dimension that goes beyond the autobiographical allusions and subjective traits
of the poet, as can be seen in the lyric entitled "Wanderer" (*Girovago*) by
Giuseppe Ungaretti:

In nessun a	In no
parte	place
di terra	on earth
mi posso	can I
accasare	dwell
A ogni	In each
nuovo	new
clima	clime
che incont ro	that I find
mi trovo	I soon
languente	languish
che	for
una volta	once already
gia' gli ero stato	I had grown
assuefatto	accustomed to it
E me ne stacco sempre	And I always tear myself away
straniero	a stranger
Nascendo	Being born
tornat o da epoche troppo	back from ages lived
vissute	too intensely
Godere un solo	To enjoy just one
minuto di vita	minute in life
iniziale	at its outset
Cerco un paese	I seek a land
innocente	which is innocent[7]

Heidegger explains that the "state of expatriation" or homelessness "becomes
a universal destiny," for if homelessness is reconsidered in the perspective of
Being-as-history, it includes all the forms of radical estrangement which
Western metaphysics has succeeded in identifying and mystifying. At this point,
"estrangement" encompasses the Marxist "alienation."

4. Sartre and Existence as "Hell"

The theme of alienation as a radically existential estrangement can also be
identified in Sartre, who sees humankind as radically estranged from the context

or human society. A person's condition of alienation is determined by the impossibility of living in the world while conserving the inviolate personal liberty. In fact, a person cannot avoid being alienated existentially since liberty is threatened or encroached upon simply by the presence of others: "Hell is other people." The inevitable reaction is flight or refusal, bound up with a feeling of deep disgust, in the face of the patent gratuity of existence, as we see in the character of Antoine Roquentin in Sartre's famous novel, *La Nausée*. It underscores that however hard humanity may strive to escape from the prison of existence, it must face the ever unstable abode with other inhabitants of this world. Sartre cannot subscribe to Heidegger's concept of "with-being." This is not the place to follow through this theme as it recurs in different stages of Sartre's work, from *The Transcendence of the Ego* through to his most important works, *Being and Nothingness* and the *Critique of Dialectical Reason*. We should, however, sketch the main coordinates of the question. Right from his first writings, Sartre faced up to the problem of the relationship between the self and others, between consciousness and the subjects external to it. Sartre later rejected the solution postulated by Edmund Husserl's phenomenological approach after finding some ideal convergences in it. In *Being and Nothingness,* Sartre returns to a systematic treatment of the relations between consciousness and intersubjectivity. Sartre's subtle analysis and descriptions of the phenomena of consciousness—those events which enable the given data to *present themselves* to consciousness, now seen as the pole of attraction for the noemes of "living experiences"—are qualified by his starting position: unreflected consciousness. This is a "solitary" consciousness, characterized by the eternal flux, slipping "through one's fingers,"[8] which is ultimately condemned to remain within its own subjectivity. Humanity exhibits an imprisonment inside the sphere of its consciousness. At each attempted escape one finds oneself alone again with one's own ego.

As a matter of fact, Sartre himself criticized the solipsism of the Western philosophical tradition, which has always sought to solve the problem of the "I-other" relationship in terms of gnoseology. He tries to transfer the analysis of intersubjectivity onto the plane of being, as Hegel earlier anticipated in *Phenomenology of Spirit,* with his "master-slave" dialectic. Sartre felt the need to escape from the solipsism of consciousness and its inference that consciousness is the only unifying pole for the world around us. Thinking does not put one in communication with another consciousness, but it is the action of the other's glance and equally of one's own glance: "This woman I see coming toward me, that man who goes past in the street, the beggar I hear singing from my window are all undoubtedly objects for me. Therefore one, at least, of the modes in which another person is present to me is objectivity."[9] In glancing at me or observing me, the other reduces me to the level of an object and nullifies my liberty, as if I were a "slave." In this perspective the original sense of "being-for-others" takes form. The other too is made a "slave," one object among many by my glance, and feels the discomfort and danger of being included and confined in my project as "being-for-me." The intersubjective relationship presents itself as a mutual exchange of limitation and negation.

Is there, then, no possibility of building a community of free human beings able to ensure reciprocal respect for the liberty of others? Sartre addressed the problem of how to cut the bond of subjection to the other, how to escape from an objectivity which is heteronomously imposed on a person. In short, is it possible to preserve my liberty and that of the other? In this context, Sartre's analysis of the process of falling in love as the first means by which the ego relates to the other while respecting personal subjectivity, without being reduced to an instrument, has attracted much attention. Yet this ideal also turns out to be utopian, because in each of the lovers there remains a subjectivity which comes into conflict with the liberty of the other. We can ignore here the description Sartre gives of the different attitudes which constitute people's attempts to escape from the purely subjective situation which is unable to give itself objectivity (such as indifference, the desire for the other's body, and sadistic behavior, all aimed at achieving the negation of the other's subjectivity). These attempts are destined to failure. The fact is that, once the ego finds it impossible to deny the other's liberty, which in any case transcends it, the subjectivity decides to set up a project or a world in which the other does not exist. The subject decides to hate its object: "This is the object which it wants to destroy, thereby suppressing the transcendence which obsesses it."[10] But in the end, even hate is destined to failure and ruin: "Its initial plan is in fact to suppress the other consciences. But even if this were possible, if it managed to abolish the other in the present moment, it would still not be as if the other had never existed."[11] In this way, the other will continue to live in the consciousness of the hater. "The triumph of hatred is transformed, in its very conception, into an obstacle. Hatred does not offer a way out of the vicious circle. It simply represents the last chance, a desperate final fling."[12]

5. Two World-Visions Contrasted

Anyone tracing a definitive profile of Sartre's phenomenological inquiries will recognize that the French philosopher affirms the radical impossibility of free subjects living together. Yet where do the fundamental conditions of existential alienation, that living with others is hellish and that the relationship with another is bound to resolve itself into a conflict, ultimately lead? We are bound to conclude that the refusal of or flight from the prison of existence or the "hell" of living with others will never permit humanity to dwell with others in the world or "inhabit the earth."

A person is seen as a homeless stranger, wandering outside the sphere of one's own consciousness until encountering the regions of otherness, only to find oneself thrown back in the narrow confines of subjectivity. People never have the possibility of inhabiting a stable abode, let alone of "cohabiting." For the Sartrean protagonist, too, Ungaretti's poetical utterance seems to ring true: "In no/ place/ on earth/ can I/ dwell."

The contemporary *Weltanschauung* (at least insofar as this is represented by Nietzsche and the nihilist school of thought) sees humanity's historic-epochal dimension as rooted in "homelessness," a radical estrangement from the day-to-day world, in which "homecoming" reveals the lack of a stable abode. This is contrasted with the worldwide view of the Ancient Greeks. The natural condition of an Athenian in the Periclean age was tó "feel at home," with oneself, at peace with existence and with the surroundings. This historicity of Greek spirit consisted in this, and the sense of tranquillity extending to both the political and metaphysical domains.

A. The Political Sphere

Consider the political sphere in Ancient Greece; it is common knowledge that there was an intimate identity of the citizen with the *polis*. The individual and the population organized into a state. The individual was not just an infinitesi-mal part of the whole, but a person who represented the life of the community, just as the community expressed the life of its separate parts. This correlation was so close that the *areté* or valor of the individual consisted in acting for the good of the *polis*. The individual was free because the *polis* itself was free. The very adjective *eleutheros*, meaning "free," not only was applied to whoever belonged by birthright to one particular race, but also indicated a person of "one homeland, that is of one territory in which one had the right to be and remain."[13] In contrast to the world of the barbarians or the Ancient East, a free man was one who could live in the territory of the *polis*, presided over by a law (*nomos*) which embraced both power and legality. Conversely, the strong link with the community did not rule out the awareness of the individual liberty. It was not until Aristotle formulated his philosophy that, the ideal of the *polis* was called into question, assigned to the "*bios theoretikos*" the highest form of autarchy, thereby destroying the close association between liberty and membership of the *polis*.

B. The Metaphysical Domain

In the metaphysical domain, we recall the integration of humankind with the whole, the individual with the cosmos, which implied the acceptance of personal destiny and adhesion to the law of universal harmony. A person in classical

Greece was not simply guided by the impulse of self-determination, but was also convinced that a person's will could be conditioned by powers which intervened from outside oneself and were identified with "destiny," *moira*. Destiny, even though it was seen as a blind and invincible force, did not exempt a person from displaying *areté*. The impulse of self-determination and the affirmation of one's personal mastery remained vital, and no hostile force, however overwhelming and ineluctable, could ever annihilate *areté* completely. The *tyché*, as Plutarch observed, "can deprive us of money, reputation, even life itself; but it is not able to make us dishonorable or evil, separate us from our true selves, or deprive us of the essential values of our innermost being."[14] Yet we must not forget that fate was conceived as the overriding order of the cosmos to which even the gods had to submit; this is why liberty consisted in accepting destiny and the law of cosmic harmony. In order to be able to subscribe to the harmonious interconnection of everything, the Greeks believed that human actions were also included in the pattern of the world's events.

However, the fact remains that humanity in classical Greece did "feel itself at home"; a person's spirit, to use the Hegelian term, was *"zu Hause* sein." There was not yet any trace of the concept of a person being in exile, a pilgrim fleeing from one land to another, forever homeless, a stranger at home.

With the passing of the Hellenistic age, the idea of the peaceful coexistence of persons with the *polis* and everything around was lost forever. As the relationship with the cosmic whole became the overriding concern, the *ekumene* took the place of the now vanished city-states. A person was no longer a citizen of a specific homeland, such as Athens: the concept of one's own land was already beginning to disappear.

At the same time, another spiritual movement helped to hasten the end of the identification of the individual with the *polis* and the idea of "feeling oneself at home": the rise and spread of Christianity. Beyond doubt, this new faith introduced the concept of a perfect reconciliation between the individual and the universal: the figure of Christ gives expression to this reconciliation. Hegel among other philosophers recognized this reconciliation. Yet it was Christianity that began to make people feel as pilgrims. There was no earthly homeland for any person. The true goal of human life is to reach in the most righteous manner possible, one's heavenly home. For this reason, that humankind should "feel itself at home," at peace with this world, became unimportant.

It was not until the nineteenth century, in Hegel's philosophical system, that the stages by which the absolute spirit, *der Geist*, could return "home," or better, "into itself," were identified. According to Hegel, consciousness continues to ignore its nature as self-consciousness by believing that its essence lies in identifying itself with the other which is absolutely transcendent, universal, and intransmutable. By contrast, consciousness is the essential or transmutable. False identification results in separation and contradictions which inevitably leads to sustained doubt and desperation. Yet the process by which the spirit takes upon itself this movement, sorting through the oppositions and writing them, is at the same time the process which enables the spirit to reach full consciousness of itself and finds the way to salvation. This salvation however, is no longer the redemption of the opposition between humanity and God but a spiritual one which saves humanity from separation and scission.

C. Hegel's Perspective

The description that Hegel gives of the "unfortunate to-be-aware" in *Phenomenology of Spirit* is too well known to do more than recall one or two general considerations. Following their scission, the individual consciousness and the other are separated by an abyss, but precisely at this point the path toward reunification can be undertaken, because both the inessential and the essential are part of consciousness, which tends to rejoin unity and nonunity. In the progress toward this reunification, the movement must necessarily be reciprocal. The universal must make itself the single universal, as is the case in Christianity. Yet while in Christianity the intransmutable or universal does take on the form of singularity, this dissolves again at once, for the historical figure of Christ rose again immediately from the dead. Accordingly, there has been no true reunification, between consciousness and "other"; for the movement was unilateral, and the scission comes to loom much larger. The Old Testament person had no knowledge of the intransmutable, while the Christian has known it and feels the burden of the scission more acutely. Consciousness sets out once more on its appointed path, but now the single consciousness has to move toward the intransmutable, the universal, whereas previously the reverse had been the case.

This is not the place to dwell on the successive stages of consciousness from pure consciousness through single essence to the self-consciousness that attains reason. I should, however, point out that consciousness has to struggle against the corporeal, the material, and the tangible. Consciousness discovers that its enemy is matter and that the flesh is, in many respects, invincible. For this reason, consciousness leaves to the Church to look after the remission of sins, and pursues its path toward the Absolute. In practice, consciousness discovers the impossibility of reuniting itself with its other, which remains something outside it. The subsequent developments of the phenomenological process of consciousness, the stages of the experience which it acquires of itself through self-consciousness, are familiar enough. I note that, at the end of its long journey, natural consciousness succeeds in elevating itself to speculative knowledge. The history of the movement of consciousness which attains self-knowledge as self-consciousness and thus as absolute spirit is a history of salvation and redemption. I am not speaking of the "immanent" dimension of Hegel's perspective or its relationship with the Christian faith. I simply wish to call attention to the movement within the system, a movement which "saves" and "redeems," by means of which the absolute spirit reaches or returns to itself, finding itself once again "at home." We have come a long way from the condition of alienation and estrangement, from being homeless and "not feeling oneself at home," as the epochal dimension of contemporary humankind.

Apart from the Hegelian perspective, has contemporary thought ever really found an answer to the question of what gives rise to human "alienation"? "Alienation" is used not only in the sense of loss of possession, whether of oneself or of the most intimate components of one's character as a free subject and member of a community, with the right to a homeland, or an abode. It is used also in Heidegger's sense of the radical homelessness of humankind as opposed to the tranquilizing banality of "commerce" with the entities of this world. Is it true to say, with Ludwig Feuerbach, that alienation is the illusion with which the individual, in creating for oneself a perfect divinity and submitting oneself to it, believes it possible to resolve the conflicts and limits of one's own finite condition? Or, with Karl Marx, that alienation is the process that takes place in the context of the capitalistic relations of production, by which a person becomes estranged from oneself to such an extent that one no longer recognizes oneself? Or again, following Herbert Marcuse, that alienation is the characteristic trait of the individual and one "dimensional" society the condition in which the critical force of reason is silenced by the force of the technological structure of society?

6. Concluding Remarks

No doubt, the equivocal and problematic nature of the term "alienation" emerges even in the reasoning of the existentialist philosopher whom we have already touched on, Jean-Paul Sartre. According to Sartre's *Critique of Dialectical Reason*, alienation, which is the counterpart of intersubjective conflict, derives from the impossibility of eliminating *rareté* (lack), or that which make a person indigent. But *rareté* is not only the product of a contingent historic-political situation, of need brought on by external necessities. It is fundamental to the identity of human nature itself, an inevitable feature which may be abstracted from the socio-economic relations:

> In reciprocity modified by rarity, the same person appears to us as his double in that he appears as radically Other (that is, as one who for us brings the threat of death). . . . Nothing, in fact—neither giant beasts nor microbes—can be more terrible for man than an intelligent, cruel, predatory species able to rival and get the better of human intelligence and whose goal would be precisely the destruction of mankind. This species

is obviously our own . . . which, whatever the society, is the abstract, fundamental matrix for all the reifications of human relations.[15]

Thus, the existential "checkmate" appears inevitable: the individual, however much one strives to present oneself as a "project" or as an "openness to the other," invariably ends up by instituting a conflicting, alienating relationship of intersubjectivity.

The Sartrean concept of *rareté* as the root cause of human alienation may be aporetic and problematic. No one would maintain that it is sufficient to do away with the society that generates destitution in order to eliminate humanity's tendency to destroy otherness. Yet this concept can serve as a useful pointer or instrument to help decipher and interpret some of the obvious manifestations of alienation which condition a large part of our present civilization. Without being afraid of slipping from the "existential" to the "substantial" plane, I have in mind, the masses of dispossessed or homeless who because of war or poverty have lost their houses, their homeland, and indeed their identity. The population of what was Yugoslavia or the refugees from Albania are among the most pressing examples, but it would not be difficult to list more.

It is legitimate to ask: what answer can we give to these peoples, to the countless individuals who claim recognition for a fundamental right to a home, as well as to a homeland? An answer does not come easily; perhaps it is not purely a philosophical question. Instead, it is an essentially political question, which needs to be dealt with in the appropriate institutions. We may try to offer some suggestions from a philosophical standpoint, in the hope that such secondary considerations may eventually clarify a definitive practical solution.

Alienation and dispersion are characteristic human experiences in contemporary society. As persons struggle to resolve intersubjective conflicts, the constancy of homelessness becomes poignantly felt as both personal and generally as the human condition. The general sense of existential homelessness affects the world's population, but it is felt, lived, through the individual's necessity to "feel at home." Such a project would inevitably include a delicate theoretical component.

We would do well to bear in mind the important considerations on this topic to be found in the works of Hannah Arendt, from *The Origins of Totalitarianism* to *The Human Condition* and *The Life of the Mind*, which promote her conviction that we have to overturn the modern concept of politics as the administration and management of society and the governing of the many by the few. Although the principle of democracy has been distorted in modern times, we should reaffirm that the domain of politics is that public domain in which people relate to each other on the basis of reciprocity and political equality, in spite of their social differences (*isonomia*), as was the case in the Greek *polis*.

It is evident that, in order to lay the foundations for the idea of direct democracy, the cultural sphere will have to play its part. There will have to be more dialogue between the peoples of different cultures. The process of emancipation must begin with nations which have suffered under the colonial yoke or were exploited by other nations. Nothing is banal in asserting that a worldwide cultural renaissance will favor the disappearance of those economic, political, and social inequalities which continually produce large numbers of destitute, homeless, and stateless people. It may appear utopian to believe in a cultural reawakening which can benefit politics, but in this case the term "utopia" is adopted in the sense of the pursuit of a future reality, with the hope of modifying the present in the image of an *eschaton* or ultimate goal. It will, however, be necessary to dedicate more attention to such stimulating prospects.

Glossary of Terminology Used

abstract self-projection	*freischwebendes Sichentwerfen*
Being-as-history	*Seinsgeschichte*
being at home	*zu Hause sein*
commerce	*Umgang*
home	*Heimat*
homecoming	*Heimkunft*
homelessness	*Heimatlosigkeit*
lighting-process	*Lichtung*
living experiences	*Erlebnisse*
nearness	*Nähe*
Non-being	*Nichts*
not true abode	*Unheimlichkeit*
ontological disposition	*Befindlichkeit*
people's self	*Man-selbst*
power-to-be	*Seinkonnen*
projection	*Entwurf*
state of expatriation	*Unheimlichkeit*
There-being	*Dasein*
To-be-aware	*Bewusstsein*
thrown-ness	*Geworfenheit*
with-being	*Mitsein*
world-vision	*Weltanschauung*

Notes

1. Rainer Maria Rilke, *Duino Elegies*, Elegy 1, vol. 69 (Frankfurt M.: Suhrkamp Verlag, 1975), p. 11.

2. See Friedrich Nietzsche, *The Gay Science* in Nietzsche's *Complete Critical Works*, ed. I. Berlin (New York: W. de Gruyter, 1973), Aphorism 125, Book 3.

3. See Martin Heidegger, *Being and Time* (Tübingen: Niemeyer, 1957), par. 57, p. 276. The translation of this and subsequent passages is mine.

4. *Ibid.*, p. 277.

5. See Martin Heidegger's *Letters on Humanism* (Frankfurt: Frank Klostermann, 1947), p. 25.

6. See Giuseppe Ungaretti, *Girovago in Vita d'un uomo. Tutte le poesie*, ed. L. Piccioni (Oscar Grandi Classici) (Milano: Mondadori Editore, 1992), p. 85.

7. Jean-Paul Sartre, *Being and Nothingness* (Paris: Gallimard, 1953), part 2, ch. 2, par. 3, p. 200. The translation of this and subsequent passages is mine.

8. *Ibid.*, part 3, ch. 1, par. 4, p. 310.

9. *Ibid.*, part 3, ch. 3, par. 2, pp. 481-482.

10. *Ibid.*

11. *Ibid.*

12. Eberhard Nestle's *Eleutheria: Studies on the Essence of Truth in Greeks and the New Testament* (Tübingen: Niemeyer, 1967), p. 135.

13. See Jean-Paul Sartre, *Critique de la Raison Dialectique* (Paris: Gallimard, 1960), p. 208.

14. Plutarch, "On Tranquility of Mind" in *Moralia*, vol. 6, trans. W. C. Helmbold, William Heinemann (Cambridge, Mass.: Harvard University Press, 1975) p. 11.

15. *Cf.* Sartre, *Critique de la Raison Dialectique*, p. 208.

Five

THE RIGHTS OF THE HOMELESS:
AN EXAMINATION OF
THE PHENOMENOLOGY OF PLACE

Patricia Anne Murphy

"Poverty is the worst form of violence."
—Mahatma Gandhi

1. Rights and Homelessness

The fact of homelessness presents a variety of opportunities for reflection. Questions of personal identity vacillate between issues of ontology and existential experience. Questions of morality are hardly separable from ontological questions, for the welfare and continued existence of persons *as* persons frequently serves as the foundation of moral inquiry. If there are rights, either legal or moral in character, which are attributed to persons, then the protection and guarantee of those rights is a moral obligation. This association to themes of just desserts entails the concept of justice, which ultimately leads to a moral ground.

A frequent argument posed in light of this landscape of rights finds the United States in a responsible position. The poor or near poor have a strong claim upon the rest of society simply because of the overall wealth of our nation. It is deplorable that some people in this country have little or no basic level of need fulfillment, considering this country's ability to satisfy those needs. To make our case, let us extend a famous argument put forward by Peter Singer[1]: If it is in our power to save someone's life with little cost to our own lives, then we are morally obligated to do so, and not to do so is morally reprehensible.

But saving someone's life is a clear and dramatic case. Protecting persons from harm, assuring their rights and privileges, providing necessary resources are less dramatic and less clearly understood obligations. Other arguments swarm around these issues. They either allude to participatory justice or to the fact that harms (both great and small) compose much of the inevitable fabric of human experience. Yet other arguments refer to incomplete images of the homeless themselves. These abbreviated visions often seize upon some trait or other of the homeless which might serve as a pre-emptive strike used to absolve the affluent of any responsibility to come to their aid. To this end, it is sometimes alleged that the homeless are: mentally ill, desirous of being homeless, of poor character, ex-convicts, substance abusers, irresponsible, lazy, opportunistic, and so forth. If I follow these arguments correctly, they purport to be portraying the homeless as somehow not deserving protection of their rights because of what they have done or who they are.

I do not take these "pre-emptive strike" arguments to be moral arguments, though they may often masquerade as such. They may be pragmatic arguments, and they may be argued further from a vantage point of utility. The presuppositions that enable these sorts of arguments, and indeed their reliance upon a social utility perspective betray a lack of true consideration of their subjects. The homeless are set apart from the rest of society, and therefore constitute some special disenfranchised subset of real society. The social utility—in the form of economic concerns, safety, or even aesthetics—that often encourages these sorts of arguments become question begging. It is the economic comfort of those who are not homeless that may be threatened. It is the middle-class neighborhoods which may be called upon to integrate persons they do not like to see into their boundaries. It is the working classes who do not want to learn that their good fortune is won at the expense of those who have in many instances lost their voices, and who are in too many ways similar to themselves. In each instance, these arguments suffer all too often from the question that should plague any utilitarian project: whose goods and benefits ought to be secured? By carefully circumscribing the recipients of the goods and services to be protected, pragmatic and utilitarian arguments can completely ignore basic ontological and ethical issues. As a result, they ascribe a sort of instrumentality to one sector of individuals, though this is done tacitly and rarely acknowledged.

But it is questions of ontology and values of personhood that in fact inform true morality. It is insufficient to say that arguments which are reducible to matters of pragmatism or social utility succeed as *moral* arguments, for they presuppose a diminished status of personhood which is the unspoken premise enabling their spurious conclusions. Once this is revealed, the inaccuracy of these arguments stands out less than their irrelevance. The majority of studies conducted on these questions find the terms "mentally ill" or "substance abuser" apply to approximately one third of the total homeless population. While we often suppose that personality disorders or various mental problems such as addictions precede homelessness, there is some recent research[2] that suggests that homelessness may aid and increase these behaviors and conditions which suggest diminished personhood.

We should encourage the continued linking of the issues of personhood and rights. But there are some clear indications that some of the permutations already suggested do not bear fruit in terms of moral reflection on the situation of homelessness. Yet I have been finding some interesting features of personhood as central and essential in considering foundational questions of rights pertaining to the homeless. The premier right is to personhood. If there are impediments to this right, then all other rights, legal or moral, cannot find their proper mark. I accept as basic assumptions in this discussion that diminished personhood is a harm which can be avoided, and that this harm constitutes a need for healing and reparation in order for the homeless population to successfully accrue further rights and privileges. The loss or diminishment of personhood is not an ontological or inherently axiological diminishment, but an existential and psychological phenomenon[3] which must be acknowledged and understood fully if we are to meaningfully address the rights of this group. We have found that proper human development requires experienced distinctions between personal space and personal place. Deprivation of these experiences has detrimental psychological effects on both children and adults.

If personhood entails a place, then a right to place emerges as one of a new class of rights which I term existential rights. A consideration of how having a place interfaces with and is a partial requisite for personhood follows. This consideration increases an understanding of the experience of homelessness, and portrays the necessity for a re-education of both the homeless and society at large. I am urging an understanding of a constellation of rights of the homeless which forms a unique ground from which more frequently anticipated rights must arise.

2. Place and Space

To speak of place is to signify, initially, the particularization of space. Physical things, of which human beings are one example, occupy space and time. While space may be reducible to physical descriptions, the concept of "place" reveals an additional dimension of human interaction with a supposed objective reality which can neither be captured by nor reduced to mere space as location. A place is a space which is invested with human significance and understanding. While an object may occupy *space*, if it is out of *place*, it cannot be located by a seeker or used for any purpose whatsoever. Hence, placefulness signifies an expanded dimension of usefulness or meaning above and beyond physical descriptions of space. While a place surely is a space, it is not only a location. I may rest assured that an object, for instance, a tool, will occupy space, somewhere, and yet I may not be able to locate it or use it if I do not know its place. Unless some regularity or particularity pertains to its occupation of space, it ceases to be a tool at all, but merely an object. Indeed by locating or placing the tool, I envision a future to the tool and my coincidence with it. I imagine a vague and primitive future, in which I shall seek it out again because of its apparent value to me.

The fact that I envision a future for the tool, however vague, imposes a layer of meaning upon the tool as object which was not there before. In "making a place for it," I increase the vast expanse of my accumulation of objects, and the placement of the tool is lodged into my memory. My universe has increased its population. Additionally, the act of placing it has enhanced the object as tool. Perhaps it was merely a rock, which I employed as a hammer. It worked so well for that purpose that I shall place it where I can get to it when I need to hammer something again. By this use, the value and identity of the rock is expanded. I confer additional ontological recognition through the vehicle of expanded existential dimension, creating a place for the object.

In the inter-human context, we create places at table, or in line, or on elevators for a variety of reasons. We expect people to eat with us, or we envision their future as including the activity of eating dinner. We may anticipate their arrival and hence already envision them as "in principle" here. It is only their physical existence which has not caught up to our expectation of them. In an elevator, there may be sufficient actual space for yet one more person to enter, and yet collecting that space together in the form of a place for him or her may take some additional shifting. We signify the value of the person to be a worthy recipient of that shared space. We particularize the anonymous and dispersed space for him or her and it becomes a place ready for his or her presence.

As a figure is partially defined by a ground, a thing or person is, in part, integrally bound to a situation. Place as particularization of space presents one dimension of the human situation. The homeless are lacking this important dimension of their situation. They lack an enduring place that is spatially defined. Other dimensions of the human situation are tied to and related to the spatial definition of place. The historical aspect of existence, in the guise of memory or anticipation of future events; the temporal aspects which are again unavoidably connected to memory and structure of discrete actions, personal psychology and systems of meaning; and the wider social integration of the human experience, each depend to some degree upon an initial place as enduring location, minimally defined in terms of space. In our reflections and conversations, we refer constantly to specific or general places. These places signify various degrees of meaning of our experience and are used as references so chronically that a normal human experience cannot be portrayed without appeal to them. Consider only a few examples:

"*This room* was filled with family and friends at Christmas."
"Uncle Mike sat *over there*."
"Father and I painted *this wall* together."
"The notches on *this door jamb* record Eve's growth this year."
"Each day she would sit by *this window* and watch the blossoms of the quince unfold."

A simultaneity of definition, both person and place, forges the meaning of lives: continuity, memories, personal identity, and reference to self and other within the context of location.

3. Place and Identity

The notion of place is indispensable in the enhancement of identity of both things and persons.

"He *placed* the basket of flowers on the table."
"We selected a *place* to plant the redbud tree."
"We will all gather over at John's *place*."
"Will you save me a *place* in line?"
"Is there a *place* for me to write?"

These various though common uses of reference to *place* or the act of *placing* reveal an understanding of rectitude and order to things. A sense of belonging or inclusion is conveyed by envisioning a place in line. By virtue of "placing" the flowers in a certain area, we present them for purposeful public viewing: they are intended for display, and hence are transformed from disparate bits of the landscape into a focus of attention. "A place to write" reveals the intentionality of the writer for meaningful activity.

Human activity and intentional life depend upon the constant envisioning and allocation of places where things are expected to occur or things are "set apart" as objects of attention. These references are interesting as they range from quite small and localized—"There is a place on the top shelf where that teacup goes"—to vast, geographically abstract and ambiguous—"This is the place that I was born and raised." Indeed it is only by reference to the concept of place that large amounts of our communications can succeed. Shared social meaning and existence require shared reference to specific locations as place.

Yet another unique feature of place or placelessness considered for analysis of human value must be mentioned. In one sense, each individual is an instance of a "portable" place. The possibility of returning to the storehouse of memories, opinions, beliefs, values, desires that endure constitutes a metaphysical place which is the only opportunity for the indexing of any possible physical space as place.[4] The person is, ideally, a place in relationship to other places.

Yet a partial or radical depersonalization breaks up the primordial place that makes up the person, taking with it the foundation for the proper relationship between itself and secondary places in the form of both, other persons as they are primordial places, and places as specific locations. The fulfillment of personhood is deeply hampered and damaged; self-image, and experience of others, is violated.

It is no wonder then, that to be without a place is to be, at least experientially, diminished in personhood.[5] Placelessness forces upon its victims a linguistic and psychological disenfranchisement. This diminishment bleeds into the social and psychological fabric of life. The co-constitutional quality of persons and the complex social construction of life are diminished if there is no place or enduring specific location which is an opportunity for the accumulation of values and memories.

Because persons are extended into space, the absence of place as enhanced continuous location is a breach in the completeness that is experienced personally as deep structure loss and socially as truncated existence. Places enable values and possessions to expand and enrich the definition and experience of identity. Places are locations where personhood can happen and flourish. Lacking a place jeopardizes the development of systems of meaning that are central for the identity of persons.

Without a place of our own the extended space and systems of value that each person is cannot happen. The dialectical relationship between physical space transformed as place and the interior psychological counterpart of a discrete and enduring image of self cannot be separated.[6] In much the same way that I earlier gave a place to the rock used as hammer, persons need the allocation of places because the endowment of place reflects value. When something is not in its place or has no enduring or particular place, we often refer to it as lost. We may conclude that place is undervalued or misplaced because forgotten. There is benefit in locating it (possibly for a first time, such as the rock that I found useful as a tool). Or, the benefit may lie in re-establishing its known location just in the case that we assign to it continuing value and hence wish to avail ourselves of it again. The spice we seek in the kitchen cupboard is unavailable and not useful to us if it is not in its place. It has a usual place because we acknowledge its usefulness and value, and thus desire to be able to locate it and use it as a flavoring when appropriate. It cannot fulfill its role as a spice if it is lost or misplaced. Similarly, people often have an essential need for place for the purposeful fulfillment of what they are as individuals. Yet the homeless and other populations suffer from a deficit in regard to place. They are existentially diminished in a crucial way.

4. No Place, No Freedom

Besides this initial level of existential harm or diminishment of the individual, there is another tier of harm which results by virtue of the social construction of reality. When we are feeling "out of place," we are uncomfortable. We do not sense an identification with the larger group. We are inhibited and limited in our freedom to be who we are most fully. We may, for instance, experience this as gratefulness that when the evening is over we can leave a particular function and get back to our own place where we belong. In these instances, the dialectic of distancing ourselves from others, and the distancing of our self from the unarticulated self, fosters and perpetuates increased social dissonance. In order to be part of the whole, we must first have a clarity of self-definition. Yet, this is precisely what the initial stage of placelessness precludes. No wonder then, that further social integration is often not accomplished. We necessarily envision in the other self the vague boundaries of the self occasioned by the absence of place. From a vantage point lacking clarity, no view is clear. Exclusivity, alienation, and fractious social structure are encouraged.

The provisions of basic rights of food and shelter reveal an acknowledgment of the value of persons at a rudimentary level. Only by virtue of understanding the precluded expectations of the homeless and the precluded felt obligations of wider society for these minimal rights can we hope to break the ever deepening cycle of existential and psychological violence which too often manifests itself in verbal and physical violence. An important part of the calculus of the complexities of homelessness is below the empirical and the pragmatic levels. An increased understanding of the structure and meaning of personhood, the sense of diminishment and oppression, the disenfranchisement that attends the experience of homelessness as "being without a place" may initiate a new approach to the attainment of rights.

Notes

1. Peter Singer, "Famine, Affluence, and Morality," *Philosophy and Public Affairs*, 1:3 (Spring 1972).

2. Lisa Goodman, Leonard Saxe, and Mary Harvey, "Homelessness as Psychological Trauma," *American Psychologist* (November 1991), pp. 1219-1225.

3. Leanne G. Rivlin, "The Significance of Home and Homelessness," *Marriage and Family Review*, 15 (1990), pp. 39-56.

4. Joseph C. Flay, "Place and Places," in *Commonplaces*, eds. David W. Black, Donald Kunze, and John Pickles (Lanham, Md.: University Press of America, 1989).

5. David A. Snow and Leon Anderson, "Identity Work Among the Homeless: The Verbal Construction of Avowels of Personal Identity," *American Journal of Sociology*, 92 (May 1987), pp. 1336-1371.

6. Frederic A. DiBlasio and John R. Belcher, "Social Work Outreach to Homeless People and the Need to Address Issues of Self Esteem," *Health and Social Work*, 18 (November 1993), pp. 281-287.

Six

HOME IS WHERE THE HEART IS: HOMELESSNESS AND THE DENIAL OF MORAL PERSONALITY

David E. Schrader

1. Introduction

For all those of us who have homes, our homes provide a place of sanctuary from the rest of the world. We have the authority to require others to leave our homes. Similarly—with the exception of special circumstances in which governmental authorities are able, for good reason, to secure search warrants— no persons outside our immediate families are entitled to enter our homes without our permission. Our homes, in short, constitute for each of us a unique domain of personal autonomy. At the same time, personal autonomy character- izes both moral personality and civic personality. At the civic level, autonomy makes a person a citizen, a full part of civil society, entitled to rights which that civil society is required to recognize. At the moral level, autonomy marks the citizen as a full-fledged part of the moral community, a being entitled to full moral dignity and full moral responsibility.

If these musings on homes and moral and civic personality are more or less correct, at least in the sense that they reflect a role that homes have played within the broad American social tradition, then the plight of the homeless ought to concern us in a unique way. If our homes are our central bastions of autonomy, then to lack a home is to lack the recognized kind and level of autonomy that a home is uniquely able to provide. Likewise, if autonomy defines both civic and moral autonomy, then anyone without a home also lacks the place in civil society that civic autonomy establishes and recognizes through our possession of a home. Therefore, to be without a home is to lack one of the central features of our society, public recognition of moral personality. In sum, the homeless are the chief non-persons of contemporary American society.

In this chapter I support the two connections I have suggested above, the connection between homes and autonomy and the connection between autonomy and civic and moral personality. The first section of this chapter will take a brief look at Aristotle and the English common law tradition, focusing on the roles they have attributed to the home and its place in society. The point of this section will be to show part of a long history of regarding the home as a bastion of autonomy wherein the holder of the home holds a kind of sovereignty against all comers, the state included. The second section will look at the role of the home in the United States Constitution as the chief locus of both privacy and autonomy, again a place wherein the holder of the home holds important immunities against the power of the rest of society. The third and fourth sections will draw the connection between this notion of autonomy and the public affirmations of civic personality and moral personality, respectively.

2. The Home in the History of Western Social Thought

Homes are places where people live. In the United States people inhabit different kinds of places, from the ranches of thousands of acres in the western plains to apartments in high-rise complexes in major urban centers, some of which include several hundred apartments to a single building. In earlier times, people lived in less dense concentration. Yet few Americans trace their heritages back to social traditions whose recent history has been nomadic. Instead, for must of us, and similarly for the dominant social ideology under which we live, homes have involved the sharing of a common and stationary place. In general, therefore, we may trace the American social ideology of the home in historical understandings of households and of real (immovable) property.

In this section I will focus on Aristotle and the English common law in order to illustrate my contention that the home has long been seen as a central locus of autonomy. For Aristotle, the household or family is the most basic unit of society. "[T]he state," he observes, "is made up of households."[1] Aristotle characterizes the family as follows: "[t]he family is the association established by nature for the supply of men's everyday wants, and the members of it are called by Charondas 'companions of the cupboard,' and by Epimenides the Cretan, 'companions of the manger.'"[2] As the references to Charondas and Epimenides show, Aristotle thinks of the family or household as those who share a "cupboard" or "manger," those who share a home. Aristotle, of course, writes in a clearly paternalistic age. He conceives of a family or household as consisting of a male together with his wife, children, slaves, and livestock. What is more essential, for my present purposes, than the particular constitution of the family or household unit, however, is that the family or household is the minimal economically viable social unit, "established . . . for the supply of men's everyday wants."[3] It is, of course, well known that Aristotle does not regard the life of a solitary individual as viable. The person who "is sufficient for himself, must be either a beast or a god."[4] We bind ourselves together into social units. The ongoing viability of society depends on social units capable of producing children. There must, then, be some minimal social unit capable of sustaining its members, some of whom are children. This minimal unit consists of people gathered around a common table, "manger," or "cupboard," comprising a household. This common table is the home.

"Property is a part of the household," says Aristotle in his *Politics*.[5] Yet only those forms of property that pertain to the maintenance of the household are natural and appropriate to the management of the household.[6] The household also has its own governance structure, which serves to manage the property of the household for the benefit of its members. The household, then, is something of a polity within a polity, or a sovereignty within a sovereignty. Given this, the home and its management lie at the heart of the household or family.

While the family exists "for the supply of men's everyday wants," the satisfaction of everyday wants is not sufficient for a genuinely satisfying human life. Our social nature impels us to form the more comprehensive association of the state to enable humans to achieve their most comprehensive level of fulfillment. Aristotle's state is essentially federal in origin. A number of households unite to form a village, while several villages unite to form a state.[7] The household, or home, we might say, is the fundamental social community within the larger and more comprehensive social community of the state. As such, the household or home is a place wherein the social good of humanity may in part be achieved.

Yet the household is more than just another social community for Aristotle. As Judith Swanson notes:

> It serves as a portal into the private. He places it at the beginning of the *Politics* both because it signals the importance of the private and because human beings first experience the private in the household. Indeed, Aristotle hints that only by experiencing household life may one progress to the many other forms of private activity that constitute part of the good life (*Nicomachean Ethics* 1142a9-10).[8]

As both a first level of human social "association" and as "a portal [from the public] into the private," the home thus becomes a first-level locus of human autonomy.

Moving forward two millennia, in the classic *Commentaries on the Laws of England*, Sir William Blackstone (1723-1780) notes that English property law exhibits a significant historical division. English law is divided into two parts: the common law that is derived from long-standing custom and from the record of decisions of the courts, and the statutory law that consists of the enactments of Parliament. Most of the law concerning personal (movable) property is the product of statutory law. By contrast, as Frederick Whelan explains:

> Most of the law pertaining to real property (of which land [and I might add, homes] is the most important example) is common law, simply because the great body of rules and precedents respecting this kind of property survives from the period before Parliament claimed the preroga-

tives of a sovereign legislature and has not been overridden by parliamentary action. The common laws "receive their binding power, and the force of laws, by long and immemorial usage, and by their universal reception throughout the kingdom" (Comm. I, 64).[9]

The laws of real property include the protection of the home wherein the law establishes "that sole and despotic dominion which one man claims and exercises over the external things of the world, in total exclusion of the right of any other individual in the universe."[10] Those laws, being in general a part of the common law of England, are established, as Blackstone notes, "by long and immemorial usage." They express a set of values that go back deep within a legal and social tradition.

The development of the law of real property within the English common law tradition constituted the development of a recognition of autonomy against the authority of society. As Kenneth Minogue observes:

> An Oriental despot was defined as the owner, not only of the land, but of all the subjects within his realm. . . . The subject of such a total, arbitrary and capricious power was helpless against his ruler and, having no secure property rights himself, was in effect the property of his ruler . . . in earlier times [from ancient Greece up to the rise of modern liberalism] the conception of the state was implicitly federal, an association of people each of whom exercised a degree of independent power; the basis of that independent power might well be seen as primarily residing in the right of property.[11]

Minogue goes on to note that the modern conception of the state has changed substantially and that "*[e]very* subject is now a citizen and is thus a member of a different *sort* of association from the civil societies of earlier times" (Minogue's emphases).[12] However, the "degree of independent power" that in an earlier time may have had its basis in property (which, of course, primarily meant real property) has even in the modern state retained the home as its center.

The English common law concerning real property has developed over a period of eight hundred years. That development has moved gradually, but inexorably, in the direction of recognizing for each person a locus of authority and autonomy in the place where he or she lives. As Charles Donahue, Jr., writes, "The mechanism by which a notion of property emerged at the end of the twelfth century . . . ended up with the free tenant as the owner of the land, in a quite modern sense, with the lord's rights limited to receipt of money payments."[13] In the sixteenth century, the copyholder—the one who lived on the property but did not hold free title to it—received most of the rights over real property that had earlier been given to the freeholder.[14] In this course of development we see a situation in which rights associated with real property establish a realm of protection around the holder of the property. The privileges and protections associated with those rights become progressively extended in the history of common law, first to the freeholders or free tenants of the twelfth and thirteenth centuries, and later to the copyholders. It is a line of development moving steadily toward recognition of a strong set of privileges and immunities held by all people in the places where they live.

While it may be true, as Minogue notes, that the modern state regards every subject as a citizen in the sense of being a participant in the political power of the state, it is far less clear that the modern state affords every subject a realm of autonomy wherein that citizen is a power to him or herself. Participation in the power of the state is very different from the possession of a realm of autonomous power. Without meaning in any sense to denigrate the importance of that participation, there is a big difference between being subject to a group of which one is a part and having a realm wherein one is subject to no one. Simple citizenship may establish political participation. It cannot, however, establish autonomy.

I hope to have shown in this section that the household constitutes a realm of autonomy in Aristotle's social thought. I hope to have established that the development of rights to real property in the English common law constitutes an important move in the direction of recognizing such a realm of autonomy for English people in the places where they lived.

3. The Home in the United States Constitution

In this third section I argue that the United States Constitution represents another step in recognizing the home as a locus of personal autonomy. The Constitution does give us a modern state, recognizing all subjects (initially at least all white male subjects) as citizens. Yet the home still attains recognition in the Constitution as a unique realm of personal authority and autonomy. That recognition comes explicitly in the Bill of Rights.

> *Amendment 3*: No soldier shall, in time of peace, be quartered in any house, without the consent of the owner, nor in time of war, but in a manner to be prescribed by law.

> *Amendment 4*: The right of people to be secure in their persons, houses, papers, and effects, against unreasonable searches and seizures, shall not be violated, and no warrants shall issue but upon probable cause, supported by oath or affirmation, and particularly describing the place to be searched, and the persons or things to be seized.

The Third and Fourth Amendments to the United States Constitution provide explicitly for security in our homes. The Fourth Amendment also speaks of our persons, papers, and effects. Both of these Amendments have been taken by the courts to provide a part of the basis for asserting a constitutionally protected right to privacy. There has been controversy over whether we have such a constitutionally protected right to privacy. One of the chief points of contention in the Senate hearings several years back over the Supreme Court nomination of Judge Robert Bork lay in Judge Bork's contention that the Constitution provides Americans with no right to privacy.

The Supreme Court decision that first spoke of a "right to privacy" was *Griswold v. Connecticut.* That case concerned the constitutionality of a Connecticut law that proscribed the use of birth control, even by married couples. The contention of the court was that the issue of whether a married couple might practice birth control lies within a constitutionally protected realm of privacy and that the state had no legitimate interest in intervening on that issue. My guess is that almost all of us would agree with the last part of that claim, that the state has no legitimate interest in intervening in the sexual practices of married adults. The point of controversy, however, lies in whether the Constitution does indeed recognize such a protected realm of privacy.

Justice Douglas's opinion in *Griswold* has been the subject of a great deal of debate, both political and scholarly. The central argument turns on the following claim: "[S]pecific guarantees in the Bill of Rights have penumbras, formed by emanations from those guarantees that help give them life and substance. Various guarantees create zones of privacy" (381 U.S. 474 at 484). Justice Douglas's language here invites controversy. Talk of "penumbras" and "emanations" sounds metaphysical in the worst sense of that term. Though the term "right to privacy" does not appear in the Constitution, the Court contended in *Griswold* that such a right is implicit in the First, Second, Third, Fourth, Fifth, and Ninth Amendments. Unfortunately, the language of Justice Douglas's opinion has done more to cloud the issues involved in that contention than it has done to clarify them. In addition to the fuzziness of talk of "penumbras" and "emanations," there is a crucial ambiguity in the reference of "those guarantees" in the passage cited above.

Judge Bork reads Douglas's opinion to claim that the "penumbras" are "formed by emanations from those guarantees" where "those guarantees" refer to the "specific guarantees in the Bill of Rights." That is a legitimate reading of the surface grammar of Justice Douglas's sentence. Judge Bork rightly concludes that such a claim could only lead to a general right to privacy by a rather odd and mystical jurisprudence.[15] An alternative reading, given by David Luban, among others, reads Douglas's opinion to claim that the "penumbras" are "formed by emanations from those guarantees" where "those guarantees" refers not back to the "specific guarantees in the Bill of Rights," but to "those [general] guarantees that help give them [the specific guarantees in the Bill of Rights] life and substance."[16] According to this reading there is nothing at all mystical or odd about Justice Douglas's reasoning. The Bill of Rights provides a set of "specific guarantees" that are based on a set of general guarantees giving citizens protection against potentially tyrannical government. Both Bork's reading and Luban's are possible readings of Justice Douglas's key sentence, although Luban's is more convincing since he sees Justice Douglas's words as giving a plausible jurisprudential argument.

It has been argued by Hyman Gross, among others, that the Court's decision in *Griswold* involves a confusion of privacy with autonomy.[17] Gross, W. A. Parent, and others regard privacy as concerned with knowledge, with "acquaintance with [one's] personal affairs"[18] or with possession of "undocumented personal knowledge."[19] *Griswold*, by contrast, is about the ability of citizens to control aspects of their own lives. The defining of moral and legal concepts is, I take it, a largely stipulative affair governed by practical considerations. What concepts do we find it valuable to identify? What conceptual distinctions do we find useful in the governing of our social lives? The distinction between privacy and autonomy that people like Gross and Parent wish to draw is a useful one. Undoubtedly the confusion of those concepts leads to difficulties as we attempt to face important social issues.

At the present time we hear a multitude of claims about the extent of a right to privacy. Does it include a right on the part of women to have abortions? Does it include a right on the part of those with deadly communicable diseases not to inform those with whom they come into contact about their diseased condition? On Gross's and Parent's definitions, the first of those issues is a question of autonomy. The second, by contrast, is a question of privacy. Fortunately, there is no need to resolve those very difficult issues for the purposes of this chapter. The concern of this chapter is with the home, and the Constitution recognizes the home as a locus of both privacy and autonomy. On Gross's and Parent's distinction, we may say that the Third Amendment protects an important element of autonomy in the home. The Fourth Amendment protects both elements of autonomy, in not permitting agents of the government to enter homes without the householder's permission, and of privacy, by restricting the government's access to information in the home.

The question of *whether* there is a constitutional right to privacy is a misplaced question. The real question is *to what extent* there is a right to privacy in the Constitution. Privacy and autonomy are not simple notions. They constitute a rather fluid set of boundaries between the self and a broader social world. Simply "to be secure in [our] persons, houses, papers, and effects" is one level of privacy. There is no question that we have a constitutionally protected right to at least that level of privacy. Beyond this obvious case, the Constitution is more suggestive than precise in what it has to say about where to draw the line between the sovereign realm of the individual or the sovereign realm of the family and the sovereign realm of the state.

Griswold also ought to show us another way in which privacy is more complicated than we might first have thought. While the issue of a couple's practicing birth control is, in all likelihood, none of the state's legitimate business, it is surely not a purely individual matter for either one of those who constitute the couple. It is instead the joint business of the couple. Likewise, the Third and Fourth Amendments do not simply assert individual rights, they assert rights of those who live in the home, in most cases a family, in some sense of that term. Recalling Swanson's interpretation of Aristotle, the home or household is "a portal [from the public] into the private." But the private cannot simply be identified with the individual. On this I will have more to say later.

What is surely beyond question, however, is that the Third and Fourth Amendments do assert some kind of realm of privacy, likewise a realm of authority and autonomy in the home. Gross may well be right that in *Griswold* the Supreme Court fell victim to a confusion of privacy with autonomy. Yet autonomy is the most centrally important issue for my present purposes. If the Court in *Griswold* should have spoken of autonomy instead of privacy, so much the better for my present case. The Constitution establishes each of us as a source of primary law in our homes. Our homes are stipulated to be places in which we and not the government have primary authority. The government cannot use our homes for the purpose of housing those whom it might need to house. The government cannot even have its agents enter our houses without our permission except under very special circumstances stipulated by special procedures.

What we see in the United States Constitution, then, is a reaffirmation of at least one important element in Aristotle's view of the household: the home is a private place that contains private activities.[20] In speaking of the home as a "private place," I do not mean to define the home as a place where we can protect information, but as a locus of private authority, of autonomy. This long-standing and venerable understanding of the home, affirmed by Aristotle and in the development of the English common law, is also affirmed as a central part of the social/political ideology expressed in the United States Constitution. In the modern state, all people are indeed citizens, participants in the process of shaping the voice of the public. Yet our modern state still recognizes that having a home, a place to go where one exercises a "sole and despotic dominion" creates a unique level of autonomy. The home provides a concrete buffer between the private world of the householders and the public world of society at large.

4. Autonomy and Civic Personality

What can it mean in the modern state to lack civic personality? As already noted, in the modern state "every subject is also a citizen." Yet we have in our own history one stark example of the absence of civic personality. That example was American slavery. The slave was not a subject of the state, but the property of his or her owner. The slave, accordingly, lacked civic personality.

The record of the slave's lack of civic personality is laid out in the decisions of American courts during the first six decades of the nineteenth century. Perhaps none of those decisions is as striking as that of Chief Justice Taney in *Dred Scott v. Sandford*. Courts commonly decide cases on the narrowest principle applicable to the facts of the case. In *Dred Scott*, however, Chief Justice Taney settles the case by affirming at the broadest level that Dred Scott, because of his African descent, lacked any of the rights granted by the Constitution to citizens of the American states: "The question then arises, whether the provisions of the Constitution, in relation to the personal rights and privileges to which the citizen of a state should be entitled, embraced the negro African race." He then answers the question by characterizing the modern history of the civic attitude that Europeans and their American descendants held toward those of African descent.

> They had for more than a century before been regarded as beings of an inferior order; and altogether unfit to associate with the white race, either in social or political relations; and so far inferior, that they had no rights which the white man was bound to respect; and that the negro might justly and lawfully be reduced to slavery for his benefit. He was bought and sold, and treated as an ordinary article of merchandise and traffic, whenever a profit could be made by it.

Chief Justice Taney goes on to note that "no distinction in this respect was made between the free negro or mulatto and the slave."

An even clearer statement of the lack of civic status of the American slave was given by Judge Thomas Ruffin in the North Carolina Supreme Court's decision in *State v. Mann*:

> The end [of slavery] is the profit of the master, his security and the public safety; the subject, one doomed in his own person, and his posterity, to live without knowledge, and without the capacity to make anything his own, and to toil that another may reap the fruits. What moral consideration shall be addressed to such a being, to convince him what, it is impossible but that the most stupid must feel and know can never be true—that be this to labour upon a principle of natural duty, or for the sake of his own personal

happiness. Such services can only be expected from one who has no will
of his own; who surrenders his will in implicit obedience is the consequence only of uncontrolled authority over the body. There is nothing else
which can operate to produce this effect. The power of the master must be
absolute, to render the submission of the slave perfect.

This rationale in *Mann* supported the Court's ruling that the intentional
wounding of a hired slave by the hirer could not constitute a crime. The courts
in these two cases (and there were countless more cases like them) held that the
slave was "the subject of . . . a total, arbitrary and capricious power."[21] As such,
the slave was totally lacking in autonomy, having absolutely no authority over
him or herself. Consequently, the slave was wholly lacking in even the most
basic rights of citizenship. The slave was a civic non-person.
    The homeless are not slaves. There is no other person who exercises "a
total, arbitrary and capricious power" over them. The homeless are not totally
lacking in autonomy. The homeless do, however, lack a place of autonomy. I,
therefore, maintain that the homeless exercise a restricted form of autonomy,
and that the autonomy of the homeless is limited precisely in the manner dictated
by their lack of homes.
    I have claimed above that in Aristotle, in the English common law, and in
the United States Constitution, the home is recognized as a place of autonomy.
The home is a place in which the resident is not subject to the arbitrary authority
of anyone outside the home. This autonomy is possessed not only by home
owners. Renters too have a substantial level of autonomy within the homes they
occupy.
    The homeless have no such place. There is no place that the homeless can
occupy without at least the tacit permission of someone else. When they occupy
private property they occupy the property of someone else. They occupy it not
by lease, but only by the arbitrary leave of whoever does have legal claim to the
property. The legal claimant can have the homeless removed quite arbitrarily.
When the homeless occupy public property they occupy property of whose
ownership they are a part. Yet the homeless are but a small part of the public.
When the homeless occupy public property they still do so only by the leave of
whoever has legal claim to the property. Since the public owns the property, the
homeless participate in that ownership. Yet, since the homeless represent but a
small and relatively powerless part of the public, they only occupy public
property by the leave of the larger and more powerful participants of the public.
We have witnessed numerous cases in which the larger and controlling
participants of the public have chosen to withdraw that leave.
    The fact that the homeless occupy their places by leave of the public is
surely not insignificant for their status as a part of the public. The homeless have
no locus of autonomy. The autonomy that they do have, therefore, is a uniquely

contingent kind. Citizenship involves a place in society, both figuratively and, in some ways, literally. We are registered to vote, for example, by our place of residence, by our homes. Even simple participation, the hallmark of the modern state, in that sense carries vestiges of the federal conception of the state of an earlier time. It was likewise a matter of some notoriety that the homeless were generally thought to be undercounted in the 1990 census. Again, it is through homes that society gains a sense of who its members are.

Because of this relationship between autonomy and civic personality, the homeless constitute a class of people of diminished civic personality in contemporary American society. The obvious annoyance that a large part of the American public experiences toward the homeless amply demonstrates the extent to which the homeless have been marginalized. They are citizens in a sense, yet their citizenship is abridged.

That the homeless experience this abridgement of citizenship creates a dilemma for the modern liberal democratic state. A hundred and fifty years ago the United States faced a dilemma of unparalleled proportions. The institution of American chattel slavery produced a conflict between the ideal of a nation that proclaimed itself dedicated to the preservation of liberty "to ourselves and our posterity" and the reality of a large group of persons legally regarded as the property of others, hence as non-persons. I do not want to suggest that the plight of the homeless is comparable to the plight of the slave. That would be a monstrous trivialization of the horrors of slavery. Yet I do want to affirm that the homeless pose a *dilemma* of a similar kind. The modern state embodies an ideology that proclaims the full citizenship of every adult subject of the body politic. Yet the homeless constitute a body of people in our society who are marginal members at best. In other words, the canonical understanding of civic personality that is a part of the modern conception of the state contradicts the reality of civic personality being rooted in a sense of autonomy that is most centrally manifested in having a place of autonomy, a home. This dilemma can be resolved only by either abandoning the ideology of the modern liberal state and accepting that the homeless are marginal members of the body politic or by retaining that ideology and finding some way of fully granting civic personality to the homeless.

5. Autonomy and Moral Personality

The final concern of this chapter is the connection between autonomy and moral personality. I said at the outset that "to be without a home is to lack one of the central features of our society, public recognition of moral personality." Again, it may be useful to start with the institution of American slavery to illustrate how the moral personality of a group of people can be denied. Note, for example, that Chief Justice Taney said in *Dred Scott* that those of African descent "had no rights which the white man was bound to respect." This was not merely a claim about legal rights. Instead, it was a claim to the effect that Europeans and their American descendants did not regard those of African descent as members of a common moral community. Chief Justice Taney went on to say that "the negro might justly and lawfully be reduced to slavery." The use of "justly" in addition to "lawfully" indicates a denial of moral as well as legal personality. Likewise, Judge Ruffin recognizes with striking clarity that the relationship between master and slave cannot be treated in moral terms. The master cannot acknowledge moral personality in the slave.

Autonomy has always borne an intimate connection with moral personality. While we most strongly associate the notion of autonomy with the ethical thought of Immanuel Kant, it is by no means exclusively associated with his ethical framework. In this section I look briefly at the centrality of autonomy to moral personality in Aristotle, Kant, and John Stuart Mill. In this manner, I show that autonomy is a central feature of moral personality regardless of the ethical-theoretical perspective one happens to take. This should support my conclusion that social arrangements that restrict autonomy also restrict moral personality.

Aristotle uses a different moral vocabulary from Kant's. The place of autonomy in Aristotle's moral thought becomes clear in Swanson's discussion of privacy in Aristotle's political thought.

> The word *idios*, "private" or "one's own," usually means in Aristotle's corpus simply what is not common, public, or relative to the regime. . . . Aristotle's conception of the private includes both the household and the meaning of *idios*, but it goes beyond both; for the private is constituted of activities that cultivate virtue and discount common opinion.
>
> It is not that Aristotle never characterizes places as private; rather, in his estimation what defines a site as private are the activities that ordinarily go on within it. If the activities promote virtue uncompromised by prevailing morality, then the place is private. Similarly, the number of persons involved in an activity does not in itself determine whether it is public or private. . . . Number of agents is a determining feature of private activity only if the quality of the activity suffers when more than a limited number participate.
>
> Because Aristotle maintains that virtuous activity may require agents to make choices and that actualizing virtue may even mean right choice making, he understands the private to include the opportunity and the resources needed to make virtuous choices, or privacy.[22]

In conceiving of the private as "constituted of activities that cultivate virtue and discount common opinion" and of "activities promot[ing] virtue uncompromised by prevailing morality," Aristotle adopts a notion of privacy that centers on the development of the self. People need to make their own decisions apart from the influence of popular opinion in order to develop themselves in the direction of personal and civic virtue. This involves the possibility of holding rule over themselves, autonomy. Swanson also notes that the development of virtue involves "the opportunity and the resources needed to make virtuous choices." The ability to make such choices constitutes autonomy. The opportunity and resources to make them require privacy.

As noted in the first section of this chapter, Aristotle views the household as "a portal into the private." Life apart from a household denies a person of one of the important sets of conditions required for the development of virtue. The lack of a home, therefore, robs a person of one of the prerequisites for the possession of a full moral personality. I want to emphasize again here a point I raised initially in speaking of the United States Constitution. Note that Aristotle also denies that privacy is a simple matter of individuality. He gives numbers significance only to the extent that they affect the outcome of choice making. When the person loses control over his or her activity to the group, privacy is lost. Obviously that loss of control becomes a larger risk in a sizeable group. Yet it is still the control of the activity, autonomy, that is the crucial factor in enabling activity promoting virtue. Autonomy, for Aristotle, is a necessary condition in the full development of moral personality.

The importance of autonomy to moral personality in Mill's moral vision is much more direct. In *On Liberty*, Mill writes, "He who lets the world, or his own portion of it, choose his plan of life for him has no need of any other faculty than the ape-like one of imitation. He who chooses his plan for himself employs all his faculties."[23]

It is only in the exercise of choice, in making determinations for oneself, that the human being develops and exercises his or her full humanity. Mill's emphasis on the importance of liberty for the development of full moral personality is so well known that it should require no significant documentation or discussion. To be a fully developed human being is to exercise the capacity for choice. People who lack some of the conditions for self-determination or important elements of autonomy will inevitably be limited in their ability to achieve full moral humanity.

For Kant, "*Autonomy* is ... the ground of the dignity of human nature and of every rational nature."[24] Kant views autonomy as "the Idea *of the will of every rational being as a will which makes universal law*."[25] Here too it follows that people who lack some of the conditions in which they can function as law-giver also lack some of the conditions of moral personality. The home, then, as a locus of autonomy, is a condition necessary to one's full development as a member of the moral community. This idea is further borne out in Kant's discussion of property in *The Metaphysical Elements of Justice*.[26]

The conclusions of this last section are difficult. Aristotle, Kant, and Mill all regarded autonomy as an essential condition for full moral personality. Commonsense morality equally holds that autonomy is an essential condition for full moral personality. Does that force a conclusion that the homeless are defective in moral personality? Not necessarily. To the extent that our dominant social ideology regards homes as primary loci of autonomy, that social ideology must find it difficult to recognize full moral personality in the homeless. The homeless thereby come to be accorded in our society both the civic and moral status of non-persons. To the extent that our society is structured so as to make the home a primary locus of autonomy, our society hinders the development of full moral personality in the homeless.

The subtitle of this chapter is "Homelessness and the Denial of Moral Personality." I chose that subtitle to assert that we tend to deny the moral personality of the homeless. This claim has two senses. First, we tend to deny their moral personality in the sense that we are often inclined simply to wish they would go away or we pretend that they aren't really there. In this first sense our denial is constituted by our disinclination to admit that the homeless share in our moral community. Second, we maintain social conditions which deprive the homeless of autonomy, which fails to help them establish a place to develop moral personality.

If my analysis of the plight of the homeless in American society is correct, then our society faces important problems. At the level of civic personality, we face the problem of how to define our notion of full membership in our civic community in such a way as to include the homeless. Can a society in which property notions play a central role in civic life find for the homeless a locus of autonomy other than the home that will serve for the homeless the autonomy-protecting role that our homes play for the rest of us? At the level of moral personality, how can we, as individuals, be moved to recognize moral personality in the homeless? The homeless are not wholly lacking in moral personality. Yet they are lacking in one of the central aspects of autonomy that generates public recognition of moral personality. This personal side of the problem may well be the easiest aspect for us to resolve. Finally, at the level of social structure, how can our society establish conditions of life for the homeless that will facilitate rather than frustrate the development of moral personality? Perhaps more fundamentally, can such conditions be established at all?

I do not pretend to have answers to these problems. The personal problem is one that we can address in the same way that human beings have had to address the problem of recognizing the moral personality of those regarded as non-persons in the past. We can work to look for the humanity of the homeless, and to facilitate conditions in which we may see their moral personality. The structural problems are far more difficult. As I have argued, the peculiar autonomy-creating role of the home is deeply embedded within our traditions of social and political analysis. I am not optimistic about the ability of our traditions to deal with the problem of homelessness. I have tried to suggest the shape of the problem. It must be up to others with greater imagination to suggest the shape of the solution.

Notes

1. Aristotle, *Politics*, 1253a, in *The Basic Works of Aristotle*, ed. Richard McKeon (New York: Random House, 1968).

2. *Ibid.*, 1252b.

3. Aristotle, *Nicomachean Ethics*, 1099b, in *The Basic Works of Aristotle*, ed. Richard McKeon.

4. Aristotle, *Politics*, 1253a.

5. *Ibid.*, 1253b.

6. *Ibid.*, 1258a.

7. *Ibid.*, 1252b.

8. Judith A. Swanson, *The Public and the Private in Aristotle's Political Philosophy* (Ithaca, N.Y.: Cornell University Press, 1992), p. 30.

9. Frederick G. Whelan, "Property as Artifice: Hume and Blackstone," in *Property: Nomos* 22, eds. J. Roland Pennock and John W. Chapman (New York: New York University Press, 1980), p. 115.

10. *Ibid.*, p. 118.

11. Kenneth R. Minogue, "The Concept of Property and Its Contemporary Significance," in *Property*, eds. Pennock and Chapman, p. 5.

12. *Ibid.*, pp. 5f.

13. Charles Donahue, Jr., "The Future of the Concept of Property Predicted from Its Past," in *Property*, eds. Pennock and Chapman, p. 37.

14. *Ibid.*

15. Robert Bork, *The Tempting of America* (New York: Simon and Schuster, 1990), esp. pp. 95-100.

16. David Luban, "The Warren Court and the Concept of a Right" (unpublished manuscript), esp. pp. 22-30.

17. Hyman Gross, "Privacy and Autonomy," in *Privacy: Nomos* 13, eds. John W. Chapman and J. Roland Pennock (New York: Lieber-Atherton, 1971), p. 181.

18. *Ibid.*, p. 169.

19. W. A. Parent, "Privacy, Morality, and the Law," *Philosophy and Public Affairs*, 12:4 (Fall 1983), p. 269.

20. Swanson, *The Public and the Private in Aristotle's Political Philosophy*, p. 10.

21. For the superb discussion of this conflict, see Frederick Douglass, "The Dred Scott Decision," in *The Life and Writings of Frederick Douglass*, vol. 2, ed. Philip S. Foner (New York: International Publishers, 1950), pp. 407-424.

22. Swanson, *The Public and the Private in Aristotle's Political Philosophy*, pp. 1f.

23. John Stuart Mill, *On Liberty* (Indianapolis: Bobbs-Merrill, 1956), p. 71.

24. Immanuel Kant, *Groundwork of the Metaphysic of Morals*, trans. H. J. Paton (New York: Harper and Row, 1964), p. 103.

25. *Ibid.*, p. 98.
26. Immanuel Kant, *The Metaphysical Elements of Justice*, trans. John Ladd (Indianapolis: Bobbs-Merrill, 1965), esp. pp. 64f.

Seven

HOMELESSNESS, VIRTUE THEORY, AND THE CREATION OF COMMUNITY

Keith Burkum

1. Homelessness and the Question of Community

I live in New York City. It may seem forward to begin this chapter on such a personal note, but it is part of the thematic of this discourse to maintain that the place within which thought occurs must figure more prominently in our reflections which we label "ethical." In this essay I stress the need for the establishment and maintenance of local communities within which we can articulate goals or *teloi* which can give specificity to the virtues necessary to the ethical life. Only within the context of the shared life of people in a particular place can we develop a sense of the proper ends of life. The "virtues" which are a proper focus of Virtue Theory receive their shape from the end that they serve. This end emerges from the phenomenological character of the neighborhood or local community. It is strange that this emphasis on the emergence of the *telos* from the local occurs within an essay that is presented under the rubric of Neo-Aristotelianism. However, it will be my contention that this is appropriate both in terms of the methodology and doctrines of both the *Nicomachean Ethics* and the *Politics* as they can best be appropriated in our historical period.

Homelessness provides a context for this discussion. Homelessness is present within the great cities of America, such as New York, in a way that it is not within suburbia. It is not that there are no homeless people in the suburbs, nor that these people are attended to with greater awareness in the cities as opposed to the suburbs. Instead, homelessness shows itself in New York to a much greater degree than in suburban places. Typically, the structure of suburbia continues to prevent any evidence of homelessness from appearing within its space. Walking the streets of New York, we can encounter features of homelessness that are crucial to this inquiry. First, homelessness is not just the condition of lacking a home in the sense of a "roof over one's head." It is the situation of one who does not participate in the "sphere of membership," as Michael Walzer puts it in *Spheres of Justice*.[1] It is the condition of not being acknowledged as belonging to society. Although in some technical, theoretical sense, these people share the same rights as everyone else, in practice we act as if they do not even exist. This lack of acknowledgment is most appalling. It is a violation at the most fundamental level of human experience. Within Neo-Aristotelian views, membership in the community is a necessity for human existence. Homelessness as a form of nonmembership does more than violate ethics. It denies a person the possibility of participating in a form of life in which ethical judgment takes place. Residents of New York live a sort of public life that suburbs prevent their residents from experiencing. We constantly encounter people walking about engaged in every possible activity which is legally permitted, and even some that are not. Although people tend not to spontaneously engage with one another, there is a common understanding of the way in which each is exposed to the other as fellow pedestrians in a large city. Those who are homeless do not share in this publicity and are, as such, without a place and invisible.

The heightened publicity of the large city brings into the sharpest possible relief the lack of the homeless person's membership in society. It is not that people who are not homeless fail to notice those who are homeless, but rather the homeless are not included in the public space of the non-homeless. People just walk by the homeless "as if they did not exist." A symptom of this is found in the tendency of many people who are homeless to be increasingly aggressive when they choose to ask for money from passersby. Another set of indications along this line is the many ways in which homeless people act which seem to bespeak their perception of how they are not part of the publicity of the city's society. For example, many people who are homeless position themselves on the sidewalk with placards that identify their homeless situation and argue for the legitimacy of their homelessness. It is as if they are seeking permission to "be there" since they do not belong to the publicity of the majority. So often these people do not verbally engage with those walking by and do not attempt to confront them. Whether or not the homeless confront this public, their presence on the street is usually reactive and reinforces the facticity of their nonmembership in society.

Not only the lack of money or social resources leads to homeless people's homelessness. In fact, many homeless people have some resources and acquire a number of possessions. In addition, a kind of community often forms amongst homeless people, helping them survive. The majority see homeless people as nonmembers on the grounds of their lack of a concrete place to call home. The majority increasingly blames the poor for their poverty, but their poverty did not cause the perception of nonmembership of the homeless. Despite the use of money in particular as the measure of all things in our society, the relative lack of it did not accord the homeless the status of nonmembers. Instead, the majority sees these people as homeless and, therefore, as nonmembers in society. Literally it is the lack of resources, both financial and social, that causes the homelessness of people. But our focus here is on the socially-constituted nature of human reality, a situation of nonmembership within society.

By speaking of the nonmembership of the homeless I do not mean to suggest that ethically sensitive people ought not to attend in a central way to alleviating the social and financial needs of homeless people. Indeed, it is part of the argument of this essay that Virtue Theory strongly mandates the support of these people through the exercise of the virtues of liberality and justice on the part of those who are ethically sensitive. Instead, an approach which would offer such support without addressing the question of membership is fundamentally flawed.

Finally, the issue of membership is no simple matter. Many people who hold membership within the larger society do not receive the full range of distributive justice with respect to goods and services. The situation of women comes to mind here with respect to equal opportunity in terms of employment in certain areas of the economy. Also, some people are considered members of the larger society in the abstract sense but are not accorded membership in any of the local communities within the larger majority population. This is the plight of many minority groups—such as the African-American community. By attending to the question of membership in the case of the homeless, I am in no way minimizing the centrality of the concern for justice with respect to the needs of other groups.

2. The Neo-Aristotelian Stance

My thoughts here are worked out from a Virtue Theory which is Neo-Aristotelian. Virtue Theorists have recently proposed that such a theory—derived from the traditions of the virtues from the ancient and medieval periods—is relevant in the current era. There are crucial differences between the classical accounts belonging to Aristotle and Aquinas and between the classical and contemporary views. Some of these differences are doctrinal and others are presuppositional in nature. Reflecting the difference between a classical and a contemporary view, someone like Michael Slote offers a "virtue ethics" whereas Aristotle articulates a philosophical theory for a "tradition" of the virtues. Following Alasdair MacIntyre, I hold that "a philosophical theory of the virtues is a theory whose subject-matter is that pre-philosophical theory already implicit in and presupposed by the best contemporary practice of the virtues."[2] I agree with MacIntyre's statement with respect to the classical traditions of the virtues but am skeptical of its relevance to contemporary accounts. Aristotle's theory outlined the philosophical groundwork for a "practice" of the virtues that structured his society and gave it coherence. His account was a theory and yet more than a theory in that it was anchored in the social embodiment of its subject-matter. It is appropriate, then, to consider Aristotle to be speaking for a "tradition" of the virtues. Although someone like Slote appeals to "our common-sense thinking about the virtues,"[3] Slote's view is largely wishful thinking at best. I would maintain that there is no "common" practice of the virtues which is the source of coherence in the larger American society. Hence, there is no immediately available basis for the kind of thinking to which Slote appeals. Later in this chapter, I will have occasion to offer a defense of this claim.

A tradition-based approach to the virtues is the most rational one. I will not provide a full defense of this position except to say that the fundamental intuition regarding a virtue-based ethics is that the *telos* of the Good Life is to bring about a society which produces certain kinds of people with specific desirable character traits. To speculate about the proper shape of such people with little or no precedent available within one's social nexus lacks an indispensable concrete, empirical basis. Here, I follow Aristotle's lead in holding that "we must begin with things evident to us."[4] Metaphysical assumptions, which usually play a strong role in such an ethics, cannot provide the whole of the content. Yet, if there is no immediate prospect of a common understanding of the virtues in the larger society, all is not lost. With MacIntyre, I believe that it is both possible and necessary to work for the "construction of local forms of community within which civility and the intellectual and moral life can be sustained."[5] Such communities, in their process of formulation, might well look for guidance to past practices of the virtues found in Aristotle's culture. However, there is no historical necessity for such local communities to look to past traditions. Some of these might develop different and even incommensurable tables of virtues.

In this chapter, I am articulating a form which the practice of the virtues could take with respect to a specific type of community, part of whose constituency is homeless people. It is beyond the scope of this chapter to carry out this task completely. Instead, I am attempting to identify those features of a possible practice of the virtues which would relate to the needs of the homeless in their homelessness. Following Aristotle's stress on the unity of the virtues, this account properly fits into a much larger account of a possible life of the virtues that might obtain within an urban environment such as New York. This is peculiar in that a single, univocal practice of the virtues has not fully emerged yet in this place and perhaps only portions of such a life are present. After all, I have just criticized Slote for theorizing about the virtues without an adequate concrete grounding in the life of some community. My position must not be confused with this. By localizing my inquiry, I am able to focus on incipient and developing practices within the community which may provide the basis for an emerging life of the virtues. In addition, by locating this reflection within the context denominated *Aristotelian*, I am attempting to learn both from the thought and experience of one compelling effort to pursue the life of the virtues in the past. Yet, by understanding this reflection as "Neo-Aristotelian," I indicate the obvious and not so obvious ways in which the Aristotelian precedent cannot and should not be applied even as one might follow the central principles or structures of this way of thinking. For example, even as I repudiate Aristotle's notorious views on the legitimacy of "natural" slavery, I find something instructive even here for our discourse on homelessness.

However, at this point it would be fair to inquire as to the value of this reflection even if it is correct. Given the teleological orientation of this discourse, how effective would it be in addressing the concerns of the homeless? After all, Aristotle in his context could coherently identify his ethical reflections as contributing to "political science" and as helpful to rulers who governed actual *politai* within which the life of the virtues was extant to some extent. Is this merely intellectual speculation or, worse, an improper effort by a philosopher to impose a pattern of behavior upon people without their consent? Communities in this society have a strong commitment to the notion of equality and this effort to specify some possible form for the life of the virtues in my community may be unacceptable elitism. In response to this let me say the following. The issue of the proper role of the philosopher both within the larger democratic society and one's local community is a large one that must be addressed by any ethicist, regardless of perspective. The question of the relation of the ethicist's reflection to the larger society, for the Neo-Aristotelian, must be set aside for the reasons identified above. In addition, I would observe that as we approach the end of the century it appears that the larger society, to the extent that it even exists beyond the bureaucratic level, has a thin commitment to sweeping equality for all. This is evinced in the retreat in the present political climate from the values of the Civil Rights Movement and Affirmative Action, for example. In general, this thinness is threatening to us all and must be addressed. Such a posture is consistent with a Neo-Aristotelian stance, I believe, because although the perspective is not a form of egalitarianism, the effect of the application of characteristic principles within this view is to promote important kinds of equality. As for the charge of elitism, within the context of the local community, the philosopher can and should play a role in helping to clarify and shape the understanding of the Good and, consequently, the virtues but this is not the primary task of leadership in a community. Nor is it the case that such reflection, by itself, produces the instantiation of a proposed form of life. After all, Aristotle never supported the idea of the philosopher-king. The ethicist, however, can help to stimulate the development of a community's form of life by engaging as many people within the community as possible in an ongoing dialectical inquiry into the proper goals of the community and how best to achieve them.

3. The Contrast with Kantianism and Utilitarianism

Let us return to the issue of homelessness as a state of nonmembership in the community, and let us consider it from the vantage point of Neo-Aristotelianism. In the *Politics*, Aristotle holds that "the state belongs to a class of objects which exist in nature, and that man is by nature a political animal; it is his nature to live in a state."[6] Aristotle, based on his metaphysical views, considers it essential for a human being to live within a human community. Notice, then, that Aristotle directly addresses membership in his account of ethics and politics (for him these are really the same inquiry). For Aristotle, many persons who have membership within the *polis* lack citizenship and the full range of legal rights that today we insist upon for all persons regardless of their differences from the majority or the group in power. We would never accept such views. Neo-Aristotelian perspectives would reconceptualize the metaphysical underpinnings of the theory of human nature so as to reject slavery and to regard women as equal citizens of the community. Although this is not the place to argue the details, Aristotle's restriction on the scope of citizenship is rooted in metaphysical mistakes which must be corrected without losing the insights into the life of the virtues which his work provides. For example, Aristotle claims in the *Politics* that men should rule women because the "deliberative faculty in the soul" is "inoperative" in women.[7] Therefore, women cannot rule through reason, which, according to Aristotle, is the only way just rule can be administered. A Neo-Aristotelian view would show how the facts of human nature are different and that there is a fully-functioning rational capacity within women which is equal to men. Aristotle does assert that "the government of a state is rule over free and equal persons,"[8] and Neo-Aristotelian views, to be adequate, must accord all human beings the status of "free and equal." To retain the views regarding women, for example, Aristotle would betray his own naturalistic methodology. It is correct to claim that "in dealing with any phenomena dependent on natural growth we must always look to nature's own norm,"[9] but in the case of the status of women, Aristotle misinterpreted the norm. It is perfectly coherent within the rubric of Aristotelian thought for the dialectical methodology to carry us to doctrines opposed to those originally held within the Aristotelian system.

At the same time, I am not claiming that Neo-Aristotelian views must become radically equalitarian. There are different domains within a community which are not political, in Aristotle's broad sense of the term, where leadership is not always properly shared in an equal way. Within the *polis*, not everyone is equally suited to provide all the different kinds of leadership needed. Yet, citizenship ought to be accorded to all without exception. However, a person must first have membership before exercising citizenship. It is striking that Aristotle's emphasis upon membership as essential to human life is so great that he considers even slaves to be part of the *polis*. This membership is represented in the perverse but telling assertion that "the slave is in a sense a part of his master, a living, but as it were a separate, part of his body."[10] Membership is the *sine qua non* of human existence. Not "membership" in some vague collective like the modern nation-state. Such "membership" is too abstract and does not satisfy an essential human need for participation in a local community. For Aristotle, even the slave has membership in the household of the master and the *polis* is an organic community that grows out of households. Modern ethics and political thought lack emphasis on the need to live in a rational and just local community. This emphasis is central to adequate accounts which are Neo-Aristotelian. This contrasts with the well-known versions of Kantian theory and utilitarianism, with its various formulations of act- and rule-based approaches to ethics.

Consider the situation in Kantianism. A person can give the appropriate regard to the mandate of the Categorical Imperative and even seek the Kingdom of Ends without ever paying attention to the question of membership in an empirical community. Indeed, the emphasis upon the noumenal level in Kant's discussion of the formulations of the Categorical Imperative mandates that empirical membership not be an ethical issue in that such membership threatens to introduce an element of heteronomy into the discussions of the duty of the individual. Even in the overtly political work *Eternal Peace*, Kant derives the mandate belonging to an empirical community from the threat present to my autonomy in a state of nature where the presence of those not bound to a civic order is a constant danger to everyone around them. Hence, Kant proposes the "postulate" that "all men who can mutually affect each other should belong under a joint civic constitution."[11] If some group of individuals cannot affect us, as may be the case with the homeless because of their exclusion from the publicity of the city, then moral mandate lacks a basis.

Even that formulation of the Categorical Imperative which requires that I treat the other "always as an end, never merely as a means"[12] does not mandate the extension of membership. It would mandate the non-abuse of the homeless as well as the requirement that they receive the just distribution of goods and services in the larger society. It is not at all clear that I must work to provide for someone else a home and the sense of membership in my community. Here the objection is possible that when people accept the nonmembership of the homeless, they treat homeless people as means and not as ends in that their view of the homeless makes their experience of their communities more comfortable. They may find homeless people "undesirable" and not want to consider them as part of their communities. Their acquiescence in the nonmembership of the homeless would then be a means to an end. The problem with this, ultimately, is that empirical membership is a socially constituted phenomenon and as such cannot be mandated within the sway of the authority of the individualist-based ethics we get out of Kant. From the vantage point of the phenomenological account of homelessness offered earlier in this chapter, Kantianism has no basis for the articulation of the urgency for the extension of membership to homeless people into our local communities.

According to utilitarianism, all of the lamentable abuses of the homeless could be sanctioned under various construals of the Utility Principle. Most likely even sweeping proposals to ensure the welfare of these people would be supported under this type of theory. It is not hard to imagine that careful analysis of the current situation in the larger society would lead the utilitarian to provide housing for the homeless as part of the best way to maximize pleasure or satisfaction within the larger society. However, it is hard to see how such a theory could unequivocally support a mandate for membership at the level of the local community. Giving a homeless person housing does not automatically extend membership in the local community. Even when the theory approaches the issue from the vantage point of preference-satisfaction, the question of membership would have to be calculated out on the utilitarian calculus like any other decision. Even if, in most cases, a mandate for membership emerges it will not have the moral authority that it does within a Neo-Aristotelian view. Further, the calculation may have unexpected consequences. Perhaps many homeless, after a period in this status, would no longer desire membership in any of the establishment communities. The media often cite anecdotal cases in which homeless persons refuse critically needed help—in freezing weather, for example—not just for fear of the violence of the homeless shelters in New York, but also because they do not want anything to do with the other communities. They presumably want to be left alone. Perhaps their attitude is an all-or-nothing one in which they wish to have membership or else they choose to have no connection to others who are not homeless. The calculation simply would not have any obvious result, and this does not comport well with the strong ethical sense that it is unacceptable for the homeless to lack membership. Again, their membership is the *sine qua non* of a Neo-Aristotelian approach.

4. The Ends of Community and Membership

What has emerged at this point is that membership in a local community is crucial to human existence and the lack of it is central to the situation of homeless people. It is the unique strength of Neo-Aristotelian views that this need for membership is addressed within such account of ethics. The lack of such an emphasis in views such as Kantianism and utilitarianism reflects, perhaps, the excessive individualism of modern life which MacIntyre's so ably identifies in *After Virtue*. However, in keeping with the teleological emphasis of Neo-Aristotelian thinking, if we need to extend membership to the homeless into our local community, then we must work to articulate the *telos* or end for the sake of which the community exists. In order to bring someone into a community, the community must first know the purpose his or her membership will serve. This purpose probably coincides, to a great extent, with purpose all the others serve in the community—especially if equality is a value. But, the community is not a mere conglomeration of individual purposes, so there must be some purpose or set of purposes for whose sake the community exists. By articulating the purpose, we would be able to meaningfully experience membership and extend it to others.

The issue of the ends of the local communities is, in fact, a deep problem. Many social entities in the urban context may appear to be communities but lack this status. Many organizations conveniently permit individuals to preserve their isolation and protect their financial stake in the real estate market. For example, many housing cooperatives in New York City are not communities even though many people live together in the same building. These organizations often serve to insulate individuals or their families from all the others in the city. Also, there are social organizations which are communities but serve unethical ends. A drug gang might be an example of this situation. Members of a police precinct who become "rogue" cops would also furnish an example.

Operating out of the Neo-Aristotelian rubric, I believe there needs to be an end for the sake of which a community exists and this end must make some rational sense in terms of the largest possible context of significance—the end or goal of human existence. The goal of human existence might not be metaphysically construed. It might be conceived mainly in narrative or mythological terms. The philosophical status of the end of human existence is a complex issue I cannot really explore here. I submit that an ethically responsible local community would seek to articulate its end in terms of attempting to support the larger end of the Good of the human community. Further, the articulation of both ends ought to be dialectical, and I think the methodological precedent of Aristotelian thought is well worth following. A person must begin with the current views of the Good in the community and assemble the social and behavioral facts that can, with the use of dialectics, lead to a better articulation of the Good for the community and the human species. A person must concretize this conception through the construction of a table of virtues.

There are many communities and potential communities within an urban center like New York. Some of these are ethnically based, some are religious, and others are rooted in place or neighborhood. Articulating their ends in terms of some human end would provide local communities with reason not to so profoundly ignore the complete nonmembership of the homeless. I realize that this emphasis upon the Good of humanity is more universalist than Aristotle allows. However, it is consistent with the methodological direction of the working out of this way of thought given what we know and experience in the modern world. The mandate for membership would not fall on each community equally or in the same way. The community of police officers in a precinct might see ways to respond to the needs of the homeless in ways that are different from that of a neighborhood association. What is crucial here is that regardless of the type of community and its specific *telos*, if that community operates according to the broad methodology which Neo-Aristotelian views describe, then it will suffer incoherence if it continues the current profound indifference to the nonmembership of the homeless. If ethically responsible, local communities were revived in a place like New York and their pursuit of their ends was seen in the larger context of the human Good, then not only would concrete specific needs of the homeless be more likely to be addressed, but real membership would be extended as well. An individual might hold membership in several communities at once which would give rise to a level of complexity not envisioned by Aristotle. To address this is beyond the scope of the chapter, but the problem would not be insuperable as long we have a primary community identification that operates methodologically along the lines suggested. The great urban centers of this society arguably suffer many of their problems on account of either the lack of a *telos* or the inability on the part of the larger American culture to articulate one. This has resulted in a large moral vacuum within the space of the cities, and the resuscitation of the local communities within them could lead to a reconstitution of the city as a more humane institution.

5. The "New" Virtue of Liberality

Neo-Aristotelian thinking can aid a local community's efforts to inquire about its ends by applying specific accounts of the virtues Aristotle discusses, as far as possible, to our own situation. It would present concretized possibilities with respect to the possible form of the Good Life for a community which could engage its inquiry dialectically. As a brief illustration, consider the virtue of liberality and its application to those of us with money who are confronted by a panhandler. The virtue is defined as the "mean with regard to wealth" and concerns both the "giving and taking of wealth." Strikingly, the term "wealth" is defined as "all the things whose value is measured by money."[13] I am, then, obliged to give to the homeless but not to my own impoverishment. We should not act upon the feeling we sometimes have that we should just hand over all of our money to the many people who are requesting help. However, such a feeling characterizes the liberal person, according to Aristotle. Aristotle does state that it "is highly characteristic of a liberal man also to go to excess in giving, so that he leaves too little for himself. . . ."[14] He says that those who err by giving too much are not as morally problematic as those who give too little.[15] However, this virtue in its application should not be one-sidedly paternalistic. Note that, according to Aristotle, the taking of wealth by those below the "mean" also constitutes an exercise of virtue.

The liberal person gives "to the right people, the right amounts, and at the right time, with all the other qualifications that accompany right giving."[16] Hence, we are not to give just to appease a guilty conscience or to stop the homeless person from pursuing us. Instead, there is to be a specific, rational basis for giving within a specific community. Membership makes possible knowing the specifics of the other's need and provides the basis of liberality. People who are not homeless and are ethically sensitive often feel at a loss as to what and how to give. We now see the ultimate source of this in the fact that we do not share in a community together. This Neo-Aristotelian analysis can help us account for the confusion of our current experience and point to its humane resolution.

Notes

1. Michael Walzer, *Spheres of Justice* (New York: Harper Collins Publishers, Inc., 1984), p. 28.

2. Alasdair MacIntyre, *After Virtue* (Notre Dame, Ind.: University of Notre Dame Press, 1981), p. 139.

3. Michael Slote, *From Morality to Virtue* (New York: Oxford University Press, 1995), p. 104.

4. Aristotle, *Nicomachean Ethics*, bk. 1, 1095b5, trans. David Ross (New York: Oxford University Press, 1983).

5. MacIntyre, *After Virtue*, p. 245.

6. Aristotle, *Politics*, bk. 1, ch. 2, trans. T. A. Sinclair, Penguin Classic edition (New York: Penguin Books, 1983).

7. *Ibid.*, bk. 1, ch. 13.

8. *Ibid.*, bk. 1, ch. 7.

9. *Ibid.*, bk. 1, ch. 5.

10. *Ibid.*, bk. 1, ch. 6.

11. Immanuel Kant, "Perpetual Peace," in *The Philosophy of Kant*, ed. Carl Friedrich (New York: Random House, 1977), p. 436.

12. Immanuel Kant, "Metaphysical Foundations of Morals," in *The Philosophy of Kant*, ed. Carl Friedrich, p. 178.

13. Aristotle, *Nicomachean Ethics*, bk. 1, 1119b20.

14. *Ibid.*, bk. l, 1120b30.

15. *Ibid.*, bk. l, 1121b10.

16. *Ibid.*, bk. l, 1120a25.

Part Three

INTERNAL AND EXTERNAL
HOMELESSNESS IN CHILDREN

Eight

COMMUNITY, ETHICS, AND HOMELESSNESS

Michael Parker

1. Introduction

Homelessness enters people's lives, if it does so at all, through their television screen or their newspaper or perhaps, if they live in one of our larger cities, through personal contact with homeless people on the street. However, given the increasing incidence of homelessness in the countries of Western Europe and the United States, few people can fail to be aware that it exists as a problem in their community and in the way of life of those around them. In this sense youth homelessness presents itself *de facto* as an issue of concern and a problem for the whole community.

The existence of homelessness raises a number of ethical and social issues which must be confronted: by the homeless themselves, by their relatives, by those professionally involved, by governments, and by the public at large (British Charity Shelter, 1992). In this chapter, I investigate the ethical dimension of homelessness and look at its relation to the nature of community and communal responsibility. The chapter falls into four parts. In the first, I introduce the problem of homelessness among children, partly on the basis of my own experience and partly on the basis of recent empirical research. In the second part, I elaborate some of the ethical and social issues raised by the problem. In the third part of the chapter, I look at what philosophy says about the ethical issues raised and give pointers toward a conceptual framework which might help in the clarification of such issues. I look at the role an ethics of "community" can play. Finally, I propose some practical ways in which we might begin to eliminate some of the underlying causes of homelessness among children.

2. Youth Homelessness

The number of homeless children is increasing. The effect of homelessness upon the lives of young children intensifies the ethical issues relating to homelessness. Despite the substantial and growing number of children who currently run away from home or supervised care, to become homeless, there is no consensus about their rights nor about the allocation of responsibility for their protection. This lack of consensus is itself one of the causes of the increase in homelessness among children, for it allows children as young as nine or ten to "fall through the net" and end up living on the street. This is witnessed in major cities and, increasingly, rural towns and villages (Strathdee, 1992).

On the face of it, the solution to the problem of homelessness might be seen to lie simply in getting people off the streets. This can be a worthwhile activity and the British Government's Rough Sleepers Initiative was a positive move in this sense (Strathdee, 1992). However, we need to ask why so many children end up on the streets in the first place. This question retains its importance even when the street is substituted by an emergency shelter. Although every homeless child has his or her own personal story to tell, homelessness has less to do with the details of the individual's biography, tragic as this may be, than with the social and legal context in which the tragedy unfolds. For it is ambivalence about the resolution of central questions of responsibility which creates the holes in the net through which children at risk fall.

In most cases children live and grow up with those family members who take responsibility for them from birth. This usually means the child's biological family, or perhaps a stepparent. A significant number of children, however, spend their childhood in the care of foster parents, social workers, or adoptive parents. Whichever of these is the case, under normal circumstances children usually remain the responsibility of their families throughout their childhood. This relationship of dependence ends naturally, though not without difficulty, as the child becomes an adult and achieves something like independence.

The first step on the way to a child's becoming homeless inevitably involves the breakdown of these forms of support. There are three general ways in which this might come about: (1) In 1990, approximately 30,000 children aged seventeen or under ran away from their family home in England and Scotland (National Children's Home, 1992). (2) The same year 13,000 children ran away from the care of local social services. (3) Children also become homeless when their parent or legal guardian evicts the child from the household. The British charity Centrepoint's in-house statistics for April through September 1993 show that 22 percent of those interviewed said that they left home because they were told to leave.

Most runaways cite arguments within the family as a significant reason for running away from home (Strathdee, 1993). Most are in their mid-teens. This is inevitably a time of transition and some conflict for most children as they move from dependence towards independence and adulthood. The conflicts which occur at this time do not all lead children to leave home, and most get resolved one way or another within the family itself. There are times when as a teenager it is tempting and natural to want to run away but probably wrong to do so. There are also, however, times when it is right for a child to seriously consider running away from home or from care. Recent accounts in the news of cases of the sexual and physical abuse of children and of their severe neglect by parents, and indeed by social workers, often make one wonder why these children did not run away sooner.

That a child might give a variety of reasons for considering leaving home or care is clear in the cases I have described, but whatever the circumstances, it must be difficult for a child to decide whether to stay or run away. It is fair to say that, in general, children find it hard to leave home even when the mistreatment they have suffered has been extremely serious. Children will often stay in an abusive situation for many years before gaining enough courage, or perhaps fear, to leave. Family loyalty, fear of homelessness, and the threat of punishment, even in abusive families, are so powerful that if a child does run away and stay away, we can assume that something was indeed wrong. Research by the National Children's Home (1992) suggests that just over three-quarters of those children who do run away from home or care return of their own accord within forty-eight hours. Research also shows that of those who turned up at Centrepoint's nightshelter in London, 31 percent said that they were running from abuse (Strathdee, 1993). Considering the difficulty of talking about such things with strangers, the numbers are probably higher than this.

The question of when it is right for a child to run away from home or care does not admit a conclusive answer. The decision about whether or not to leave has to be the child's. It is a decision which has to be taken seriously by those who encounter such children. Children run away because they have been denied the opportunity to participate in defining their own identity and the nature of the relationships they have with those around them. That they have run away is sufficient ground for concern. For they have chosen the dangers of the street over those of home.

Most children who run away from home or from care stay in their local area, but all are at serious risk. Research by the National Children's Home (1992) suggests that 98 percent of runaways stay in their local area (as defined by police area boundaries). We can imagine the places they end up sleeping and the dangers they face in doing so. These dangers are increased by the fact that they will know that if they present themselves at a police station or at a nightshelter, they run the further risk of being returned to the "care" of those from whom they have run. Perhaps they have run away before and have been returned. For this reason runaways have been at particular risk. Until recently in the United Kingdom, under Section 2 of the Child Abduction Act (1984), it has been an offense for anyone to take away or detain someone who is under sixteen years of age, and this has meant that agencies working with runaways have faced the risk of prosecution if they did not hand them over to the police. An obvious consequence of this has been that those children who are afraid of going home or afraid of the police have commonly ended up on the street. They have fallen through even the safety net provided for other (older) homeless people by the voluntary organizations.

When runaways arrive at a nightshelter they are both frightened and tired and tend to have little reason to believe they can trust adults. The balance between staying with unknown adults in a hostel and sleeping rough on the street may be extremely fine, given the child's experiences. This means that in an on-off interview or even within the space of a day, hostel workers are often unlikely to hear a runaway child's rationale for leaving home let alone any details of the place of refuge. The child's fear at this stage may simply be the result of nights on the street or of experiences since. It *may* turn out that the reason for leaving home is insufficient ground for not to being returned fairly promptly. But this is not always the case. It may turn out that this child, for example, was subjected to years of horrendous abuse by those responsible for his or her welfare and may have been terrified into keeping this secret. If the child is saying nothing, or perhaps nothing other than not wanting to go home, what ought hostel workers to do? In practice, the immediate physical and emotional welfare of the child will provide a priority and this will involve an assessment of the long-term interest of the child, arrived at on the basis of what the child does reveal to trusted parties, those who are working on his or her behalf. But, such a process takes time, and for this there must be a "safe place" where a child might be helped to feel at ease and encouraged to tell the whole story. Section 2 of the Child Abduction Act of 1984, however, has meant that in the United Kingdom, such places have until recently been illegal.

In addition to the legal context, the existence of a "refuge" of this kind raises ethical questions about the rights of parents and other agencies. While it is sensible that the primary and immediate responsibility of those who encounter runaways ought to be the child's safety, they must also be subject to responsibilities *in addition* to those they have to the child. The hostel and its employees are in addition responsible to a wider community which includes the police, the social services, and indeed the child's parents or guardians. In many cases, if not all, these responsibilities will pull in opposite directions, and this tension creates a number of practical ethical problems for those who encounter runaways. Given that the child has in fact chosen to run away, to what extent ought parents or carers continue to be allowed access to the child? Ought hostel workers be able to "hide" children from their parents or guardians? Ought the parent or carer ever be able to demand that the child is returned home immediately and, in cases where this is ruled out, ought the parent know where the child is and be allowed to have contact? There will be occasions where a child is making accusations of sexual abuse, for example, when the question of the parent's or parents' right to manage their own affairs and the lives of the children concerned will have to be thought through carefully. The details of any case can be assessed only in the light of the facts of that case, but it might be argued that, in these more serious cases, the parent or carer ought *not* to be allowed, in the short term, to see the child. For, in such cases, it may be important to keep the child's location a secret from them in order to prevent his or her once again becoming a victim.

Yet there will be occasions of other kinds of mistreatment, when the family ought to be able to maintain a certain amount of contact and, possibly after some counseling, acquire the right to be reunited. There may, further, be far fewer serious cases of disputes where the child ought to be returned to the family or guardian as a matter of course.

In the short term, however, having discovered a particular child at risk, it may well not be possible to decide quickly which of these descriptions applies, and this in itself poses an ethical dilemma. For if it is argued on the one hand that families ought only to lose their right to manage their affairs, in cases of the first kind and, as is often the case at the early stage, there is no actual evidence of any kind (other than the fact that the child has run away from home), should the hostel's primary responsibility then not be to return the child immediately to his or her family? The right to have the child returned to the parent or carer if nothing incriminating comes out is the least that can be demanded. Having come indirectly into contact with the hostel, parents and carers also have a right to be treated fairly in its work. Their right to be contacted and told that the child is well is beyond dispute, but should they have any rights in addition to these? This is the other horn of the dilemma. For the claims of parents and guardians, important as these may be, need to be weighed against the fact that there may well be reason to believe the child to be at risk *from* her family or guardian. How are we to balance the child's need for refuge against the rights of the parent or guardian?

The need for a resolution of this dilemma and of these ethical questions is clearly of great urgency. For the current ambivalence creates a situation in which children, fearing that they will not be taken seriously and fearing that they will be returned to those from whom they have run, are avoiding contact with those who, under different circumstances, might be able to help them. In this way, this ambivalence can be said to be a contributing factor to the problem of runaways who are homeless and consequently at risk.

3. Ethics and Communities

The problem of homelessness can in the end be solved only by concerted practical and political measures. Finding the right practical measures depends upon first laying open the ethical and conceptual landscape which informs our understanding of this particular social problem, thereby making policy decisions more visible. Here philosophy is able to make a distinctive contribution.

If philosophy is going to make a useful contribution to such ethical debates, however, it must avoid detachment. Philosophy often proposes to stand aside from the everyday processes of dialogue and negotiation which together constitute the means by which people work out meaningful ways of living together. Moral philosophers, believing, rightly, that the putting aside of one's own interests must be central to ethics, have sometimes implied that the making of objective moral judgments must involve finding a standpoint outside the community and in this sense outside what it is to be human. They have attempted to achieve this in many ways. Some have advocated the adoption of the position of an Ideal Observer who must, by standing aside from the affairs of the world, attempt to take on all preferences, interests or pleasures and make a decision on the basis of satisfying the greater number of these (Williams, 1985). Others, particularly John Rawls (1972), have suggested that a position ought to be adopted behind a veil of ignorance from where an approach to ethical problems could be arrived at by the drawing up of an impartial contract or set of rules. However, approaches which depend on this kind of detachment tend to obscure the truth that issues such as homelessness are problems for us precisely because of our social embeddedness, that is, because we are human and because both homeless people and ourselves are part of the ways of life from which we draw our identities.

Philosophy, then is of more use in practical affairs when instead of encouraging us to step back from the problem at hand, it is willing for us to get involved more deeply with these problems in their specificity.

I have, throughout this chapter, referred to homelessness as a problem for "communities." Before looking at homelessness itself, I need to say a little about what I mean by a "community" here. When asked by a philosopher, such a question is often once again a demand that we step back from what it is to be human, but the definition I have in mind is a practical one and one which I believe most people would acknowledge. A "community" is an entity constituted by all those people who have to work out meaningful ways of living together. The nature of these negotiations may vary both in form and in intensity but the existence of negotiation of some kind is fundamental to the possibility of social, and of individual, life itself. This "negotiational" account of community allows for the sense of degrees of community or identification which we all tend to feel (Parker, 1995). Within the family, people enter into complex and extended negotiation about a whole range of aspects of how to live meaningfully together (or separately) *as* a family. A great sense of reciprocity often arises, even in disputes. Feelings of community within the family are often by far the strongest sense of community many people are likely to experience. Even within the family however, decisions about communal life cannot be isolated from the individual's sense of also belonging to a wider community. This might be a matter, for example, of deciding whether to recycle our refuse in response to our concern for future generations, or in contrast, it might be a matter of dealing with accusations of abuse when social workers and police arrive on the doorstep in the middle of the night to take our children away. In the modern world, via television, there is also a sense in which, for example, homeless children on the streets of Soho become *de facto* members of our community. Do we join a charity, give a donation, worry about the safety of our own children or simply ignore the problem? Any of these may be meaningful ways of responding to a newly arrived-at sense of being human beings together, of sharing in a community or a range of communities.

It is important to recognize that this conception of community is not an attempt to reduce moral concerns at the social and political levels to those at the level of the individual. It is, instead, an attempt to bring into view the social and political aspects of the individual moral landscape. Our relation to the homeless is not that of the philanthropist of liberal individualism. We are, as *individuals*, fundamentally and essentially participants in networks of communal relations/ negotiations, and as such our actions and choices are essentially moral and social. We draw and negotiate our identity as individuals according to our embeddedness in such a social and moral environment.

Accounts of ethics which are based in notions of "community" face a common difficulty in that they tend to have difficulty explaining just what would be wrong with, say sexual abuse, if a particular community happens to see it as right. The problem arises because communitarian approaches tend to see the community as the primary source of notions of goodness and the rights of individuals as secondary to the maintenance of communal life. Such criticisms of communitarianism are valid. Any useful ethical approach must be capable of upholding the rights of individuals *against* their community (for a fuller account of the dialogue between communitarianism and liberalism, see Bell, 1993). By defining "community" as consisting of those with whom I enter into negotiation about how we are to live meaningfully together, I tie it to both the importance and the meaningfulness of an individual life and to the existence of *both the community and of the individual*, for meaningful dialogue between the two. I see the identity of persons as bound up, to some extent, with their ability to engage in meaningful relationships with others, having been thrown by birth and circumstance into networks of relationships within which they must negotiate both their identity and the meaningfulness of the world around them.

In the previous paragraph I introduced the concept of "rights" and described some of the problems which arise from abstract interpretations of rights in contrast to stressing the notion of "community." While philosophical discussion of the concept of "rights" has a relatively short history linguistically, rights belong to a well-established tradition of ethical reasoning (Almond, 1991). Their origins can be traced to the recognition by the Stoic philosophers in Ancient Greece that the actual laws in a particular community might be seen to be unjust when contrasted with a "natural law" which does not have its origin in a single particular community, and to which everyone has access through individual reflection. For this reason, the concept of "universal human rights" which grew out of the "natural law" tradition has often appealed to those who have felt themselves to be oppressed. It may be argued that it is this appeal to universal human rights transcending any community that makes it possible to uphold the rights of individuals *against* their community. It must be admitted that in recent years the concept of universal human rights has come to play an important role in the practice of international relations and in the critique of government.

While the appeal to universal human rights has great power in a pragmatic sense, how far can one intelligibly identify "rights" with the concept of individuals over and above their communities? To what extent does it make sense to talk of human beings, and consequently their rights, transcending community in this way? I argued earlier that it is not possible to conceive of individuals who are able to step outside of their community. The intelligibility of the concept of universal human rights, insofar as this is understood in terms of the rights of the universal individual, rests upon the possibility of a similar detachment of the individual from human concerns. For it requires an appeal to something like the concept of an "inner person" independent of social context. The appeal to universal human rights in this individualistic sense is made possible and necessary by the contrast between the needs of the community and those of this "inner person."

However, as I pointed out earlier, any approach which demands the detachment of the person from his or her community and consequently from all meaningful interaction with others requires us to lose sight of the fact that human concerns are *concerns for us* just because of our social embeddedness, because we are human and because our humanity is framed by the fact that we share in ways of life from which we draw our identity. It is our social embeddedness which makes it possible for us to *be* individuals. For it is in our social interactions that we negotiate our identity and it is here also that we play our role in the maintenance and transformation of our community. Both individuals and communities appear to be made possible by their interrelatedness and their interaction (Vygotsky, 1978).

In the light of these considerations, any satisfactory analysis of rights must begin from the recognition that rights are to be located neither in the individual nor in the community, but in the nature of the ethical negotiations between them. Ethical problems arise with respect not simply to individuals or communities in themselves but to the forms of negotiation they undertake to work out meaningful ways of living together. This means that if there is to be a justification of the use of a vocabulary of rights, this can not lie in a commitment to the existence of an abstract individual but must lie instead in a commitment to particular ways of living with others, to particular ethical ways of living. We can see how such a commitment might lead to a different analysis of rights in a more socially embedded language. It would comprise, on the one hand, a positive right for individuals to have an active role in the creation of a meaningful identity for themselves in their negotiations with others, and on the other hand, a complementary negative right not to be objectified in such negotiations, that is, not to be fixed by it despite oneself.

Such an account could lead to an enriching of the link between the question of who can be the subject of a right and the question of the duties which such rights imply for others. For consideration of the link between duties and rights in this context must again bring one back to communities, that is to the idea that both rights and duties are tied in some sense to the nature of our relations to those with whom we have to work out meaningful ways of living together: our community.

This is not necessarily a narrow or restrictive conclusion. The extended concept of community which I described earlier included not only members of a person's immediate family, town, culture or nation, but all those with whom it is necessary to work out meaningful ways of living together. While this allows for the notion of degrees of community which most people feel, it is also a reminder of the fact that we do have meaningful relations with a community, whose constituency is diverse and extended, and that these wider relations bring with them responsibilities and difficulties the nature of which has to be worked out. This is why homelessness is a problem for everyone.

For this issue, then, the concepts of the "social embeddedness of individuals," "community," and the "negotiation of meaning" are fundamental, and we should prefer them to a theory of rights framed in individualistic terms. It leads not to the call for freedom *from* community but to the call for the right to a *voice within a community*. It is for want of a voice that children run away from home or care in the first place and it is the fear that their voice will not be heard that forces them to remain at risk. It is their community which denies them that voice.

4. Concluding Remarks

Homelessness enters the lives of most people indirectly, on their television or through the reading of newspapers, or perhaps they encounter homeless people in the street. When this happens, homeless children become *de facto* members and victims of our community and hence a problem for us. As participants in such a community, we acquire a duty to do what we can to bring about the empowerment of the children concerned. Our responsibility depends upon us, the nature of our lives and our ability to intervene. For communities and the dialogues between those within communities have a dimension of power which determines that responsibility cannot itself be equally distributed.

Homelessness is also and primarily both a personal issue for the children involved and their families and a professional issue for those who come into contact with the homeless through their work (hostel workers, the police, social workers, hospital staff, and others). Some of the problems raised by homelessness for those concerned are unique to this social issue; the combination of working with children, on the edge of the law and often against the wishes of the child's legal guardians gives rise to a range of problems not previously encountered. For many, the idea of third parties becoming involved in the relations between a family and its members or between the social services and a child in its care will be worrisome. However, if we ignore this possibility, we will pay the price of a continuing rise in the number of children on the street. Children, indeed all people, ought to be able to participate, that is to have a voice, in the everyday processes of dialogue which constitutes the means by which people work out meaningful ways of living together and out of which they draw their identities. It may be the failure to allow children to take their full part in such processes, and the fact that they feel this so deeply, that causes them to run away in the first place. If so, it may be the continued denial of this right that encourages them to stay away from those who might otherwise help them.

What is required is the establishment of a forum where children will feel safe and where they will be able to begin to participate in the dialogues which frame their lives. In the United Kingdom, the Children Act of 1989 has made it possible for approved agencies, subject to stringent supervision, to work for a limited period with children who run away in the ways I have indicated. This can only be a good thing. However, in 1994, the Centrepoint Glaxo Refuge for Children in London was still the only example. Establishing such refuges would not stop children from running away from home or from care, nor would it stop them ending up on the street, but it would ensure that once there they would quickly have access to the safety and support necessary to establishing something like a healthy lifestyle.

Youth homelessness itself will continue unless we reconstruct the nature of family life and life in our community in general in such a way that children and indeed all people feel themselves to be participating in the development of their own and their community's way of life instead of feeling like its victims. Perhaps the true measure of whether or not a person's work with a child or a parent (or anyone else for that matter) has been ethical is the extent to which they come through the experience feeling that their story has been heard and that they have been taken seriously.

Works Cited

Almond, Brenda. 1991. "Rights." In *A Companion to Ethics*, edited by Peter Singer. Oxford: Blackwell.

Bell, Daniel. 1993. *Communitarianism and Its Critics*. Oxford: Clarendon Press.

British Charity Shelter. 1992. *Homelessness: The Facts*. London.

Button, Eleanor. 1992. *Rural Housing for Youth*. London: Centrepoint.

National Children's Home. 1992. *Runaways: Exploding The Myths*. London.

Parker, Michael. 1995. *The Growth of Understanding*. Brookfield, Vt.: Ashgate.

Rawls, John. 1972. *A Theory of Justice*. Oxford: Oxford University Press.

Strathdee, Radience. 1992. *No Way Back*. London: Centrepoint.

———. 1993. *Children Who Run*. London: Centrepoint.

Vygotsky, Lev. 1978. *Mind in Society*. Boston: Harvard University Press.

Williams, Bernard. 1985. *Ethics and the Limits of Philosophy*. London: Fontana.

Nine

PSYCHIC HOMELESSNESS

René A. C. Hoksbergen

1. What Is Psychic Homelessness?

In 1992 at the Adoption Centre of the University of Utrecht, the Netherlands, we ended a research project that had lasted more than ten years. We were confronted with growing numbers of problems between adoptees and their adoptive parents. More and more often these problems resulted in residential treatment of the adoptees. We approached the social workers, the parents, eighty adoptees aged fifteen to twenty-one years, forty of whom had the experience of residential treatment, and a control group. Using the concept *psychic homelessness*, I am not adding a new concept to the Diagnostic and Statistical Manual of Mental Disorders. I want to draw attention to the phenomenon that I have run into too often with adolescent adoptees.

When someone says "I have a home" or speaks of "my home," the expression means that the person feels secure under a certain roof, feels safe, and has an obvious emotional bond with that home and the people who live there. Nancy Newton Verrier (1993) gives many significant examples in her book *The Primal Wound*. Some adoptees say that they feel as if part of themselves is missing or that they are experiencing a big empty hole inside. Many adoptees told Verrier that no matter how close they are to their adoptive parents, the children reserve a space for the mother who gave birth.

In social psychological terms we are talking about the in-group or reference group (Rabbi, 1992), the group with which the person identifies, with which the person has satisfying relationships, and whose norms and values, to a certain extent, become those of the person. David Krech, Richard S. Crutchfield, and Egerton L. Ballachey (1962, p. 102) define the reference group as:

> Any group with which an individual identifies himself such that he tends to use the group as a standard for self-evaluation and as a source of his personal values and goals. The reference groups of the individual may include both membership groups and groups to which he aspires to belong.

Discussion is confined to the relationship between the adoptee and the adoptive and biological families. Both groups are what I call micro-reference groups from the adoptee's perspective. The adoptive family is the most prominent and therefore most important micro-reference group for the adoptee. As the adoptee grows up, the biological family turns out to have a reference function as well. Sometimes this is the reference group "to which one aspires to belong." This can become apparent from fantasies but also from concrete actions. Think of questions that the child asks and information the child acquires! Do motives for searching not stem from this "aspiring to belong"? An adopted child gets (adoptive) parents who want to have a child and who are desperately longing to welcome him or her into their home and heart. They want to give their new family member all the safety, sense of security, attention, and love that he or she needs.

This is quite different from what has generally been the case with what we, in Europe, call "the homeless," that is, people without any psychological and/or physical settlement. Research on the homelessness in the Netherlands shows that the homeless were often neglected in their youth, unwanted and rejected in the first years of their lives. Seventy percent of the homeless have spent some time in children's homes. They experienced deficient safety, love, and security with their biological parents. Early childhood neglect is one common characteristic. These children grow into people who, due to psychological reasons (not cognitive reasons), are not able to live and function independently in society.

Some characteristics of the homeless indicate why these people hardly have any chance in society. They have a fundamental distrust of themselves and others, and because of this they cannot easily develop normal relationships. Homeless persons experience intimate emotional bonds as a threat and are not able to deal with emotional processes. Their general lack of a sense of identity is shown in various ways: limited insight into their own possibilities, muddling of fantasy and reality, insufficient impulse control, great need for attention, amoral behavior, and fear of failure, sometimes combined with high demands on themselves. They are often strongly manipulative, and they show externalized problem behavior such as stealing, sexual provocation, and vandalism. Their limited planning ability leads them to live from day to day. The homeless are people who often combine their feelings of psychic homelessness with physical homelessness. They are insecurely bonded and often have a high measure of animosity toward their environment. This picture is similar to that in the United States.

If home-life circumstances for adopted children are relatively favorable, must we still give them special care and attention? Is psychic homelessness such a frequently occurring phenomenon for adoptees that measures must be taken to assist those adoptees who suffer from it? Looking at some of my research results, I have to respond affirmatively. Many before me in the United States have repeatedly and thoroughly demonstrated that adoptees need special care.

What I am concerned with here is homelessness in the psychological sense, with *psychic homelessness*. By this I mean the experience of individuals' not completely belonging in the family in which they are growing up, that is, in which they spend most of their youth. This causes insufficient bonding and a feeling of rootlessness. Foreign or interracially adopted children also feel torn between two cultures, suffer from the sensation of being "in between" people. This feeling of in-betweenness, however, can be found to an extent in all adoptees, independent of their race. For this reason, I have distinguished between being culturally in-between and being emotionally in-between. Being emotionally in-between applies to all adoptees to different extents. One of the consequences of this complex experience of social reality can be that the nearest micro-reference group (the adoptive family) has a weaker and possibly ambivalent identification function for the adoptee. Some adopted children will experience a strong sense of homelessness, and others will not have such strong feelings. Important life experiences, such as having children or witnessing the death of parents, have a big influence on this sense of homelessness. We should take into consideration that homelessness or feelings of being torn out by the roots are characteristic across different groups.

2. Psychic Homelessness for Different Groups

Psychic homelessness can have serious effects. We must discover how to prevent it. Psychic homelessness affects many groups of people. The first group is comprised of people born of an unwed mother who grow up in a children's home and later on as stepchildren or foster children. Some of these people have no idea who their natural parents are. In the Netherlands, an increasing number of people are rebelling against secrecy. Among them is Riet Monteyne, a woman in her forties who in 1989 conducted a thirty-one-day hunger strike to prevent the destruction of adoption records, among which were her own, with background information on children who had lived in children's homes. In 1992, a middle-aged woman filed a lawsuit against her mother, who refused to identify her father. This was the first court case with such a charge. In the second group I place people who grow up on the mother's side of the family but who do not know the identity of their father. In some cases, even the mother does not know who the father was. Included here are the increasing numbers of those born by artificial insemination and *in vitro* fertilization. This group makes up nearly 5 percent of all Dutch residents. Divorced couples create a special subgroup. The care-taking parent, usually the mother, often wants nothing more to do with her ex-husband. For her children she regards her ex-husband as a non-person, even though he is their father. Later in life, during adolescence or adulthood, many of these children start searching for this other parent.

The third group, the population which is the subject of this essay, is made up of fully adopted people of Dutch or foreign origin. In 1993, there were approximately 20,000 adoptive children of Dutch origin and approximately 21,000 adoptive children of foreign origin. Abandonment of children has almost completely disappeared in countries like the Netherlands, Belgium, and

Scandinavia since 1970, resulting in a steady yearly decrease in the number of children put up for adoption. Since 1982 only two to five children per one million inhabitants were up for adoption. In the United States (and in almost all other countries), this number is much higher, although the exact numbers since 1975 are not available (Pierce and Vitillo, 1991).

3. Homelessness and Foreign Adoption

People who grow up in a completely different family from the one into which they were born (Dutch adoptees), or who even originate from a completely different region or ethnic group (foreign adoptees), will often experience a measure of psychic homelessness.

Foreign adoption has become a worldwide phenomenon that is closely related to important historical events. As a consequence of World War II, many orphans from Germany and Austria were moved to the United States. Mixed-race children from South Korea and Vietnam found their way to homes in the United States as well, including those removed dramatically in the so-called "babylift" from Saigon in 1975. Many mixed-race children, mostly from South Korea, also came to European countries.

Over the past decades, television has kept us up to date on disasters, which time and again move married couples to open their homes to adoption. Recently, this has also been the case with the children conceived by the terroristic rape of Bosnian women. In this way adoption of children from South Korea was started in 1969, and by 1992 there were 3,762 South Korean children in the Netherlands, and about 100,000 in the United States.

Since 1975, some 800 to 1,000 children have been adopted annually by Dutch families (Table 1). In 1992, twenty-three countries were involved, among which the most important are Colombia, India, China, and Brazil (Table 2). Although in this context no international statistics exist, approximately 25,000 children annually, mainly from Asia and South America, go to the West for adoption. The United States accounts for as many as 10,000 foreign adoptions each year (Bachrach *et al.*, 1990).

4. Homelessness

In the above, I have explained what I mean by homelessness and its relation to *psychic homelessness*. The first period of life of foreign adoptees sets in place the feelings of being alone. To what extent does affective neglect and being unwanted lead to feelings of psychic homelessness during adolescence and in adulthood? Can we assume that children who were affectively neglected during the first two months after birth or during the first few years, and who were not able to develop an attachment to their parents, literally and figuratively do not feel at home in this world, that they feel like strangers among people? Which aspects in their lives lead adoptees to identity problems and feelings of psychic homelessness? The *age and health condition during placement* of these children are important factors (Hoksbergen, Spaan, and Waardenburg, 1988). If we look at the *situation at the time of arrival* of children six months and older, we can state that the majority of these children have been neglected psychologically or physically. Some have also been abused and maltreated. A pattern of behavior with these children can cause great difficulties for the adoptive parents. Because of their early lack of safety and security, children often grow to distrust all adults. This can be manifested by the inability to bond. The child has difficulty bonding and feeling safe with his or her new parents. Strongly adverse behavior, social isolation, and excessive desire to please are symptoms that identify these children's attitudes as socially disturbed. In the Netherlands and in Belgium the term "bottomless pit syndrome" (Egmond, 1987, p. 131) is often used as short indication of this particular socially and emotionally disturbed behavior. When further specifying what this means, however, we often miss the experience of psychic homelessness.

The Belgian Association for Parents of Bottomless Pit Syndrome Children sums up clearly in its trimonthly magazine, *What Now*, the symptoms of the syndrome (*What Now*, 1994, p. 31):

1. This existence has no real basis. It is just like a bottomless pit! You put endless amounts of love, attention, and care into it, but seldom get anything back.

2. The syndrome often appears in older adoptive children whose past history is insufficiently known. But it appears just as often in natural children, foster children, or stepchildren, who for some reason lacked basic trust in their parent(s).

3. There is little or no sense of self-respect and no trust in adults. As a result there is a deeply rooted fear of establishing solid relationships. There is a strong tendency to make multiple contacts. Because of this it is difficult for such children to sense the problems of others.

4. They experience the intimate emotional bonds within the family as a threat. There is more appreciation for the shallow attention from others than for the personally aimed attention from a few dependable persons. There is a constant struggle for power between the care-taking parent(s) and the child, a struggle that is not perceptible for outsiders. Besides, the child is able to turn emotions on and off as if on command.

5.   The devastation caused by the earliest experiences of "pain" or "being unwanted" staggers belief. This lack of basic trust during the first years of life often expresses itself in the urge to be destructive of self or those nearest (parents). Other expressions of this aggression can be cruelty towards animals, vandalism, insomnia, provocative sexual behavior, and running away, in short, an insatiable hunger for attention.

6.   Brakes or thresholds are practically non-existent in the child. The development of the conscience did not get a good start.

7.   The child exhibits survival behavior and apparent adjustment. The child is a genius at observing, assessing, and manipulating those around him. There is a strong tendency to play both parents and other family members off each other.

8.   The child continually feels frustrated.

9.   The child has little sense of time and space. Learning disabilities often arise, despite normal intelligence.

10.   The initial phase is usually characterized by incredibly well-adjusted behavior, without homesickness. Over time, the behavior towards the care-taking parent(s) becomes increasingly rejective. The initial behavior, however, is maintained towards others, sometimes even towards the parent who does not directly take care of the child.

The diagnostic survey of children with bottomless pit syndrome almost completely corresponds with what Hans Keilson (1979) concludes in his research on 204 Jewish foster children. In the group of children who were under five at the time they were separated from their biological parents (71 children), but also frequently in older age categories, Keilson most often observed neurotic effects on character. That is to say that there is a possible neurosis (non-malicious, mild form of a psycho-social disorder) that is deeply anchored in the person and therefore difficult to cure. Symptoms are: great insecurity, contact disorders, paranoid attitude, and psychopathiform conduct disorders. This last term was introduced by Theodore Hart de Ruyter and Leo N. J. Kamp (1972). It refers to behavior that bothers the child but that is especially experienced as disturbing or unpleasant by the environment. Such behavior is mainly aimed towards the outside world (acting-out). Violent and primitive aggressive impulses against the outside world are apparently indulged in an uninhibited fashion, and guilt feelings seem to be practically non-existent (De Witte, 1990).

The micro-reference group can also belong to this outside world. Likewise, Keilson saw in his Jewish group significant loyalty and identity problems, that can lead to serious crises especially during adolescence. Many Jewish children were placed with childless married couples. This offers strong support to the hypothesis that children who were neglected at a young age will often experience *psychic homelessness* later in life. That is, they have problems with bonding and feeling attached. If they show this at all, they do so often in a neurotic fashion. Consider these two examples.

A. Victims of World War II

We can read about examples of these unrealistic emotional feelings in the 1992 special issue of *ICODO INFO*—a publication of ICODO, a Dutch organization devoted to helping victims of war—entitled "Jewish Underground Children from Back Then." Emmy Kolodny was born in 1939 and went into hiding in several households between 1943 and 1945, after which she returned to her mother (her father had been murdered). When she was an adult, she first moved to Israel and then to the United States. She wrote an article entitled "Who Am I?" for the special issue mentioned. Thus concludes her story:

> I do not feel as if I ever found a home. When we were children we were always told that we had to be grateful, because we had others to thank for our lives. "You are lucky to be alive" was something we heard often. Ever since 1945, when we came "home," I have lived with feelings of guilt that I survived the persecution. To this day I feel the pressure of the yoke on my shoulders of the unwanted responsibility for the fact that I am alive.

B. Peter

A typical example of an adopted child who experiences psychic homelessness is Peter. Peter does not really feel at home in the Netherlands. His acting-out behavior is an extreme example, but genuinely representative of psychic homelessness among some foreign adoptive children. Peter is the son of a European father and a black mother. At the age of six, he came from a foreign country with his three-year-old brother to his childless Dutch adoptive parents. He lived at different addresses in his country of origin, but he had no negative memories of his mother. He never knew his biological father. After the normal period of adjustment, Peter behaved reasonably well. Socially speaking, things were going well too, although at school he had a hard time keeping up. His language development began to lag behind, and he was barely able to finish technical training. Peter is quite reserved by nature, but until his twentieth birthday, he fared reasonably well. His parents had no complaints about him. He was honest, diligent, and trustworthy, and he had a good relationship with his father, who was fond of him. Later on, though, his father told me that he never had the feeling that he could see through Peter completely. Sometimes a wall seemed to exist between Peter and the outside world. Peter had no friends. The subject of adoption was somewhat problematic in this family. The fact that their children might have problems concerning their adoptive status doesn't seem to have occurred to the parents. For years, Peter was unwilling to talk about adoption. His parents did notice, however, that as Peter grows older, more objects and articles from his native country appear in his room. He also began to withdraw into himself more often. He had a girlfriend, but he did not discuss his background with her.

When his parents approached me, things had gone seriously wrong with Peter. The process of withdrawal had become of disturbing. Disagreeable facts had furthered this process. His brother had run away and gotten into trouble. Peter was not able to find a good job, likely as a result of discrimination. People called him names on the street. His limited knowledge frustrated him as well. The first time I approached him, communication was only possible by way of notes that he handed to me in silence. As a matter of fact, neither his parents nor I were able to see much of him at all. Dinner had to be put in front of his door at times. It had been like this for several weeks. One day, things took a turn to the worse. He suffered from a complete blackout, and in that state he seriously threatened his parents. Peter had to be involuntarily admitted into a psychiatric clinic. After a week, I visited him at his request. He wanted to know more about his background, about his biological parents, and about the reason why he was put up for adoption. He wanted to emigrate to his country of origin. He claimed he did not feel Dutch nor did he feel a bond with his parents. He wanted to leave the clinic as soon as possible. Peter found being locked up ridiculous, and he did not feel comfortable with the other patients. He wanted to track down his biological family. He told me frankly that he only felt bound to his unknown background and that he had always felt this way. He felt strongly about his father but saw him more as a friend. He found his adoptive mother important as a practical care-taker and not as a mother. The way Peter saw it, his mother lived far away.

When Peter was discharged from the clinic, the possibility arose of making his dream of finding his natural parents come true. He stayed away for two months and traveled across the country, trying to find information about his relatives. He did not succeed, but he did gain insight into his situation as a little boy, because the last children's home in which he lived still existed. During an extensive conversation with Peter a few weeks after his return, I noted that several changes had occurred: (1) The mystique of his country of origin had disappeared. Peter now talks about it in realistic terms in both negative and positive ways. He wants to visit the country more often, but does not want to emigrate there. (2) He had become calmer and seemed more or less to accept his place in our country. He plans to move somewhere else in the Netherlands and live independently. (3) He had told his adoptive parents all about his trip. His relationship with them had normalized. (4) It frustrated him tremendously that he was not able to find out anything about his relatives. He plans to continue his painstaking search through the useful contacts he established. Finally, (5) he encountered a somewhat older sister who was adopted in Europe as well, without their knowing about each other's adoptions.

After three years passed, Peter had visited his country of origin; next he found relatives and in the meantime has found suitable employment in the Netherlands. There has been no more question of psychotic behavior. In the end, he is more communicative and enjoys a normal relationship with his parents. His feelings of not completely belonging have diminished, but they have not disappeared. He still does not feel like he is a real son of his adoptive parents, nor does he feel completely Dutch. But the positive part of the story is that Peter has learned to live with the peculiarities of his life.

5. Assistance

Adoptive parents will hopefully obtain more information on the effects of neglect and abuse that develop into serious forms of psychic homelessness. Hopefully, we will be able to advise parents on how to deal with some conduct disorders caused by neglect during early childhood while they adjust to adoptive status. The conduct disorders can be significant. Just like the physically homeless, adopted children placed out of home, for instance, show a strong tendency toward aggression. On the items "stealing" and "fighting" on the Child Behavior Checklist, they scored respectively twelve and ten times higher than the control group (Geerars, Hart, Hoksbergen, 1991, p. 58). The chance of becoming lonely is an obvious characteristic of the homeless and ranked high in their response. For instance, only about 25 percent of these youths have any contact with the adoptive family. If we bear in mind that one can assume that adoptive children generally have less contact with other family members, the chance of psychic and physical homelessness is great.

The chance of isolation is greater for adoptees than for other people. We should realize that the married couple rather than the whole family chooses adoption. There is no self-evident and socially obliging bond between relatives. Stronger ties with the nuclear family can be established if the other relatives admit the adoptee into their midst as a family member. One condition for this is that the adoptee and the family are able to get along. It is safe to assume that when there are big family problems, then the chances of the adoptive child getting along with the rest of the family are slim. The chance for what I call "adoption-isolation" is great.

Some adoptees experience support from just one relative with whom they get along well, despite the possibly of great problems with the adoptive parents. Likewise, we should think of the loyalty problem adoptees have. They have feelings towards two sets of parents, and the parents with whom they grow up can feel this as threatening to their parenthood. Adoptees often realize this and try to take up a stronger loyal position to their adoptive parents. This is one of the reasons that some adoptees start the search for their biological family only after their adoptive parents have died. It is likely that this loyalty problem is also closely related to the phenomenon of *psychic homelessness*. I advise adoptees who are in doubt to search.

6. Searching

I assume that the feelings of psychic homelessness correspond closely to the motives of searching. This is precisely what we see in the life of our adoptee Peter and what twenty-year-old Rita tells us before she leaves for Nepal to meet her biological mother: "I think that I will only be able to settle down once I see her again." But Rita was already nine years old when she came to live with her adoptive parents. Maricella, a fifteen-year-old, visits her country of origin, Guatemala, with her adoptive father. After the first intense emotions of seeing the familiar places that she left seven years ago, she has to admit that she has become a stranger to Guatemala, although she says she feels more at home there.

Over the last few years, the media have regularly publicized stories of youths or adults who found or one or both of their parents again. Through all the stories and examples I have presented, there are common characteristics of the situations. First, the effects, irrespective of the person's character, are dependent on life experience, the relationship with the adoptive parents, how the experience of adoptive status is felt, and the reaction of the biological parents. Secondly, the results are often therapeutic. A person wants to meet a blood relation and is searching for one's own identity. The need can be great and its fulfillment can bring a certain calm. However, when the search is only partially successful, or if the encounter is too charged with negative emotions, new psychological problems such as confusion and feelings of abandonment may emerge. This is the case where a traced biological parent refuses any contact. This risk exists, and therefore I recommend using a professional intermediary. A certain amount of follow-up care is also recommended. Research has shown that most encounters go off well, but the expectations and behavior of the adoptees are different from those of the biological parent(s), and therefore in most cases the effects of meeting each other are different as well. The search is in itself an active process of coming to terms with the individual's own identity. If it is valid to compare adoption to post-traumatic stress disorder, it might be necessary to search simply in order to gain control over negative symptoms.

According to DSM IV (Faumann, 1994), the essential feature of a post-traumatic stress disorder is that some characteristics (fears, nightmares, over-sensitivity to sounds, dreams, perception disorders) develop following events that one experiences as traumatic. The third finding is that encounters with or a visit to the country of origin can stimulate the adoptee to learn to live with the generation break and with feeling "in-between."

7. Conclusion

In 1987, when Aruna Bandling was twenty-one years old, she started the search for her mother in India. As a six-year-old, she came from a children's home in Bombay to a young Swedish couple. Her answer to the question whether she sees herself as Swedish or Indian is, "I am not Swedish, I am not Indian, I am nothing." Such a reaction may seem extreme, but I am afraid that it reaches the heart of the matter. Adoptive children can run into big problems with their identity and with receiving a satisfying and especially a tranquilizing answer to questions such as: "Who am I actually?", "Who am I in your eyes?", "Am I still the same person I was before the adoption?"

I see several responsibilities. Diminishing the adoptee's feelings of psychic homelessness is a great responsibility for the biological parents, the adoptive couple, or for the social worker. Once comfort with the feeling of homelessness is achieved, the adoptee can feel more at home in his or her social surrounding.

Society carries great responsibility as well. An adoptive system built on sentimentality and secrecy, that too often pits birth and adoptive parents against each other, an adoptive system unable to acknowledge the simple human right of adoptees to have access to their own life history is also a main reason for feelings of psychic homelessness for so many adoptees. Let us fight for adoptees in the United States to have the same rights and possibilities as other human beings.

Table 1

DUTCH AND FOREIGN CHILDREN PLACED FOR ADOPTION BETWEEN 1970 AND 1993

YEAR	I NUMBER OF DUTCH CHILDREN	II NUMBER OF FOREIGN CHILDREN	I + II TOTAL NUMBER OF PLACED ADOPTEES
1970	747	142	889
1971	568	159	727
1972	396	203	599
1973	328	316	644
1974	214	619	833
1975	171	1,018	1,189
1976	157	1,125	1,282
1977	142	1,105	1,247
1978	144	1,211	1,355
1979	143	1,287	1,430
1980	104	1,594	1,698
1981	99	1,161	1,260
1982	77	1,045	1,122
1983	66	1,365	1,431
1984	63	1,099	1,162
1985	72	1,137	1,209
1986	63	1,292	1,355
1987	39	872	911
1988	49	577	626
1989	30	642	672
1990	52	830	882
1991	49	819	868
1992	42	618	660
1993	42	574	616
	3,857	20,810	24,667

(Table continued)

Table 1 (continued)

**DUTCH AND FOREIGN CHILDREN PLACED FOR ADOPTION
BETWEEN 1970 AND 1993**

YEAR	III TOTAL BY LAWYER- ASSIGNED	IV TOTAL NUMBER OF BORN ALIVE	V STEP-PARENT ADOPTIONS
up to 1969	6,877		
1970	1,209	238,912	
1971	1,155	227,912	
1972	1,292	214,133	
1973	1,260	194,993	
1974	1,679	185,982	
1975	1,535	177,876	
1976	1,492	177,090	
1977	1,720	173,296	
1978	1,544	175,400	
1979	1,798	175,000	
1980	1,901	181,300	106
1981	2,543	178,600	518
1982	2,365	172,070	559
1983	1,937	170,240	535
1984	1,840	174,440	462
1985	1,619	177,000	356
1986	1,781	184,300	365
1987	1,963	186,676	367
1988	1,629	186,647	408
1989	1,265	188,979	372
1990	1,174	197,965	415
1991	1,338	198,665	359
1992	1,451	196,734	356
1993	998	195,748	396
	45,365		5,574

Table 2

MOST IMPORTANT COUNTRIES FOR INTER-COUNTRY
ADOPTIONS IN THE NETHERLANDS BETWEEN 1970 AND 1992

COUNTRY	NUMBER OF ADOPTIONS			TOTAL NUMBER
	1990	**1991**	**1992**	

Total number of adoptions to 1990 is 17,969

COUNTRY	1990	1991	1992	TOTAL NUMBER
Austria	-	-	-	291
Bangla Desh	-	-	-	495
Bolivia	1	-	3	5
Brazil	91	111	57	637
Chile	2	3	-	202
China	-	-	26	26
Colombia	208	169	181	3,124
Costa Rica	1	10	-	54
Dominican Republic	1	2	-	46
Ethiopia	33	33	49	189
Germany	-	-	-	97
Greece	-	-	-	576
Guatemala	3	3	1	8
Haiti	19	-	12	204
Hungary	3	5	4	18
India	92	77	71	2,436
Indonesia	-	-	-	3,071
Israel	3	3	3	14
Jordan	-	-	5	5
Korea	6	9	11	3,762
Lebanon	-	1	-	327
Mauritius	-	-	-	52
Peru	4	6	-	184
Philippines	13	12	10	138
Poland	22	40	29	139
Romania	4	23	2	30
Sierra Leone	4	1	5	11
Sri Lanka	263	228	97	3,128
Suriname	17	25	9	105
Taiwan	17	31	38	136
Thailand	19	23	17	253
Yugoslavia	-	-	-	82
Others	4	4	3	391
TOTAL	830	819	633	20,236

Works Cited

Andersen, R. S. 1989. "The Nature of Adoptee Search: Adventure, Cure, or Growth?" *Child Welfare*, 68:6 (November-December).

Aumend, S. A., and M. C. Barrett. 1984. "Self-Concept and Attitudes Toward Adoption: A Comparison of Searching and Nonsearching Adult Adoptees." *Child Welfare*, 63:3 (May-June), pp. 251-259.

Bachrach, C. A., P. F. Adams, S. Sambrano, and K. A. London. 1990. "Adoption in the 1980's." *Advance Data from Vital and Health Statistics of the National Center for Health Statistics*, no. 181 (5 January).

Brodzinsky, David M., and Marshall D. Schechter, eds. 1990. *The Psychology of Adoption*. New York: Oxford University Press.

Brodzinsky, David M., Marshall D. Schechter, and Robin Marantz Henig. 1992. *Being Adopted: The Lifelong Search for Self*. New York: Doubleday.

De Stem. 1992. "Valkenhorst-kinderen eisen algemeen recht op kennis afstamming. Pesoonlijke zieligheid mag geen rol spelen." 15 October.

De Witte, Herman F. J. 1990. "Ontwikkelingspsychopathie en Psychopathiforme Gedragsstoornissen (Conduct Disorders)." In *Leerboek Kinder-en Jeugdpsychiatrie*, edited by Janny Sanders-Woudstra and Herman F. J. de Witte. Assen: Van Gorcum.

DSM-III-R. *Diagnostic and Statistical Manual of Disorders*. 1987. Washington, D.C.: American Psychiatric Association.

Egmond, Geertje, van. 1987. *Bodemloos bestaan: Problemen met adoptiekinderen*. Baarn: AMBO.

Fauman, Michael A. 1994. *Study Guide to DSM IV*. Washington, D.C.: American Psychiatric Press, Inc.

Feigelman, William, and Arnold R. Silverman. 1983. *Chosen Children*. New York: Praeger Publishers.

Fischer, Florence. 1973. *In Search of Anna Fischer*. New York: Arthur Fields.

Geerars, Hetty, Harm't Hart, and René Hoksbergen. 1991. *Waar ben ik thuis: Geadopteerde adolescenten over adoptie, hun familie, problemen, uithuisplaatsing en toekomstvisie*. Utrecht: Adoptie Centrum.

Hart de Ruyter, Theodore, and Leo N. J. Kamp. 1972. *Hoofdlijnen van de kinder-psychiatrie*. Deventer: Van Loghum Slaterus.

Hoksbergen, René. 1983. "Adoptiefkindersen bij Medisch Opvoedkundige Bureaus (MOB) en Jeugd Psychiatrische Diensten (JPD)." In *Adoptie uit de kinderschoenen*, edited by René Hoksbergen and Hans Walenkamp. Denventer: Van Loghum Slaterus.

Hoksbergen, René, Jacqueline Spaan, and Bert Waardenburg. 1988. *Bittere Ervaringen: Uithuisplaatsing van buitenlandse adoptiekinderen*. Amsterdam/Lisse: Swets en Zeitlinger.

ICODO INFO. 1992. Themanummer: *Joodse onderduikkinderen van toen* [Special Issue: *Jewish Underground Children from Back Then*]. Utrecht: Stichting ICODO, 9, 92, 2.

Keilson, Hans. 1979. *Sequentielle Traumatisierung bei Kindern: Deskriptiv-klinische und quantifizierend-statistische follow-up Untersuchung zum Schicksal der jüdischen Kriegswaisen in den Niederlanden*. Stuttgart: Ferdinand Enke Verlag.

Kessler Stichting. 1992. *Huis voor Thuislozen*. Den Haag: Kessler Stichting.

Kornheiser, T. 1983. *The Baby Chase*. New York: Atheneum.

Krech, David, Richard S. Crutchfield, and Egerton L. Ballachey. 1962. *Individual in Society: A Textbook of Social Psychology*. New York: McGraw-Hill.

Lifton, Betty Jean. 1975. *Twice Born: Memoirs of an Adopted Daughter*. New York: McGraw-Hill.

————. 1979. *Lost and Found: The Adoption Experience*. New York: Dial Press.

Paton, Jean M. 1954. *The Adopted Break Silence*. Philadelphia: Life History Study Center.

Pierce, William, and Robert J. Vitillo. 1991. "Independent Adoptions and the 'Baby Market.'" Chapter 11 in *Adoption, International Perspectives*, edited by Eva D. Hibbs. Madison, Conn.: International Universities Press.

Rabbi, Jaap. 1992. "Over het ontstaan van saamhorigheid en cohesie binnen groepen en van rivaliteit en vijandigheid tussen groepen." *Onze Alma Mater*, Leuvense Perspectieven, 46 (May).

Sorosky, Arthur D., Annette Baran, and Reuben Pannor. 1984. *The Adoption Triangle*. New York: Anchor Books.

Tahk, Youn-Teak. 1986. "Intercountry Adoption Program in Korea." In *Adoption in Worldwide Perspective: A Review of Programs, Policies, and Legislation in 14 countries*, edited by René Hoksbergen. Lisse: Swets & Zeitlinger B.V.

Tavecchio, Louis W. C. 1991. *Affectieve verwaarlozing en thuisloosheid. Een haalbaarheidsstudie naar thuisloosheid vanuit het perspectief van de gehechtheidstheorie.* Leiden: Vakgroep Algemene Pedagogiek.

Triseliotis, John. 1973. *In Search of Origins: The Experiences of Adopted People.* London: Routledge and Kegan Paul.

Verhulst, Frank C., and J. M. Herman Versluis-den Bieman. 1989. *Vaardigheden en probleemgedrag.* Assen/Maastracht: Van Gorcum.

Verrier, Nancy N. 1993. *The Primal Wound.* Baltimore: Gateway Press, Inc.

What Now. 1994. Magazine of the Belgian Association for Parents of Bottomless Pit Syndrome Children, Brussels.

Winkler, Robert C. 1983. "The Search of Adoptees and Relinquishing Mothers for Each Other." Request for Support Grant. Western Australia: University of Western Australia.

1. Photograph by Janice Agati-Abbarno, 1998

2. Photograph by Janice Agati-Abbarno, 1998

3. Photograph by Janice Agati-Abbarno, 1998

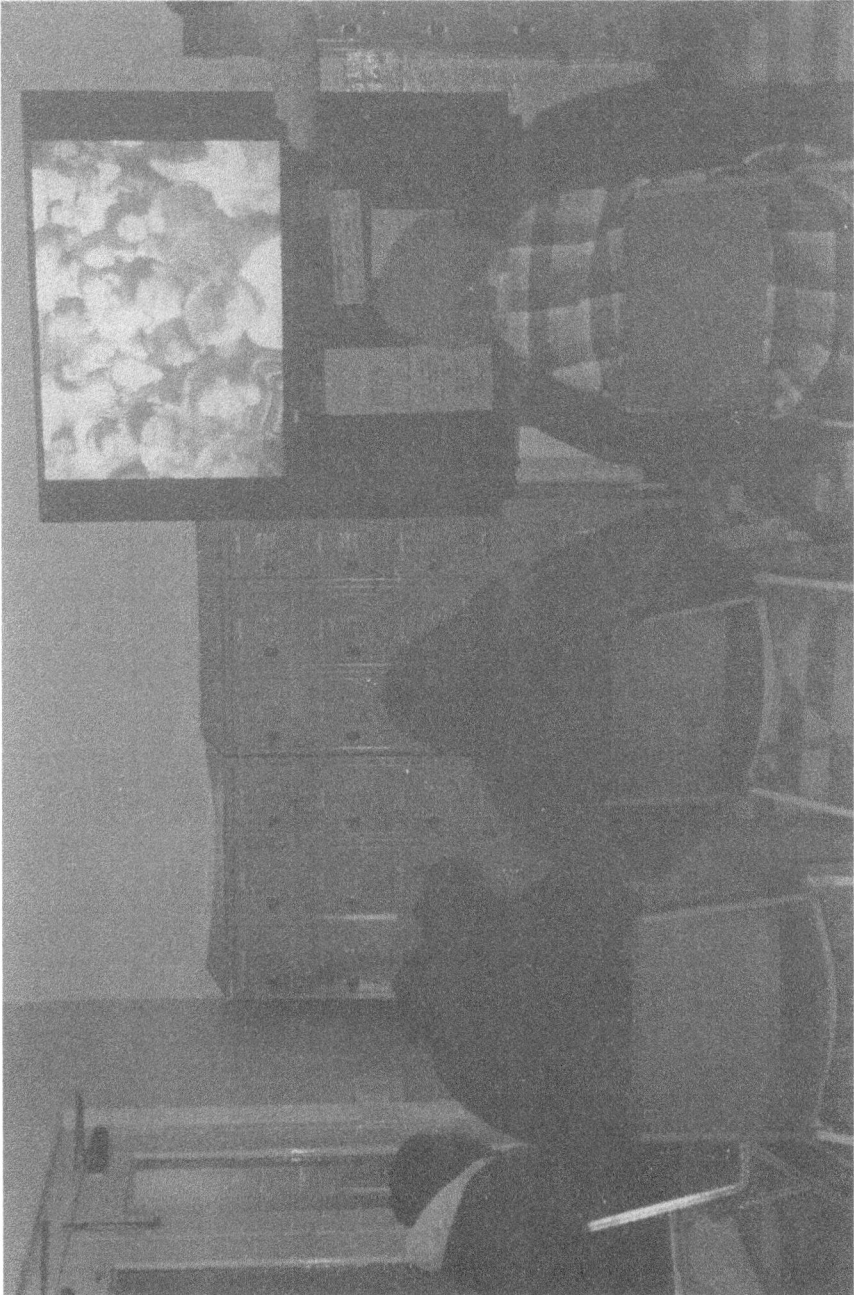

4. Photograph by Janice Agati-Abbarno, 1998

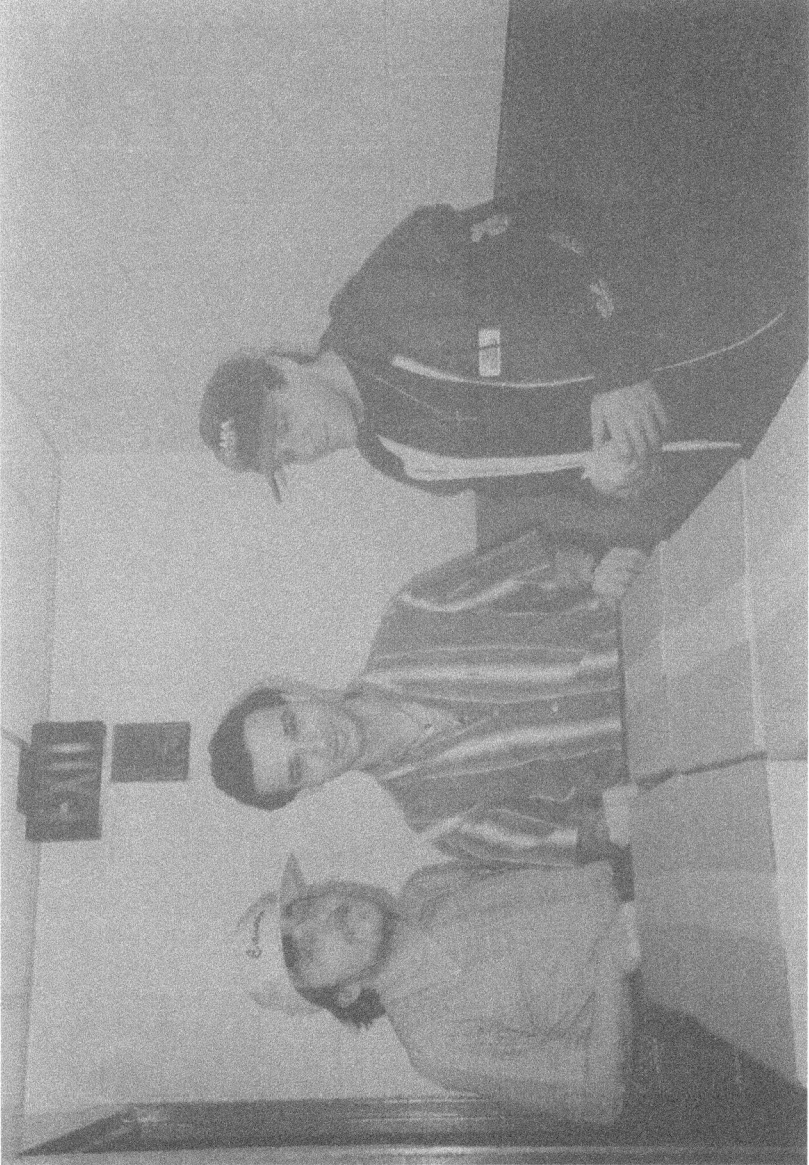

5. Photograph by Janice Agati-Abbarno, 1998

6. Photograph by Janice Agati-Abbarno, 1998

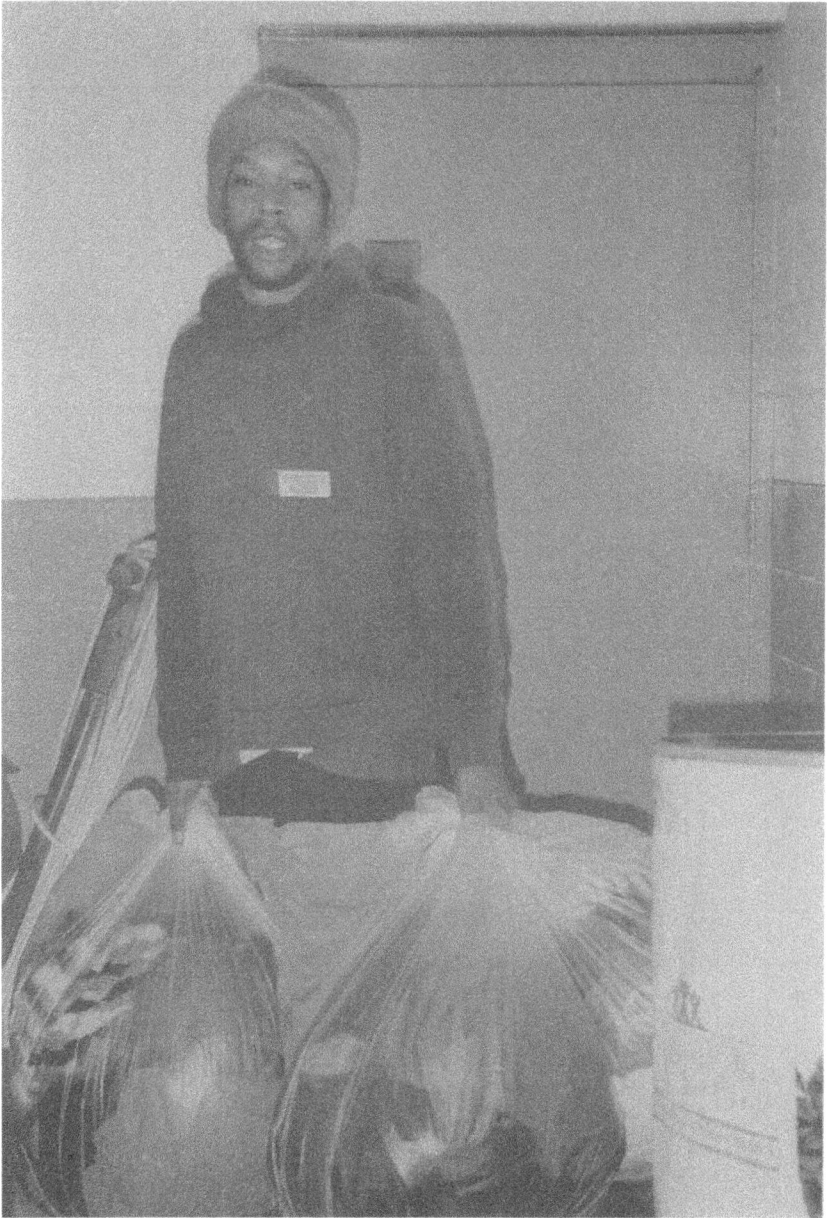

7. Photograph by Janice Agati-Abbarno, 1998

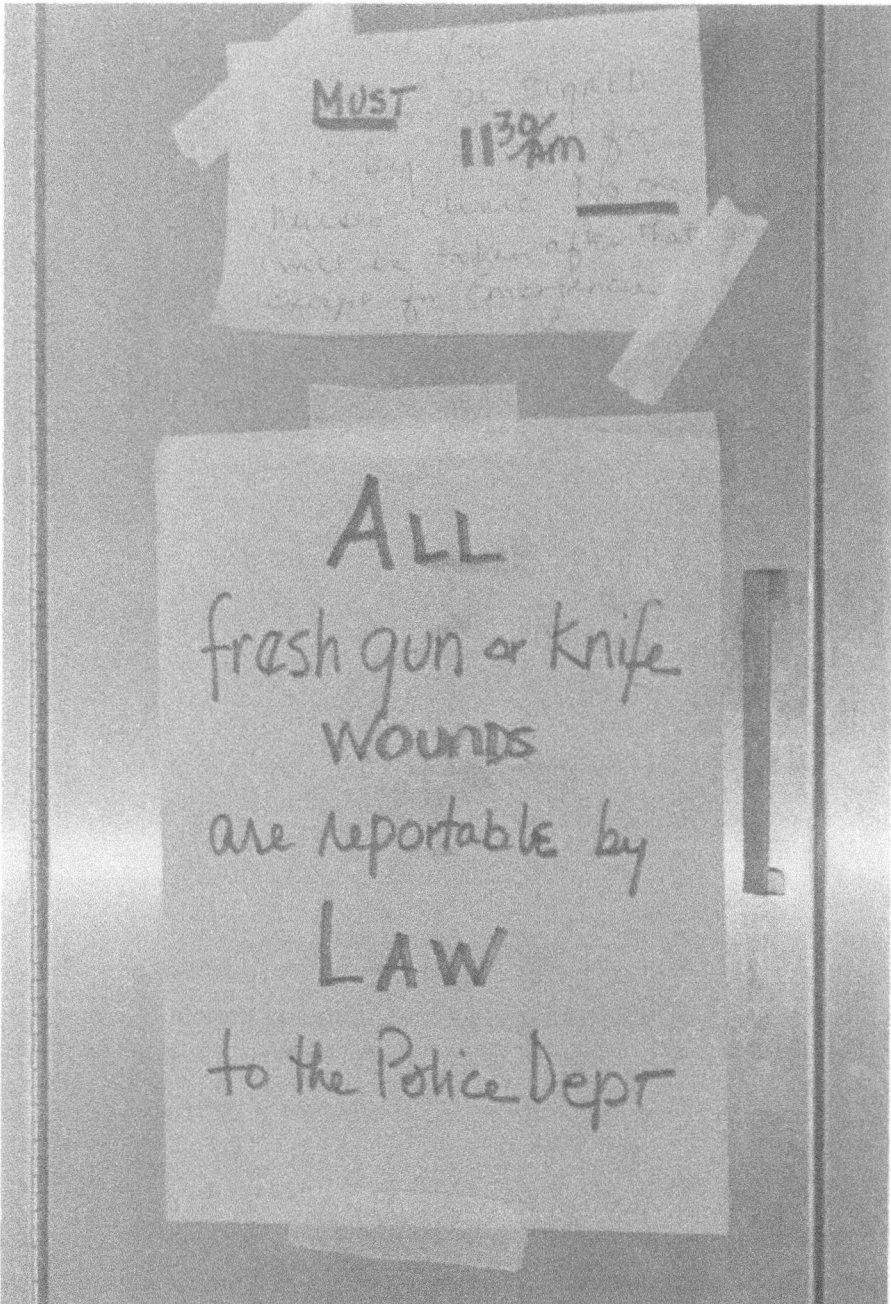

8. Photograph by Janice Agati-Abbarno, 1998

Part Four

NO HOME, NO CITIZENSHIP

Moral and Political Dimensions

Ten

THE HOMELESS AND THE RIGHT TO "PUBLIC DWELLING"[1]

Anita M. Superson

1. Introduction

While in my local public library in Chicago, I noticed a security guard who diligently patrolled the floor. He tapped with his stick anyone who appeared to be nodding off and announced in a commanding voice that there was to be no sleeping in the library. "Since when?" I thought, but then realized that there were a number of people around me who appeared disheveled and unclean, and who were probably homeless. The library could not evict these people, so it tried to deter their coming there by imposing the ban on sleeping.

The event I witnessed generated the topic of this chapter, namely, the issue of whether the homeless have a right to "public dwelling." The rights of the homeless, or homelessness in general, is a surprisingly neglected issue in the philosophical literature. Yet it is a critical issue that demands philosophical attention, since homelessness is on the rise. This chapter focuses on one small problem concerning the homeless, namely, their right to public dwelling. After examining some arguments against their having such a right, I defend the view that they do have this right. The defense rests on the facts concerning the causes of homelessness and the severe restrictions on the choices the homeless have.

2. Municipal Treatment

People need only observe the ways in which the homeless have been treated to see that this issue has already been settled in the minds of officials who have made it difficult for the homeless to live in public places. For instance, when about three hundred homeless people set up tents in Tompkins Square Park in Manhattan, the police raided the park, cracking heads at random.[2] In Berkeley, the University of California ordered repeated police raids on People's Park and evicted a soup kitchen.[3] Atlanta went beyond public parks: Mayor Maynard Jackson proposed "public nuisance" laws to give police the power to remove the homeless from vacant buildings and parking lots.[4] In New York City, police have patrolled the subway, insisting that everybody remain off the floor and on the move so as to prevent the homeless from lying on grates that emit some heat in the winter.[5] In Greenwich Village, barbed wire was placed across hot-air grates on sidewalks to prevent the homeless from sleeping in the neighborhood.[6] The homeless could not turn to cars as a refuge: Municipal Code 85.02 prohibits the use of a car as a residence.[7] One writer sums up society's treatment of the homeless, remarking that in this country, an automobile has more natural right and is more protected than a person: it can sit on a curb, and for $50 a month can get a heated space.[8]

3. Dangerousness

Several arguments emerge in the literature on homelessness in defense of the view that the homeless do not have a right to "public dwelling." Among the most common is that the homeless are dangerous and so, like criminals, should be kept off the streets. Their danger is said to stem from their being either ex-convicts or victims of mental illness.

But this argument is based on a myth. Its defenders cite John F. Kennedy's signing of the Community Mental Health Centers Act in 1963, claiming that it got the mentally ill out of institutions and onto the streets.[9] Most reports estimate that in the United States, between 350,000 and 3 million people are homeless.[10] The National Coalition for the Homeless estimates that there are 3 million homeless people in the United States.[11] There reportedly is no evidence to suggest that psychopathology was more prevalent in homeless families in the 1980s than it was in the 1970s; instead, there is evidence that the economic circumstances of families have changed during that time, as I will discuss later in the chapter.[12] It has been estimated that anywhere from 10 percent to 33 percent of homeless people exhibit some kind of psychosis, the figure being lower among homeless families.[13] This statistic is biased. The homeless often exhibit characteristics of mental illness: without food, shelter, and bathing facilities, and with constant worry about survival, they become listless, depressed, and (perhaps) sometimes violent. These are natural responses to their situation, the kind everyone would have if put in their place. These responses do not necessarily signify mental illness.[14]

If not many homeless people are mentally ill, even fewer are ex-convicts. Statistics on their prison and police records are unreliable because they are biased, reflecting petty crimes such as minor theft and crimes such as prostitution that the homeless are forced into for survival. The homeless are much more likely to be victims—not perpetrators—of crime.[15] Many are beaten sadistically, as they are open targets when sleeping in public places.[16] One homeless man sleeping in the park was doused with kerosene and set on fire,[17] and another was stabbed seventeen times by two California high school students.[18] The homeless are easy targets for criminals because of their weakened condition due to poor health as well as their "public availability." One report claims that homeless people are in very poor health: tuberculosis is twenty-five times higher among the homeless than in the general population; the homeless are ten times more likely to contract AIDS than the general public; and the homeless commonly suffer from gangrene from standing in long lines for food and from repeatedly sleeping sitting up.[19] Since the homeless are not dangerous, they are unlike criminals, so it does not follow that they should be kept off the streets.

"Dangerousness" may be in the eyes of the public; the homeless are thought to be dangerous because they *look* dangerous. But what does this mean, and is it true? Many of us have mental images of a stereotypical criminal (such as the dark, brooding man lurking in the alleys, who seems to be fast with a weapon). But many hard-core criminals do not match those images; they are people who look like ordinary folks, hardly dangerous, such as pedophile priests. We cannot infer anything about a person's character from her or his appearance. Besides, if we were going to keep all dangerous-looking people off the streets, as this argument suggests, that would include many people who in fact are *not* dangerous. If disheveled people connote dangerousness, this just shows a lack of understanding and a bias on our part similar to racism. We fear what we do not know or understand.

4. Rights as Taxpayers

A second argument has been offered by Stuart Bykofsky, a journalist writing in *Newsweek*.[20] Bykofsky argues that since his tax dollars are spent to keep the streets paved and clean, he is the landlord of those who live in the streets. He thus has the right to evict them, and eviction is what he advocates.

This rather extreme argument is unsound. Consider the following three reasons. First, Bykofsky fails to realize that many of the homeless have paid or do pay taxes. At least one-fourth of the homeless have jobs.[21] A representative group surveyed in Ohio indicated that 87 percent once held a job.[22] One report claims that nearly 40 percent of those who had been homeless for at least five years had a full-time job.[23] According to Bykofsky's reasoning, the homeless also have a right to control what kind of behavior is allowed to go on in the streets (such as, they have a right to allow people to live on the streets). Second, children constitute a significant and growing portion of the homeless. Since they cannot legally work they cannot pay taxes. According to Bykofsky's position, taxpayers can decide that children cannot live on the streets, perhaps forcing them into orphanages or foster homes away from their parents. Women also constitute a significant portion of the homeless both as single parents and divorced parties. In this day and age women are encouraged by a patriarchical system to cultivate domestic skills instead of skills that would enable them to thrive or even survive in the paid labor force. Add to this the fact that many women are the sole caretakers of their children, making it difficult for them to enter the paid work force if they cannot afford adequate daycare. It is not fair, as Bykofsky's argument implies, to deny these people landlord privileges. Third, and most important, the mere fact that Bykofsky pays taxes doesn't give him the right to decide who does or does not live on the streets, any more than it follows that because he pays taxes used to subsidize highways he gets to decide who does or does not drive on them. He could not propose, for example, the elimination of junky cars, as long as they met basic safety requirements. Not all tax-paying entails ownership. Some taxation is designed to make life convenient for everyone, not to bestow rights to certain goods. Thus, the argument from taxes is unsuccessful.

5. Offensiveness

A third argument against the right to public dwelling lurks behind the first two, and it concerns offensiveness to others. Both Bykofsky and John Leo have argued that the homeless contribute to the demoralization and destabilization of entire communities.[24] Since, it is claimed, homeless people take over park benches, relieve themselves in sandboxes and on the street, and emit bad odors as a result of not washing themselves for weeks, people are offended by their presence. Their offensiveness outweighs any right they may have to public dwelling. The recent case of Richard Kreimer, a homeless man from New Jersey, exemplifies this line of reasoning. Kreimer was told to leave a public library because of his body odor, which other patrons found offensive. In order to aid in his eviction, the library kept a record by means of a surveillance camera of Kreimer entering the building. At issue was the violation of Kreimer's civil rights; he was awarded $250,000.[25]

The argument at issue does not disambiguate the meaning of "offensiveness." There are at least two kinds of offense: physical and moral. Consider physical offense. The argument is that because the homeless are physically offensive, their right to public dwelling is outweighed by the interests of those offended. In response, it is admittedly difficult to live up to standards of personal hygiene in the United States if one does not have access to running water. At least some (and perhaps a fair number of) homeless people manage to keep themselves clean even under the worst circumstances by using public restrooms or shelters or places of business. We all know people who are not homeless, but who fail to meet our standards of hygiene. Nothing about one's physical state follows from the fact that one is homeless or not. If anything, the argument from physical offense is an argument to provide public restrooms for those who want access to running water without their having to patronize a place of business. But it is not a good argument for singling out the homeless and denying their right to public dwelling.

Consider next *moral* offense. The argument is that because some people are morally offended by the homeless, their right to public dwelling is overridden by the interests of the offended. Joel Feinberg has defined taking offense to include the following characteristics: "a) I suffer a disliked state, and

b) I attribute that state to the wrongful conduct of another, and c) I resent the other for his role in causing me to be in the state."[26] Feinberg goes on to say that in order for there to be an offense, it is necessary that there be a wrong, not (just) that the victim feel wronged: there will be a wrong when an offended state is produced in the victim without justification or excuse. According to Feinberg, even if the conduct is wrong, the offense must be weighed against the interests of those engaged in wrongful conduct, in this case, the homeless.

Defenders of the moral offense argument believe that the homeless are guilty of either (1) being free-riders, or (2) simply being present in public places.

People who believe that the homeless are free-riders might think, "Why should I have to struggle in life, working hard day in and day out, when these people can sit around in a park all day begging for money and other handouts?" It is a common belief that the homeless prefer to remain homeless because it is easier to beg for handouts than to work at a job.

To determine whether public dwelling is wrongful conduct because the homeless are free-riders, we need to look at who the homeless are. Aside from the few who have a history of mental illness and the few who abuse drugs and alcohol, the homeless include Vietnam veterans, the physically disabled or chronically ill, the elderly, single parents (usually women), runaway and abused children, female victims of domestic violence (many of whom are pregnant), immigrants, and those who are the victims of bad luck.[27] One survey showed that 26 percent of those whose longest residence in the year prior to request for shelter was as primary tenants in their own apartment had been "battered or threatened with violence by a boyfriend or spouse."[28] According to one source, only 4 percent of one thousand homeless people surveyed could fall into the category of "lazy, shiftless bums."[29] Several sources state that families are the fastest growing group of homeless.[30] This list alone should be sufficient to dispel the myth that the homeless are free-riders, as defenders of the moral offense argument believe, and for this reason their conduct is not wrongful.

6. Economic and Political Background

An examination of both the causes of homelessness and the choices of the homeless reveals that their very presence in public is not wrongful. Most of the problems of the homeless were exacerbated during the Reagan administration. The statistics are staggering. Sources report that under the Reagan administration, federal subsidies for low-income housing were reduced anywhere from 60 to 77 percent.[31] Two and a half million units of low-income housing have disappeared since 1980.[32] The units were either converted to condominiums, demolished, abandoned, burned, or taken over for offices in downtown areas.[33] Between 1970 and 1983, single-room-occupancy units (SROs) in cheap hotels that were used to house the homeless fell by 89 percent in New York, and 88 percent.in Atlanta.[34] Nationally, by 1990 there were 8.5 million households for 4.3 million available and affordable rental units, leaving a shortage of 4.2 million units.[35] To put these figures in perspective of the national budget, in 1980, for each dollar spent on national defense, 19 cents were authorized for subsidized housing. This number was reduced to *only 3 cents* by 1987.[36] In the mid-1980s, more than 5.8 million households spent over one-half of their income on shelter.[37] From 1973 to 1983, median rent rose 137 percent, while median family income rose only 79 percent; for those whose annual income was less than $3,000, rent was over 60 percent.[38] We cannot expect this situation to improve, since the poorest fifth of the nation had a 24 percent increase in their taxes between 1980 and 1984.[39] Since 1968, the number of children living in poverty increased by 3 million, but welfare benefits to families decreased 35 percent.[40] The minimum wage remained at $3.35 per hour between 1981 and 1988, though the cost of living during that time rose by one-third.[41] In his first two years in office, President Reagan also reduced the number of beneficiaries of Supplemental Security Income (for the indigent aged, blind, or disabled), Aid to Families with Dependent Children, Daycare, Medicaid, HUD appropriations for subsidized housing,[42] and school feeding programs.[43] Since 1981, over one million people lost eligibility for food stamps, and benefits were decreased to 47 cents per meal.[44] In 1985, the *New England Journal of Medicine* reported that 35 million Americans did not have some form of health insurance.[45] Given these statistics, it is clear that the poor have only gotten poorer. People forced to choose between food and shelter or other such "luxuries" as health care, do what they must to survive. Yet Reagan once remarked that the homeless were homeless *by choice*.[46]

These statistics might be sufficient to convince some people that the homeless have a right to public dwelling, since their choices have been severely restricted by elements beyond their control. Yet diehard supporters of the moral offense argument, even if they come to disagree with Reagan's view that the homeless are homeless by choice, might still insist that the homeless do not have a right to public dwelling. Instead, they should be put away in shelters. Indeed, neither the United States Constitution nor any State Constitution guarantees a right to shelter. Private institutions such as religious organizations provide more shelters than either federal or state governments.[47]

But one has only to hear about life in a shelter to realize that it really is no option. One shelter in Washington, D.C., was full of vermin, had broken windows and large holes in the walls, and only one working shower for five hundred men.[48] Shelters run by Rescue Mission and the Salvation Army allow a person to stay only two nights, and require him or her to listen to sermons and to pray.[49] In all shelters the schedule is regimented. Inhabitants must get up at 5:45 a.m. and, after a quick breakfast, must return to the streets. The lights go out early at night, and talking is prohibited. Crime exists, as younger people prey on older, weaker people. Inhabitants have little or no privacy, no place to relax and be themselves. There is no guarantee of receiving meals. Most shelters provide only one small meal a day, and people must line up as if they were in prison to get it. Restaurant allowances obtained by some inhabitants cannot be used to buy groceries because there is no kitchen, and hot plates are not permitted. But since the allowance is so small, if it is used in restaurants, it is sure to run out in a hurry.[50] The atmosphere in shelters is depressing. As one homeless person put it, "the shelter makes you crazy, like you're one of them."[51] But this person need not worry, for there is a thirty-day limit for federal support for families in welfare hotels.[52] This person will soon get out.

Once individuals are in a shelter, it is difficult for them to improve their living situations. Inhabitants are not allowed to save money in bank accounts. They must spend a good deal of their time traveling far in order to get rent checks to hand over at the front desk. Those who would be the best candidates for helping them get out cannot do so. In Hotel Carter in New York, families and friends have to pay to visit their loved ones in the shelter. If their families are poor to begin with, shelter residents cannot expect to seek their help in establishing a better living situation than what they have. Thus, conservatives are wrong to think the homeless have not exhausted their familial resources. Poverty in the families of the homeless, coupled with abuse of some kind, hardly makes returning to the family an option for many homeless people.[53] There is little promise of getting out of a shelter and into public housing; one source reported a waiting list of 200,000 names and eight years.[54]

Obviously, the choices of the homeless are quite limited. Shelters provide little freedom, not much relief, and a depressing atmosphere. There is no home to go back to, since all the homeless lack money and cannot afford housing. The choice is housing *or* food. Public housing (as opposed to temporary shelters) is not always obtainable, and it offers a plethora of its own problems. For instance, Cabrini Green in Chicago is plagued by gangs, with shootouts. Recently there has been a rash of children on their way to school or outside at play killed in gang crossfire.

It would be very difficult for the homeless to improve their situation by effecting changes in the political climate of the country. As a rule, circumstances make it unlikely that they will band together as an organized group with a cause. Even worse, it is difficult for them to vote in elections because they lack a permanent address. In New York City, a federal judge ruled that they had a right to vote if they met age and citizenship requirements, and allowed them to use the addresses of sidewalks, park benches, and post office steps.[55] A similar ruling was made in Washington, D.C., where the Board of Elections and Ethics ruled that "a fixed abode can be outside the confines of the home," allowing two homeless men who lived on heating grates to vote.[56] On the other hand, in Santa Barbara where a group of homeless people lived together under a tree, the city tore down their mailbox so that they could not register to vote. This happened after a group of about four hundred of them marched in protest to the Reagan ranch.[57]

The severe restrictions on the choices of the homeless are brought on by a capitalistic system, one that allows people to prefer living on crime-ridden streets because it is their best option. This fact is striking when viewed in light of what life on the streets is like. Aside from being vulnerable to crime, the homeless have been restricted in many ways. For instance, though the Supreme Court ruled in 1972 that street-begging was not illegal unless it became harassment,[58] the Transit and Port Authority in New York banned panhandling in subway stations and bus terminals,[59] and Mayor Jackson in Atlanta proposed licensing panhandlers in order to chase them out of the business district.[60] The right to eat has also been restricted. The West Beach Community Association in Santa Barbara "put a measure before the city council that would outlaw the removal of food from garbage cans without the owner's permission."[61] In Fort Lauderdale, the city commissioner suggested putting rat poison on the local garbage, but later retracted the suggestion and proposed instead chlorine bleach.[62] Though certain benefits cannot be denied a person because she does not have a permanent address, a Los Angeles County supervisor voted to require homeless in that city who lacked identification to be fingerprinted and photographed before qualifying for welfare.[63] The homeless have been denied access to adequate health care. Even if they receive medical treatment for their ailments, it would be difficult for them to follow needed prescriptions, as many of them lack access to running water and a clock.

7. Conclusion

Based on the alarming statistics and facts presented here, I conclude that public dwelling on the part of the homeless is *not* wrongful behavior because it certainly is *not* without justification or excuse. The homeless *are* justified in public dwelling, given the severe restrictions on their choices about where to live. The moral offense argument is unsound.

The statistics cited above can be used to argue that even if public dwelling *were* wrongful behavior, the behavior nevertheless should be allowed because any offense it causes is outweighed by the interests of the homeless. The statistics reveal that the situation of the homeless is caused by the system under which they live, and that it is the system that severely restricts their choices and threatens survival in many circumstances. Forbidding public dwelling would limit the choices of the homeless even further, by forcing them into restrictive and depressing shelters, or back into undesirable (and sometimes life-threatening) home-life situations. The interest of the homeless in surviving, and in having a decent quality of life, outweighs the offense others experience. It would be morally wrong to forbid public dwelling. In the end, the homeless have a right to "live" in public places, a right that outweighs the interest others have in not being physically or morally offended.

If my arguments are sound, they will have shown something minimal. It does not follow from the fact that the homeless have a right to public dwelling that they have a right to *shelter*. A fuller defense of the rights of the homeless would establish a right to shelter; being provided with shelter is more desirable than merely being able to live on the streets. Though some effort has been made to provide shelter, much more needs to be done.

The solution to the problem of the homeless inhabiting public places depends on how we perceive the problem. We must look to the *causes* of homelessness. I suggest that homelessness is caused foremost by a lack of money, along with, of course, the fact that cost of living is high and that the capitalist system does not provide sufficiently for people who are unlucky. If we recognize the real cause of the problem, instead of attributing it to people's being lazy, or mentally ill, and so on, our attitude towards the homeless in public places is likely to shift to one of tolerance. We will no longer perceive them as dangerous, or as being in our way, or as eyesores, but as victims of the system. Once this is admitted, we will come to view their presence in public places not as *their* problem but as *our* problem.

Notes

1. This chapter is a version of a paper presented to the Society for Philosophy and Public Affairs at the American Philosophical Association, Central Division Meeting, April 1993. I thank Joan Callahan for providing me with the opportunity to organize and participate in the session.

2. John Leo, "Homeless Rights, Community Wrongs," *U.S. News & World Report*, 107 (24 July 1989), p. 56.

3. Sarah Ferguson, "Us vs. Them: America's Growing Frustration with the Homeless," *Utne Reader* (September-October 1990), pp. 50-55.

4. James Baker, "Don't Sleep in the Subway," *Newsweek*, 117 (24 June 1991), p. 26.

5. Jonathan Kozol, "Slow Descent into Hell," *Time*, 129 (2 February 1987), pp. 26-29.

6. Charles Krauthammer, "When Liberty Really Means Neglect," *Time*, 126 (2 December 1985), p. 103.

7. Anne Fadiman, "A Week in the Life of a Homeless Family," *Life*, 10:13 (December 1987), pp. 31-38.

8. Chester Hartman, "Why They Have No Homes," *The Progressive* (March 1985), p. 27.

9. Krauthammer, "When Liberty Really Means Neglect."

10. Peter Marin, "How We Help and Harm the Homeless," *Utne Reader* (January-February 1988), pp. 36-47.

11. See William R. Breakey and Pamela J. Fischer, "Homelessness: The Extent of the Problem," *Journal of Social Issues*, 46:4 (1990), pp. 31-47.

12. See Kay Young McChesney, "Family Homelessness: An Introduction," *Journal of Social Issues*, 46:4 (1990), pp. 191-205.

13. Marin, "How We Help and Harm the Homeless," p. 39. See also Marybeth Shinn and Beth C. Weitzman, "Research on Homelessness: An Introduction," *Journal of Social Issues*, 46:4 (1990), pp. 1-11.

14. See Charles Grigsby *et al.*, "Disaffiliation to Entrenchment: A Model for Understanding Homelessness," *Journal of Social Issues*, 46:4 (1990), pp. 141-156.

15. *Ibid.*, p. 103.

16. John Leo, "Harassing the Homeless," *Time*, 125 (11 March 1985), p. 68.

17. Neal Karlen and Daniel Pederson, "Attack on the Tree People," *Newsweek*, 104 (24 December 1984), p. 20.

18. Jonathan Kozol, "A Reporter at Large: The Homeless and Their Children, Part II," *New Yorker*, 63 (1 February 1988), pp. 36-67.

19. See Gary L. Blasi, "Social Policy and Social Science Research on Homelessness," *Journal of Social Issues*, 46:4 (1990), pp. 207-219.

20. Stuart D. Bykofsky, "No Heart for the Homeless," *Newsweek*, 108 (1 December 1986), pp. 12-13.

21. Jacob V. Lamar, "The Homeless: Brick by Brick," *Time*, 132 (24 October 1988), pp. 34-38.

22. "The Homeless: Out in the Cold," *Newsweek*, 106 (16 December 1985), pp. 22-23.

23. Grigsby *et al.*, "Disaffiliation to Entrenchment," p. 151.

24. Leo, "Homeless Rights, Community Wrongs," p. 56.

25. This data was presented on American television (20 March 1992). I thank Thaddeus Superson for bringing this to my attention.

26. Joel Feinberg, *Offense to Others* (New York: Oxford University Press, 1984), p. 2.

27. Marin, "How We Help and Harm the Homeless," p. 39. See pp. 40-41. See also *Time*, 126 (2 December 1985), pp. 27ff. See also James D. Wright, "The Worthy and Unworthy Homeless," *Society*, 25:5 (July-August 1988), pp. 64-69, esp. p. 66. See also Shinn and Weitzman, "Research on Homelessness: An Introduction," pp. 4-5.

28. Beth C. Weitzman, "Pathways to Homelessness Among New York City Families," *Journal of Social Issues*, 46:4 (1990), pp. 131-132.

29. Wright, "The Worthy and Unworthy Homeless," p. 69.

30. See, for example, "A Family Down and Out," *Newsweek*, 109 (12 January 1987), p. 44.

31. Marin, "How We Help and Harm the Homeless," p. 38, and Lamar, "The Homeless: Brick by Brick," p. 34.

32. *Ibid.*

33. Jonathan Kozol, "Are the Homeless Crazy?" *Harper's*, 277:1660 (September 1988), pp. 17-19.

34. Patricia King, "Help for the Homeless," *Newsweek*, 111 (11 April 1988), pp. 58-59.

35. Kim Hopper, "Homelessness Old and New: The Matter of Definition," *Housing Policy Debate*, 2:3 (1991), pp. 757-813.

36. Kozol, "The Homeless and Their Children, Part II."

37. Marjorie Hope and James Young, "Sinking into Homelessness," *Commonweal* (15 June 1984), pp. 368-371.

38. McChesney, "Family Homelessness," p. 193.

39. Hartman, "Why They Have No Homes," p. 27. See also McChesney, "Family Homelessness," p. 192.

40. Kozol, "Are the Homeless Crazy?" p. 17; McChesney, "Family Homelessness," p. 192.

41. Lamar, "The Homeless: Brick by Brick," p. 34.

42. McChesney, "Family Homelessness," p. 193.

43. Hope and Young, "Sinking into Homelessness," p. 369.

44. *Ibid.*, p. 370.

45. Jonathan Kozol, "A Reporter at Large: The Homeless and Their Children, Part I," *New Yorker*, 63 (25 January 1988), pp. 65-84.

46. Peter Marcuse, "Why Are They Homeless?", *The Nation*, 244 (4 April 1987), pp. 426-429.

47. See Lauren M. Malatesta, "Finding a Right to Shelter for Homeless Families," *Suffolk University Law Review*, 22:3 (Fall 1988), pp. 719-746.

48. "Holiday Inn for the Homeless?", *Newsweek*, 106 (8 July 1985), p. 44.

49. Marin, "How We Help and Harm the Homeless," p. 44.

50. Kozol, "The Homeless and Their Children, Part II," p. 50.

51. Kozol, "Slow Descent into Hell," p. 29.

52. Jerry Adler and Lisa Drew, "Saving the Children," *Newsweek*, 111 (25 January 1988), pp. 58-59.

53. See Jeffrey A. Meyer, "Establishing a Right to Shelter: Lessons from Connecticut," *University of Bridgeport Law Review*, 11:1 (1990), pp. 1-29.

54. Kozol, "The Homeless and Their Children, Part II," p. 51.

55. Marcia Z. Nelson, "Street People," *The Progressive*, 49 (March 1985), pp. 24-29.

56. "Homeless in D.C. Win Right to Vote," *Jet*, 66:16 (25 June 1984), p. 28.

57. Karlen and Pederson, "Attack on the Tree People," p. 20.

58. Eric Pooley, "Beggar's Army," *New York*, 21 (29 August 1988), pp. 31-37.

59. Ferguson, "Us vs. Them," p. 51.

60. *Ibid.*

61. Karlen and Pederson, "Attack on the Tree People," p. 20.

62. Leo, "Harassing the Homeless," p. 68.

63. "Homeless in L.A. County Must Be Fingerprinted to Qualify for Welfare," *Jet*, 70:3 (7 April 1986), p. 9.

Eleven

NO SHELTER EVEN IN THE CONSTITUTION? FREE SPEECH, EQUAL PROTECTION, AND THE HOMELESS[1]

Uma Narayan

1. Introduction

In recent years the numbers of destitute and homeless people in the United States has greatly increased, accompanied by an increase in hostile public sentiments against the homeless. There are increasing reports of serious physical attacks directed at vulnerable homeless persons.[2] Ironically, many laws and policies pertaining to the homeless are designed to legally hound and harass them and to clear them out of public spaces instead of providing protection. In this chapter, I criticize some of these laws and policies directed at the homeless. I focus on two sorts of laws and policies, both of which seem designed to remove the homeless from public spaces. First, I look at laws designed to ban begging in public spaces, such as the New York Transit Authority's ban on begging in the subways, and Atlanta's proposal to keep panhandlers out of the business district.[3] Secondly, I examine a cluster of "public nuisance" laws and policies, some of which seem designed to literally remove the homeless from public parks, vacant buildings, parking lots and public libraries, and the rest to "discourage" the homeless from obtaining shelter or sustenance in public places.[4] Examples of such policies include proposals to place barbed wire on hot-air grates to prevent the homeless from securing warmth, and to put rat-poison in local garbage to deter the homeless from looking through it for food.[5]

I argue that on *moral* grounds these laws and policies *ought* to be unconstitutional. I begin with a consideration of laws that would ban begging and argue that a *morally adequate* interpretation of the First Amendment would support the conclusion that any legal ban on begging is unconstitutional. I explain why our legal tradition of First Amendment interpretation does not treat begging as protected speech, but argue that this legal tradition is open to moral criticism. I then go on to make moral arguments as to why laws and policies that do not directly involve issues of speech, but instead deny the homeless a right to make use of public spaces, also ought to be unconstitutional. I proceed as a moral and social philosopher reflecting on constitutional issues, though I make moral arguments of a sort that seem appropriate in the context of constitutional discourse.

2. Free Speech, Audience Interests, and a Legal Ban on Begging

A major debate over the constitutionality of laws banning begging revolves around whether begging deserves First Amendment protection. The reasoning of Judge Altimari of the U.S. Court of Appeals for the Second Circuit exemplifies one side of the debate in his opinion in *Young v. New York Transit Authority*. He expresses "grave doubt" as to whether begging is "sufficiently imbued with a communicative character to justify constitutional protection."[6] Arguing that the object of begging is the transfer of money, Judge Altimari concludes that "[s]peech is simply seen as not inherent to the act; it is not of the essence of the conduct."[7] We can see the other side of the debate in the arguments of Helen Hershkoff and Adam Cohen, who argue that begging is "simply a spoken appeal made by one human being to another" and conclude that a law banning begging only seeks to punish one form of conduct, communication.[8] I agree that begging is an act of communication in that it involves both communicative intent (the beggar minimally intends to convey a request for charity) and communicative *content* (the beggar communicates a definite message, that he or she is in need and would like the material assistance of the person solicited).[9]

The issue is not whether begging necessarily involves words or not; one might successfully beg in silence, using the mute appeal of holding out a tin cup or an empty hand. It is also not enough to show that begging is an act of communication, since the important issue is whether begging involves *valuable communication* of a sort that should be constitutionally protected. After all, burning the flag may involve no words, but is protected as valuable political expression under the First Amendment.[10] In what terms can we understand the communicative value of begging? We most often analyze the value of speech in terms of the auditor's interests. I shall therefore start by asking what value begging, as a communicative request for charity, may have for those to whom it is addressed.

Many of us regard a request for charity as an occasion that permits us to perform minor acts of moral merit. We do not necessarily claim that begging may have value to members of its audience by providing an occasion for smug moral satisfaction. Knowledge of our social context, the extent of homelessness and destitution, the inadequate social provisions that foster such an extent of destitution, our empathy for plight of the homeless, all lead us to regard an appeal for charity as a chance to do something for a fellow human being, while being critical of the structures that produce such need and destitution. Some of us may also be moved by religious injunctions that remind us we are our brother's keeper and which enjoin moral responsiveness to human suffering. Some may not have such favorable attitudes to assisting the homeless. However, communication need not have value to *all* members of its audience in order to warrant protection; it suffices that a significant portion of its audience consider it valuable. Those who find no moral value in responding to a fellow citizen in need are free to decline their assistance.

I have thus far analyzed the communicative value of begging to its audience in its narrowest sense, one that presupposes little about "wider messages" that may be communicated by such requests. Some "wider" messages might in fact be communicated. The plaintiffs in *Young*, a group of panhandlers in New York City, testified that their solicitations often led to conversations with passersby, in which they explained what it was like to be homeless and advocated the cause of the homeless. Even when such conversations do not ensue, a request for charity might draw our attention to the existence of the homeless, and lead to significant social and political understandings about the society in which we live.

Hershkoff and Cohen have argued that begging as communication has this wider communicative value. They argue broadly that begging has "Enlightenment Value," contributing to the emergence of truth from the free exchange of ideas, and "Democratic Governance Value." So begging contributes to the welfare of the community by enabling those who decide on issues to understand them. Although I am sympathetic to their argument, I would like to raise an objection to Hershkoff and Cohen's defense of begging as speech that has political value. A legal ban on begging is seldom *motivated* by a desire to limit political expression about the plight of the homeless. Beggars, and others, remain free to communicate everything they want about the plight of the destitute, without actually engaging in begging.

While some might call it a fantasy that actual homeless and destitute persons might have the means to educate the public about their plight without engaging in begging, bans on begging do not necessarily aim at limiting political expression about the homeless. Where a regulation prohibits a particular conduct to "protect a governmental interest that is not related to the suppression of free expression," courts evaluate the regulation using the standard set out in *United States v. O'Brien*,[11] which is referred to as the "O'Brien standard."[12] Since I discuss this standard at length later, it suffices for now to point out that arguments of the sort made by the Transit Authority—that passengers perceived begging to be "intimidating," "threatening," and "harassing," and that begging "disrupts" and "startles" passengers, creating potential for serious accidents—do in fact provide sufficient grounds for a ban on begging that legally satisfy the O'Brien standard. The argument that begging has political value to its audience does not suffice to make a ban on begging unconstitutional in cases where the ban is not motivated by a desire to suppress such political expression.

Hershkoff and Cohen's arguments about the Enlightenment Value and the Democratic Governance Value of begging as speech recall Alexander Meiklejohn's view that policies regulating speech should be evaluated by asking

whether they assist democratic debate.[13] Meiklejohn's views have been criticized for legitimizing protection of too narrow a range of speech, and commen-
tators such as D. F. B. Tucker have argued that speech that serves other
legitimate but not explicitly political purposes, such as speech that makes a
contribution to art or science, or speech that entertains, should also be recognized as serving important audience interests.[14] However, even this wider notion
of audience interests does not capture the sort of *moral* value that I have argued
begging may have for its audience. A request for charity enables some of us to
respond, in a face-to-face manner, to the need of a destitute fellow citizen, in a
way we may reasonably regard as morally valuable. We do not seem to
recognize moral value as one of the qualities speech might have for its auditors.

While what Hershkoff and Cohen call Enlightenment Value and Democratic Governance Value could conceivably be promoted without anyone
actually engaging in begging, there is something interestingly different about
what I have called the moral value that begging may have for its audience. This
"moral value" is unlikely to obtain without people's begging. One has little
opportunity to morally respond to another's need, when a prohibition prevents
the person from conveying his or her need for assistance. However, even if such
moral value for its audience were recognized as making speech worthy of First
Amendment protection, laws banning begging would be upheld under applications of the O'Brien standard. The authorities would need to argue only that
their ban on begging was not motivated by a desire to curtail speech that had
such moral value its audience, and then show that "governmental interest that
is unrelated to the suppression of free expression" is at stake.

3. Begging as Communication and Its Value to Speakers

Arguments that focus on the value of the speech to its audience fail to capture
a crucial moral dimension of the communicative value of begging: its value to
its speakers. The survival of many beggars depends on their successfully
communicating their need to those who might render assistance. Begging is
linked to the subsistence interests of beggars and is crucial to their dignity as
persons. David Richards's general analysis of the connection between free
speech, individual autonomy, and self-respect is illuminating with regard to the
particular predicament of the destitute.[15] Destitution entails a vulnerability which
impairs a person's dignity. Depriving a person of the right to communicate his
or her predicament to others and thereby seek assistance further increases
vulnerability. It defies the person's right to use his or her powers in the only way
available in order to survive.[16]

Begging as communication serves to preserve the dignity as well as vital
subsistence interests of its speakers, and subsistence interests are, morally
speaking, fundamental interests of individuals.[17] However, much of our moral

and legal discussions about the value of speech has shown an unfortunate tendency to ignore the value of speech to its speakers and its connections to preserving human dignity. If the courts were to acknowledge that begging as communication serves the vital subsistence interests of speakers, they would have to face the argument that a ban on begging impairs fundamental interests of individuals. Such a law should then trigger strict scrutiny. This would mean that such a law would be constitutional only where it can be shown that it is necessary to foster a compelling state interest, using the least restrictive means possible.[18] The demands of strict scrutiny would be much harder to meet than that of the lenient O'Brien standard, which only asks that the law further *an important or substantial government interest.* However, our constitutional tradition has repeatedly refused to recognize that various economic interests, including "necessities of life," are fundamental rights whose impairment warrants strict scrutiny. Therefore, there is little room in our constitutional tradition to invoke First Amendment protection on the grounds that a particular form of speech is tied to crucial subsistence interests of individuals, even though we can make a strong *moral* argument for it.

I will take a different tack and argue that the sorts of reasons most often given in support of a ban on begging in fact fall well short of satisfying the O'Brien standard. Therefore a blanket legal ban on begging should be deemed unconstitutional. I will focus on the sorts of reasons given by the Transit Authority in *Young* to make my case. By arguing that the O'Brien standard is not satisfied, even where a ban on begging covers only the confines of the areas regulated by the Transit Authority, I show that reasons for a more general ban on begging in public spaces are likely to be based upon suspect presuppositions concerning the destitute.

4. The O'Brien Standard and a Ban on Begging

According to the O'Brien standard, a government regulation is regarded as "sufficiently justified" when (1) it is within the constitutional power of the government; (2) it furthers an important or substantial government interest; (3) the government interest is unrelated to the suppression of free expression; and (4) the incidental restrictions on alleged First Amendment freedoms is no greater than essential to the furtherance of that interest. I shall proceed on the assumption that conditions (1) and (3) obtain in most cases where a legal ban on begging is under consideration. Regulations concerning public spaces seem within the constitutional powers of government, and such laws are seldom *motivated* to curtail free expression about the plight of the homeless. Conditions (2) and (4), however, are seldom satisfied, in any morally compelling way, according to the rationales for a blanket ban on begging in public spaces.

I will take the three broad sorts of reasons given by the Transit Authority in *Young* as typical of reasons given to support a ban on begging. The three sorts of reasons can be broadly stated as follows:

1. Begging raises questions of public safety, in that it "disrupts" and "startles" passengers, creating potential for serious accidents.
2. Begging constitutes a form of harassment.
3. The majority of passengers "perceive" begging as "intimidating," "threatening," and "harassing."

Consider the first reason. It seems undeniable that promoting public safety constitutes an important or substantial government interest. However, such a reason would justify, at most, *zoning regulations* that forbade begging in areas where risk of *concrete harm* to others exists. The Transit Authority might be justified in banning begging near trains, on or near escalators, and so forth. The plaintiffs in *Young* said that they were quite willing to abide by reasonable zoning regulations, such as those barring them from begging near ticket counters, escalators, and even on the subway cars themselves. However, while such considerations of public safety might justify some "time, place, and manner" restrictions on begging, it does not justify banning begging in all areas owned by the Transit Authority, let alone a blanket ban on begging. In great many public spaces, such as public parks and the central areas of subway terminals, being solicited by beggars poses no substantial risk of harm. A complete ban on begging therefore does not satisfy the second clause of the O'Brien standard, since the ban secures no important or substantial government interest.

What of the second reason, that begging constitutes a form of harassment of the individuals solicited? If begging did constitute a form of harassment, a ban on begging would plausibly serve an important or substantial government interest, thus satisfying the second clause of *O'Brien*. However, no compelling reasons exist to support the conclusion that begging *per se* constitutes a form of harassment. While some acts of begging may be conducted in a manner that constitutes harassment—for example, where the person solicited is persistently followed, impeded in his or her movements, or threatened upon a refusal to give —nothing about begging *simpliciter* makes it harassment. Begging often does not incorporate these aspects of harassment and is conceptually distinct from harassment. Many beggars do not harass. And most harassers are not beggars. We already have laws that deal with harassment, and banning begging hardly begins to address harassment. More importantly, it is not fair to curtail important liberties of a whole group of people on the grounds that *some* of them engage in harassment.

Interestingly, in *Young* the Transit Authority argued that begging on its premises was intrinsically a form of harassment, even if beggars did not actually do anything explicitly confrontational. Arguing that in the crowded subway environment, passengers feel captive, the Transit Authority contended that "in the subway environment, begging is inherently aggressive, even if not patently so."[19] Judge Altimari concurred that in such environments, begging would be inherently "experienced as transgressive conduct."[20] Such arguments are bothersome, since they would provide grounds for banning begging in precisely those spaces that offer greatest opportunities for solicitation. However, I do not find such arguments convincing. I find it difficult to understand what makes one human being asking another for charity "inherently aggressive" when such request is made in a crowded space. In crowded public places like the Transit Authority premises, there are people selling newspapers and other commodities, people asking for the time or for directions, people pushing past in a hurry to get where they are going, people playing music, proselytizing, having fights or loud conversations, and people soliciting for organized charities. It is hard to see why otherwise unabrasive requests for charity are any more unpleasant or "intrinsically aggressive" than these various activities that make up the milieu in any crowded urban environment. I argue that no good reason exists to consider begging "intrinsically harassing" and that a ban on begging on these grounds should fail the second clause of *O'Brien*, since it serves no important or substantial government interest.

The argument that begging is "intrinsically harassing" is additionally problematic, because it tends to be supported by the third of the reasons I set forth previously, that people "perceive" begging to be "threatening," "harassing," and "intimidating." That reference to people's perceptions supports the assertion that "begging is intrinsically harassment" is revealed in the U. S. Court of Appeals' conclusion in *Young* that the Transit Authority was not discriminatory in banning begging while allowing organized charities to solicit because "[n]owhere in the record is there any indication that passengers felt intimidated by organized charities."[21] People's "perceptions" cannot be used as a basis for arguing that begging is "intrinsically harassing" and that it should therefore, be banned.

The Transit Authority supported its case for banning begging by reference to a study conducted by them that allegedly proved that beggars were perceived by passengers to be a major "quality of life" problem in the subway system. They claimed that the study showed "that beggars are perceived to pervade the subway system and that the ridership considers the presence of beggars as a significant problem."[22] Several points need to be made. The Transit Authority did not make clear what exactly the passengers were asked. For instance, if a survey were taken in which people were asked whether they considered beggars to be a "quality of life" problem in the subway (or, in the streets, the parks, the neighborhood, for that matter), likely many would answer "yes," even if they did not deeply object to the presence of the destitute. This would not necessarily mean that they would support a ban on begging in order that they might have a better quality of life. The Transit Authority never established that a majority of the public in fact supports a ban on begging. Reports suggest that as many people booed as cheered when police initially enforced the ban and forcibly removed beggars from subways.[23]

Besides, even if a majority of the public did perceive beggars to be a "quality of life" problem and consequently supported a ban on begging, it would not necessarily justify such a ban. We need to morally evaluate the reasons people might have for their negative attitudes toward the destitute. I will consider a number of reasons that might be at work and argue that they are all morally problematic.

First, public antipathy may be motivated by stereotypes that the destitute are lazy and shiftless and by beliefs such as that expressed by Ronald Reagan, that the homeless choose to be homeless.[24] Second, antipathy may rest on views that the homeless are "crazy" and "dangerous."[25] That these beliefs are false generalizations based on negative stereotypes can be demonstrated by looking at the empirical evidence available in books such as Peter Rossi's *Down and Out in America*.[26] Those individuals among the homeless population who engage in criminal acts or pose a public danger because of mental health problems should be dealt with by the existing mechanisms that are used for dealing with any of us who are criminal or dangerous. To stigmatize a whole group of people because of the actions of some of its members is unfair. After all, women who have frequently been harassed by non-destitute men both in the subway system and in a variety of public spaces are (quite rightly) unlikely to inspire public policy initiatives to have all men removed from the subways if they were to complain that the presence of men adversely affected their quality of life!

Third, negative public sentiments against the homeless might be due to people perceiving the destitute as "public nuisances"—people whose destitute presence makes public spaces less enjoyable, comfortable, or aesthetically pleasing for those who are better-off. It would take the disappearance of the destitute from public spaces, and not just their refraining from begging, to alleviate such sensibilities. Support for laws against begging, like many other laws directed at the homeless, may often be inspired by the belief that the homeless would disappear from public spaces if denied the means to shelter and subsist within them. It is hardly worth belaboring that something is morally appalling about sensibilities that reduce fellow human beings to "eyesores" and "public nuisances." Nor must much more be said for those who would protect their tender sensibilities by arranging things so that the destitute "disappear" from the orbits of their lives, with no concern for their subsequent well-being. I can sympathize to a degree with people feeling resentful at having to deal with problems that they believe society as a whole should provide the means to relieve. While I believe such resentment might well be justified, it should be directed at society's failure to do what it should for the destitute, not at the destitute themselves. The more affluent should respond by supporting more assistance for the destitute. Responding by attacking the present, inadequate support for the destitute is reprehensible.

I believe that justifying a ban on begging on the basis of morally problematic public sensibilities, on stereotypes, prejudiced antipathies, and misplaced resentment, violates what Richard Mohr calls the Dreyfus Principle. The principle says "[s]tigmas that are entirely socially induced shall not play a part in our rational moral deliberation," and rules out using discriminatory sentiments held by people as a good reason for institutionalizing further discrimination.[27] I would use Mohr's Dreyfus Principle to argue that pandering to morally problematic sensibilities cannot constitute an "important or substantial government interest," in any context. Therefore, a ban on begging whose reasons refer to such problematic sensibilities cannot be judged as satisfying the second clause of the O'Brien standard in any morally acceptable sense.

However, our legal traditions and current legal practice do not oblige or even encourage subjecting allegedly "important or substantial government interests" to moral scrutiny. As an unfortunate result, no constitutional restraints are placed on the state that prohibit the state from referring to morally problematic sensibilities as bases for substantial state interests that may then be used to prohibit morally innocuous conduct by others. So, my moral critique of laws banning begging that are based on morally problematic sensibilities is unlikely to constitute a compelling legal argument that such a ban is unconstitutional. I would therefore like to follow up with two further lines of moral argument. The first contends that in contexts where the state has failed to adequately provide for the welfare rights of the destitute, the destitute have the right to freely make peaceful use of public spaces in order to secure their subsistence. The second contends that the destitute ought to be considered a "suspect class" under the Equal Protection Clause of the Fourteenth Amendment.

5. Public Spaces, Subsistence Interests, and the Homeless

I will begin with some general moral considerations about the homeless, and the use of public spaces. I am deeply sympathetic to arguments, such as those made by Anita Superson, that under existing social conditions, there is good reason to recognize that the homeless have a "right to public dwelling."[28] I would like to further add moral weight to this conclusion by pointing out that government policies, through acts of both omission and commission, are shared in the creation of large numbers of the destitute. The acts of omission include failures to provide adequate welfare support, health care for the mentally ill, and public education of a sort that equips people for employment. Acts of commission include military involvement in Vietnam and elsewhere, leaving many veterans among New York City's homeless with physical and/or psychological problems that impede them from supporting themselves. United States economic and tax policies are certainly responsible for a situation in which 44 percent of the jobs created between 1980 and 1988 paid poverty-level wages and a situation where 0.5 percent of households own 45 percent of all the wealth. Government policies are also responsible for changes in the housing situation. For instance, 87 percent of single-room-occupancy hotel units (SROs), which formerly housed a large number of New York City's homeless, were demolished or converted between 1970 and 1982, and much of the conversion was made attractive by city tax abatements.[29]

Superson has analyzed the problematic nature of the reasons given in support of recent policies which share the goal of removing the destitute and homeless from public spaces.[30] Additional problematic forms of reasoning may be at work that make these policies seem justifiable. Those who support these policies probably start with the idea that "public spaces" should exist for the "public good." They then proceed to leave out the serious subsistence interests of the homeless in their concrete determination of the "public good." This is attributed to the dominant picture of the "standard citizen" who is seen as having a legitimate interest in "public spaces." This is the picture of a citizen who has a private dwelling and a means of subsistence that does not require begging in public places. This picture facilitates the assumption that public places do not exist to provide means for citizens to shelter or subsist but exist to facilitate their ability to go about their lives, with convenience, comfort, and enjoyment.[31] The "standard citizen" picture helps to rationalize the failure to give adequate moral weight to the vital interests of destitute citizens, while giving disproportionate moral consideration to the considerably less serious interests of better off citizens.

I would hardly wish to deny that in an ideal world, all citizens would have the dignity and privacy made possible by having a private dwelling. In an ideal world, park benches would be spaces for relaxation and not beds; transit facilities and public libraries would not be places where people went to stay warm; and garbage would be undisturbed by those looking for scraps to eat. What I object to is the assumption that we live in the sort of world where we can reasonably expect these things and where we can judge those who use public spaces in this manner as people who lack civic sense. I object to perceptions of the destitute that reduce them to public nuisances who have no entitlements to be in or use public spaces, and who can be made to magically disappear by acts of legislative conjuring. What I object to are policy responses to the homeless that are motivated simply by the desire to remove them from public view, exemplified in these memorable words of columnist George Will:

If it is illegal . . . to litter the streets, frankly it ought to be illegal for people
. . . to sleep in the streets. Therefore, there is a simple matter of public
order and hygiene in getting these people somewhere else. Not arrest them,
but move them off somewhere where they are simply out of sight.[32]

We need to recognize that the destitute are fellow citizens going about the
business of trying to survive in the only ways open to them. This use of public
spaces to secure their vital subsistence interests warrants constitutional protection in certain contexts. We have constitutional guarantees because certain
interests of individual citizens need to be insulated from the negotiations of
democratic politics, from the possible tyranny of the state, as well as from what
John Stuart Mill called the tyranny of the majority.[33] The subsistence interests
of the destitute are not only serious interests of individuals but are interests that
are unlikely to be protected via the political negotiations of democratic politics.
The destitute not only lack independent political clout, but are an unpopular and
disliked group whose interests seem unlikely to be supported by the voters or the
officials they elect. These interests fit the profile of the sorts of interests of
individuals that typically warrant constitutional protection. I shall consider
different ways in which such protection might be offered.

Recognizing basic welfare rights would afford such constitutional protection by making them rights that would be constitutionally enforced if the
legislature failed to provide them. Rodney Peffer has argued that there is no
conceptual mistake in talking of fundamental rights to well-being and that
recognizing such rights would help us better account for our moral deliberations
in a variety of cases.[34] He understands such rights to well-being as "a category
of rights conceptually connected to our basic needs as human organisms . . .
rights to the things we require if we are to survive and to have any sort of a life
worth living."[35] James Sterba has argued at length that there is conceptual room
for welfare rights in a variety of political perspectives.[36] I am sympathetic to
such arguments for welfare rights and inclined to believe that the role the state
plays in rendering people unable to provide for their own subsistence obligates
the state to provide for them. However, while I think such arguments are morally
feasible, I want to explore a different sort of argument for constitutional
protection of the subsistence interests of the destitute.

Most of the constitutional rights we recognize are rights to freedom from
various interferences, and not rights to the provision of means to satisfy
important individual interests. I side-step arguments for recognizing basic
welfare rights (rights to the provision of means of basic subsistence) as constitutional rights and set out an argument based on freedom from interference.
I argue in terms of a right to freedom from certain forms of state interference
that impede the attempts of the destitute to subsist in a context where there is a
failure to provide adequately for their subsistence. The following moral

principle should govern a nation's laws and policies: When the state fails to provide for the basic subsistence needs of some of its citizens, those affected should at least enjoy freedom from any laws and policies that pose impediments to citizens' achieving subsistence by means of the non-dangerous and peaceful use of public spaces, unless there is a compelling reason for any such law or policy. By peaceful uses, I mean uses that do not constitute acts of violence against other citizens. If this principle were operative, any law or policy that would prevent destitute citizens from subsisting via the use of public spaces would have to describe what *compelling reason* justified it, and why it was serious enough to override the subsistence interests of the destitute. Such laws and policies could not rely on appeals to the fact that some of the better-off regarded the presence and activities of the homeless in public places as a nuisance, becoming frightened even by non-threatening conduct on the part of the destitute.

Since 1937, a dichotomy has existed in constitutional judicial review of classifications. In one group, classifications are employed in economic and general social welfare regulation. In the other, they touch upon what are recognized to be "fundamental constitutional values." Classifications of the first sort will be upheld so long as they can be shown to relate to a legitimate function of government. Classifications of the second type, however, will be subjected to "strict scrutiny" and upheld only if they are necessary to promote an important or compelling end of government. Accordingly, the courts will uphold legislative actions that burden poor persons—unless, of course, they involve the abrogation of otherwise recognized fundamental rights—as long as the action has some rational relationship to a legitimate end of government, an easy standard to meet.[37]

The Supreme Court in some cases has refused to subject to strict scrutiny legislation that burdened poor persons by affecting their receipt of government subsistence benefits or other welfare benefits, public housing, access to the judicial process where no fundamental right is involved, or the allocation of public educational opportunities based on wealth.[38] The Court's refusal is explained thus: "It is apparently the view of the majority of the justices that there is nothing in the judicial function that makes them institutionally capable of deciding economic policy as to the allocation of income and wealth through the review of legislative classifications."[39]

However, the sorts of cases in which I think that legislative actions that burden the poor should be subject to strict scrutiny differ in important ways from these previous cases that the Court has refused to subject to strict scrutiny. First, the legislative actions I am concerned with are not about the distribution of income and wealth; so the Court is not being asked to make economic policy decisions about the allocation of income and wealth.[40] In fact, the legislative actions I am concerned with do not involve the provision of any of the means of subsistence. Instead, I am concerned with actions that impede the destitute from securing their own subsistence. Second, the legislative actions I am concerned with are not actions that burden the poor in general, but are actions that impede the desperately poor, the destitute. Third, I am not arguing for strict scrutiny to be applied to the entire range of policies that may have any adverse impact on the desperately poor. I argue for the narrower class of actions that prevent the destitute from peacefully using public spaces to provide for their vital subsistence interests, in the absence of adequate legislative provisions that would secure these interests. Considerations that have deterred the Court from subjecting some of the previously mentioned cases to "strict scrutiny" do not apply here. Given that such considerations do not apply, laws that fall into this narrower class should be subjected to strict scrutiny and be deemed constitutional only when a compelling state interest is at stake.

6. Equal Protection and the Homeless

Another moral argument for subjecting to strict scrutiny laws and policies that affect the subsistence interests of the destitute can be made by invoking the Equal Protection Clause of the Fourteenth Amendment. I believe there are good reasons to treat the homeless and destitute as a suspect class for Fourteenth Amendment purposes. Laws that are explicitly targeted at the destitute or have a disproportionate impact on their ability to secure their subsistence interests should be subjected to strict scrutiny, and they should be upheld only when they are necessary to secure compelling state interests. The best articulated theory of the conditions that must be satisfied to consider a group to be a suspect class lie in Justice Brennan's opinion in the *Regents of the University of California v. Bakke* decision. The first two criteria, which he refers to as "the traditional indicia of suspectness," are as follows: First, the group must be "saddled with disabilities, or subjected to a history of purposeful unequal treatment"; second, it must be "relegated to such a position of political powerlessness as to command extraordinary protection from the majoritarian process."[41] I believe that ample empirical evidence can be invoked to make a strong case for the view that the destitute are a politically powerless and an unpopular minority and thus satisfy the traditional criteria for considering a group a suspect class.

Justice Brennan also declares that a suspect class must constitute a discrete and insular minority. Do the destitute fail to constitute a discrete and insular minority? Should their discreteness or insularity matter in terms of treating them as a suspect class for purposes of legislation that impedes them from securing their own subsistence via the use of public spaces? I understand the Supreme Court's use of the term "discrete minority" to mean "constituting a minority group whose members are clearly and distinctly visible as members of that group." The destitute in our society constitute a minority; so that is not at issue.

Since I am addressing the *destitute* and not the poor in general, I argue that they do constitute a discrete minority, since being destitute marks the appearance of people in immediately obvious ways. Exceptions number fewer than people whose membership in a racial group is not obvious. I understand the Court's use of the term "insular minority" to mean "constituting a minority group whose members permanently retain their identity as members of that group," where group membership is an "immutable characteristic" of its members. Are the destitute an "insular minority" in this sense? Obviously not. People acquire membership in the class of the destitute. Presumably, some people escape membership in that class by a change in fortune, though I suspect that many who acquire membership in that class do not ever leave it. However, the fact that being destitute is not an "immutable characteristic" should not matter for the purposes of the sort of constitutional protections I am arguing for. I am arguing for constitutional protection against laws and policies that impede the subsistence of all of those who are destitute at any particular given time, whose destitution makes them members of a politically powerless and disliked minority. When a individuals become destitute, they acquire membership in this vulnerable class; if they cease to be destitute, they no longer need the protection extended to this class. In short, I fail to see why "insularity" is morally relevant or should be a pre-condition for constitutional protection being accorded to a vulnerable group.

Since *Bakke*, the Supreme Court has been moving away from according strict scrutiny under the Fourteenth Amendment only to classifications that are suspect in that they involve discrimination against a discrete and insular minority that is politically powerless or historically disliked. The Court has declared all racial classifications to be inherently suspect, even if they are designed to benefit racially disadvantaged minorities.[42] I do not understand the logic behind subjecting racial classifications to strict scrutiny, even when they do not discriminate against politically powerless or disadvantaged minorities, while withholding strict scrutiny from laws and policies that target a politically powerless and unpopular minority, the destitute. Furthermore, since *Bakke*, the courts have upheld "strict scrutiny" for cases that involved a racial classification but did not involve any of the restricted list of rights they have previously recognized to be "fundamental rights" (mostly rights connected to voting, criminal appeals, and inter-state travel). The Court would not explicitly have to declare subsistence rights to be "fundamental rights" in order to subject the sorts of cases I have in mind to strict scrutiny if they recognized that the destitute constitute a "suspect class."

It makes moral sense to subject to strict scrutiny laws and policies that impede the destitute from peacefully using public spaces in order to secure their subsistence, declaring them unconstitutional unless they can be shown to serve a compelling state interest. I believe strict scrutiny should apply to all laws and policies which would affect the homeless, even when they do not explicitly mention beggars or the destitute and homeless. With regard to race, laws will be subject to strict scrutiny even when they do not explicitly involve a racial classification. For instance, a zoning ordinance may be found to be unconstitutional if it can be proven that the purpose and effect of the ordinance is the exclusion of a racial minority from a residential area.[43] The courts will even test a law "in its application." For instance, in 1886 a law which prohibited the use of wooden buildings for hand laundries was found as an unconstitutional racial classification in its administration when all Chinese persons who owned such laundries were forced to give up their businesses, while all non-oriental persons with similar laundries were granted exemptions.[44] I advocate a similar approach to laws and policies that indirectly affect the subsistence interests of the destitute, whether in purpose and effect, or in administration.

The poor may have always been with us, but most of the recent laws and policies concerning the homeless seem to involve the desire to move the destitute and the homeless somewhere else. Their plight seems to elicit not compassion but resentment and legislative harassment. They are perceived, not as fellow citizens struggling to survive under desperate conditions, but as blots on our landscapes and destabilizers of our communities. I would be only too happy if popular public attitudes toward the destitute and homeless changed for the better, providing fewer political incentives for these sorts of laws and policies. But I am far from confident that better public attitudes towards the destitute or better provisions for their basic needs are around the corner. As long as the destitute remain vulnerable, deeply disliked and politically powerless, constitutional protection of the sort I have described is not only morally compelling, but in keeping with the basic political reasons we have constitutional protections at all.

In 1819, Chief Justice John Marshall spoke eloquent words which resonate in the context issue:

> Let the end be legitimate, let it be within the scope of the constitution, and all means which are appropriate, which are plainly adapted to that end, which are not prohibited but consist with the letter and spirit of the constitution, are constitutional . . . we must never forget, that it is a *constitution* we are expounding.[45]

Notes

1. Shorter versions of this chapter were presented at a session on "Homelessness and the Law" organized by the Society for Philosophy and Public Affairs, New York, and at the American Philosophical Association, Central Division, Chicago, April 1993. My

discussion of attempts to legally ban begging draws on my earlier paper, "Begging for Justice: Free Speech, Equal Protection, and a Legal Ban on Begging," in *The Bill Of Rights: Bicentennial Reflections*, eds. Yeager Hudson and Creighton Peden, *Social Philosophy Today*, no. 8. I would like to thank Jennifer Church, James W. Hill, Jesse Kalin, Molly Shanley, Andrew von Hirsch, and Iris Young for their helpful comments on various drafts of this chapter.

2. See "Attack on the Tree People," *Newsweek* (24 December 1984), p. 20, and "Harassing the Homeless," *Time* (11 March 1985), p. 68, for some details.

3. See Sarah Ferguson, "Us vs. Them: America's Growing Frustration with Homelessness," *Utne Reader* (September-October 1990), for details.

4. For details, see *U.S. News and World Report* (24 July 1989), p. 56, and *Newsweek* (24 June 1991), p. 26.

5. See "When Liberty Really Means Neglect," *Time* (2 December, 1985), p. 103, and "Harassing the Homeless," p. 68.

6. *Young v. New York City Transit Authority*, 903 F2d, May 1990, p. 153.

7. *Ibid.*, p. 154.

8. Helen Hershkoff and Adam S. Cohen, "Begging to Differ: The First Amendment and the Right to Beg," *Harvard Law Review*, 104:869 (February 1991), p. 908.

9. Narayan, "Begging for Justice," p. 152

10. *Texas v. Johnson*, 109 S.Ct. 2533 (1989).

11. *United States v. O'Brien*, 391 U.S. 367, 88 S.Ct. 1673 (1968).

12. See *Young v. New York City Transit Authority*, p. 157.

13. Alexander Meiklejohn, *Political Freedom: The Constitutional Powers of the People* (New York: Oxford University Press, 1965).

14. See D. F. B. Tucker, *Law, Liberalism, and Free Speech* (Totowa, N.J.: Rowman and Allenheld, 1985).

15. David A. J. Richards, "Free Speech and Obscenity Law: Toward a Moral Theory of the First Amendment," *University of Pennsylvania Law Review*, 123 (1974).

16. See Hershkoff and Cohen, "Begging to Differ," p. 903.

17. See, for instance, Henry Shue, *Basic Rights* (Princeton, N.J.: Princeton University Press, 1980).

18. On "strict scrutiny," see Jeffrie G. Murphy and Jules Coleman, *The Philosophy of Law* (Totowa, N.J.: Rowman and Allenheld, 1984), p. 89.

19. *Young v. New York City Transit Authority*, p. 150.

20. *Ibid.*, p. 154.

21. *Ibid.*, p. 155.

22. *Ibid.*, p. 149. Emphasis mine.

23. *The New York Times* (18 April 1991), p. 27.

24. Peter Marcuse, "Why Are They Homeless?", *The Nation*, 244 (4 April 1987), p. 428.

25. See Anita M. Superson, "The Homeless and the Right to 'Public Dwelling,'" in this volume, pp. 142-143.

26. See Peter H. Rossi, *Down and Out in America* (Chicago: The University of Chicago Press, 1989).

27. Richard Mohr, "Gay Rights," *Social Theory and Practice*, 8:1 (Spring 1982).

28. Superson, "The Homeless and the Right to 'Public Dwelling.'"

29. See Peter Marcuse, "Neutralizing Homelessness," *Socialist Review*, 18:1 (January-March 1988), pp. 69-96.

30. Superson, "The Homeless and the Right to 'Public Dwelling,'" pp. 141-145.

31. See Uma Narayan, "'Standard Persons' and 'Non-Standard' Vulnerabilities: The Legal Protection of 'Non-Standard' Interest," in *Law, Justice, and the State*, eds. Mikael M. Karlsson, Olafur Pall Jonsson, and Eyja Margret Brynjarsdottir (Berlin: Duncker and Humbolt, 1993), pp. 377-386.

32. Quoted in F. Steven Redburns and Terry F. Buss, *Responding to America's Homeless: Public Policy Alternatives* (New York: Praeger, 1986), p. 127.

33. John Stuart Mill, "On Liberty," in *Utilitarianism and Other Writings* (New York: Meridian Books, 1962), p. 129.

34. Rodney Peffer, "Rights to Well-Being," *Philosophy and Public Affairs*, no. 1 (1978), p. 66.

35. *Ibid.*, pp. 79-80.

36. James Sterba, *How to Make People Just* (Totowa, N.J.: Rowman and Littlefield, 1988).

37. See John E. Nowak, Ronald D. Rotunda, and J. Nelson Young, *Constitutional Law*, 3rd ed. (St. Paul, Minn: West Publishing Company, 1986).

38. See *Dandridge v. Williams*, 397 U.S. 508, 90 S.Ct.

39. Nowak, Rotunda, and Young, *Constitutional Law*, p. 680.

40. See *San Antonio Independent School District v. Rodriguez*, 411 U.S. 1, 93 S.Ct. 1278 (1973).

41. *Regents of University of California v. Bakke*, 438 U.S. 265, 98 S.Ct. 2733 (1978).

42. See *City of Richmond v. Croson*, 448 U.S. 469, 109 S.Ct. 706 (1989).

43. See *Arlington Heights v. Metropolitan Housing Development Corp.*, 429 U.S. 252, 97 S.Ct. 555 (1977).

44. See *Yick Wo v. Hopkins*, 118 U.S. 355, 6 S.Ct. 1064 (1886).

45. *McCulloch v. Maryland*, 17 U.S. (4 Wheat) 316, 4 L.Ed. 579 (1819).

Twelve

SOCIAL POLICIES, PRINCIPLES, AND HOMELESSNESS

Natalie Dandekar

1. On a Bombay Street

In the soft, warm evening, crowds move. Individuals stand out: women graceful and agile in *saris* or *salwar khameez*; children darting among them wearing Western tee shirts or neo-Victorian frilled frocks or pitiful rags; men strolling arm in arm wearing Western style shirts open halfway to the navel, men moving quickly in traditional *dhoti*, gleaming white, men in *pajama kurta* striding toward the bus stop. Indian style sandals, business shoes polished to mirror brightness, dainty high-heeled sandals, gym shoes of every description. The crowds move on foot. Overburdened diesel-spewing trucks and buses, motor rickshaws, motorcycles, scooters, and private cars fill the streets. Amidst the noise and the confusion, small shops close. The shopkeepers lock safety shields over vulnerable window displays. The theaters fill. Roving street vendors proffer garlands of fragrant jasmine or small cones of *kulfi*, a dessert something like ice cream made with evaporated milk.

By midnight, the vendors no longer hawk their wares. Pedestrians returning from the theater step carefully around and over sleeping humans. If you ask who these homeless people are, the answer will surprise you. Everyone knows that twenty percent of the homeless are fully employed but cannot find any place they can afford to rent. They are less lucky than residents of squatter camps, the illicitly erected tents and boxes which, like shabby mushrooms, spring up in tracts of land surrounding modern high-rises. While police may evict people in the squatter camps at any moment, the homeless on the sidewalk have nowhere to be evicted from.

Respectable citizens—working people with nowhere to call home, nowhere they can afford to rent—sleep on sidewalks by night. By day they bundle their belongings into a variety of safe storage spaces which they can afford to rent. By day they comprise roughly twenty percent of the Bombay work force.

The effort to understand homelessness numerically represents one aspect of what, following Robert Bellah (1985), I refer to as social engineering. Social engineering represents an approach to social life in which only someone with mathematically sophisticated analytic expertise is considered competent to deal with social problems. Basically, those who privilege a social-engineering approach presume that experts, after gathering the necessary numbers, can work out efficient solutions to social problems.

The reliance on social engineering is widespread both in India and in the United States, but it should be seen as an inappropriate approach to homelessness. To make this argument, I first establish three related points: (1) homelessness resembles the catastrophic accidents adherent to complex engineering systems as described by Charles Perrow (1984); (2) contemporary socio-political environments should be seen as complex systems irreducible to the categories of quantitative analysis; and (3) we in the United States and India have a forty-year tradition of trying to solve social problems with social engineering. Second, I point out why social engineering as an approach to social life is incompatible with basic principles of participatory democracy. Third, I argue that John Ladd's positive conception of responsibility can be extended in ways compatible with the principles of participatory democracy to promote more appropriate ways of connecting with homelessness.

2. Catastrophes of Complex Systems

Charles Perrow (1984) shows that when technological systems are complexly interactive, engineering at its best cannot prevent catastrophic outcomes. There are some systems in which actual failures on the part of specific individuals or groups may be, in themselves, relatively insignificant. Nonetheless, in these systems the relatively insignificant failures result in minor accidents that snowball into an unstoppable catastrophe. To the extent that Perrow's analysis can be convincingly brought to bear on contemporary environments as complexly interactive systems, social engineering must share the limitations Perrow has identified.

A. Perrow's Analysis

Focusing on technological systems at high risk for catastrophic accidents—nuclear power, petrochemical plants, aircraft, and marine traffic control—Perrow (1984) demonstrates that only some risky enterprises can be made safer. Others necessarily rely on organizational systems in which elements are so complexly interactive that engineering safeguards can never fully prevent system failures. In Perrow's terms, interactively complex and tightly coupled systems are always at high risk for catastrophe. The demands on the system are inherently inconsistent with successful management of an unpreventable coincidence of expectable, minimal failures. "[I]t is the way the parts fit together, interact, that is important," Perrow writes; "[t]he dangerous accidents lie in the system, not in the components . . ." (p. 351). In these complex technologies "failed parts cannot be isolated from other parts."

Failures on the part of specific individuals or groups are in themselves relatively insignificant. When catastrophic failure occurs, the terrible consequences are "not due per se to the individual acts or omissions of a few persons but to the accidental coincidence of large numbers of failures, no one of which would have been fatal by itself." Blaming individuals is irrelevant and inappropriate.

Perrow's formulation of the catastrophic accident has eight further defining characteristics: (1) it is sudden, or closed-ended; (2) it is marked by one specific beginning; (3) there is a point in time at which the accident per se ends, giving way to a phase in which one copes with the aftermath; and (4) the accidental accumulation of policies are so connected with one single technological system that the accident may be said to be located there; (5) these policies were developed by engineers under the (false) assumption that effects can be isolated; (6) these engineers rely upon scientific techniques notable for sophisticated mathematics; (7) system failure takes the form of a cascade of unintended and unpreventable interactions; and (8) when such unintended interactions are observed, efforts and policies designed to end the cascade fail because of other unobserved interactions.

On the basis of this analysis, Perrow constructs an argument against reliance upon engineering as a way out of the problems inherent in engineered systems of this sort. This secondary argument relies on realizing that mathematical models of safety are sophisticated but narrow; they are, he says, "cramped by the monetarization of social good. Social ties, family continuity, a distinctive culture and valued human traditions are unquantified and unacknowledged" (p. 308).

I believe that both parts of Perrow's analysis usefully apply to our understanding of homelessness as an unintentionally produced outcome of mutually interacting social policies in complex modern social environments. Since many of these social policies may be rooted in a social-engineering approach, the challenge Perrow levels at the best engineering practice also applies to our efforts to rely on social-engineering expertise to remedy the wrongs which have resulted in homelessness.

B. Contemporary Urban Systems as Complex and Interactive

City life depends upon a high level of division of labor and functional differentiation among subsystems such as the economic, the political, and the scientific. Danilo Zolo (1992) recently made several points acknowledging social complexity:

> social complexity manifests itself as the variety and semantic discontinuity of the languages, understandings, techniques and values which are practiced within each subsystem and its further differentiations. The meaning of an event experienced within one social environment—a

religious experience, for example—cannot be conveyed in the terms
relevant to the experience of a different environment—a sports club, for
instance, or an office or a nuclear research laboratory. (Zolo, 1992, p. 5)

However, even as different subsystems come to rely on semantic discontinuities,

there exist phenomena of growing interdependence between the various
subsystems. Political campaigns, for example, are nowadays conditioned
by the requirements of the medium of television, but this medium is
subordinate to legislation governing political use of the media, and both
the politicians and the television company have to submit to the exigencies
of the advertising market conditioned not only by general economic
legislation, but also by the increasingly fierce competition between
television and more traditional forms of publicity. Since they are forced to
make their prediction and projections in the absence of full information
and sufficient knowledge of the lines of interaction, the economist,
politician and social engineer have to accommodate themselves to a
significant body of "perverse effects," results they had not predicted and
which are hardly welcome to them. (Zolo, 1992, pp. 5-6)

We can easily see parallels between what Zolo here calls "perverse effects" and
the accidental coincidence of trivial failures which, according to Perrow,
characterize catastrophes in high-tech systems. But is pervasive homelessness
an accidental outcome of perverse interactions, a system failure for which no
one person or policy is to blame?

C. Homelessness and Contemporary Social Engineering

In a single collection of essays, *The Homeless: Opposing Viewpoints,* authors
single out rent control (Tucker, 1990), insufficient welfare benefits (Rossi,
1990), deinstitutionalization of the mentally ill (Krauthammer, 1990), family
breakdown (McMurry, 1990), alcoholism (Cohen and Sokolovsky 1990), or
economics (Marcuse, 1990). Other authors in the same volume argue just as
persuasively against blaming these policies (Orr, 1990). This suggests that
blame may be irrelevant, in which case we are justified in regarding homelessness as a catastrophic accident.

Homelessness is unlike the kind of catastrophic engineering accident
which Perrow has analyzed in four respects. (1) It is neither sudden nor close-
ended. (2) It is not marked by one specific beginning. (3) As a catastrophe,
homelessness has no endpoint, no point in time which can be called coping with
the aftermath. (4) Finally, the accidental accumulation of policies which
occasion and entrench homelessness do not seem to be connected with just one

system. Yet I hold these differences less relevant than the following similarities: the catastrophic consequence follows upon policies developed by social engineers under the (false) assumption that the effects of these policies can be isolated. Those who develop the policies rely upon scientific techniques notable for sophisticated mathematical manipulations. The policies result in a cascade of unintended and unpreventable interactions. When such unintended interactions are observed, efforts and policies designed to end the cascade fail because of other unobserved interactions.

D. Examples of Social Engineering

For at least half a century, Americans have approached social ills as problems amenable to social-engineering solutions. The two main welfare traditions in the United States rely on organized private charity or public support programs. But with the exception of social security, public support programs are themselves assimilated to the model of charitable aid (Blackmun, 1971). Moreover, as far back as 1949, the reliance on expert administration of charity was an assumed truth:

> In the 1949 Wechsler Children's I. Q. Test, examinees are asked "why is it generally better to give money to an organized charity than to a street beggar?" A child gained I. Q. points by choosing the answer that asserted "public charities are in a better position to investigate the merits of the case; a more orderly way of contribution for the donor." (Blau, 1992, p. 5)

As Joel Blau comments dryly, "Children who simply assert that giving to a beggar makes them feel better demonstrate a lack of innate intelligence . . ." (pp. 5-6).

In the United States today, "[n]ational polls show a near-irresistible demand . . . for solution to this blight on our national character" (Coates, 1990, p. 21). Behind the demand for a solution lies the assumption that homelessness is a single problem, and that scientific collection of data will, with proper analysis, yield policies which efficiently produce the preferred outcome.

Who are the homeless? An initial answer is almost too easily formulated: those who, although not institutionalized, cannot claim any private dwelling space as their own. However, this apparent ease of definition provides a misleading sense of understanding. We cannot even determine how many people are homeless. Nor do we understand what processes occasion and entrench homelessness. What special constraints do the homeless face? We don't know. But we are deploying resources in an effort to find out.

Various studies that attempt to count the homeless attest to the untrustworthiness of the resultant numbers (Levitas, 1990). This should give us pause.

At least we should wonder whether categorizing people in terms of one problem artificially produces an inappropriate sense of understanding. Have problems of employment, demographics, social disaffiliation, mental health, family violence, and the number of persons living below the poverty level been thus homogenized under the rubric of a housing problem? Are they now seen as subcategories, mere characteristics of the homeless. But we need to be careful about how this need plays out. As Blau has noted:

> Consensus about the composition of the homeless population is important and its absence has undoubtedly hindered the development of sensible policies. . . . Yet the debate also possesses a far less attractive side. It is one thing to make some basic distinctions about the population's makeup; it is quite another to substitute the pursuit of these distinctions for significant policy interventions. . . . [S]ocial science researchers are inevitably caught up in the growing tension between studying an issue on the one hand and doing something about it on the other. Most researchers want to help the homeless, and they understandably want this help to be based on the best possible data. But data that show the need for major new commitments of funds run up against . . . budgetary constraints. . . . Blocked by the financial obstacles to change, the research has often fed the national inclination to objectify poor people. . . . [C]haracteristics come to displace the people who possess them. (Blau, 1992, pp. 16-17)

We need to know what processes occasion homelessness. We especially need to know what processes might reasonably be expected to undo the ill-effects of the counsel processor. Beginning in 1987, the National Institute of Mental Health has provided $2.3 million to the Rand Corporation to fund a five-year study to ascertain how mentally ill homeless people in Santa Monica and on Skid Row in Los Angeles manage to find shelter. The principal investigator says the study is aimed at discovering "why and how some cease to be homeless, where do they go, how does that happen, what kind of housing is useful and what support services do they really need?" (Levitas, 1990, p. 12)

I believe we ought also to question whether homelessness is a problem amenable to solution through the application of analytic expertise to quantitative, objectively reliable data. Current re-evaluations of international development paradigms (Wignaraja, 1990; Shiva, 1988; Young, 1993; Jazairy, 1992) support the conclusion that policies arrived at through the application of analytic expertise to quantitative data have frequently led to unintended harms such as urban homelessness. Thinking about homelessness in Bombay illustrates some of the sad lessons that analyzing years of development now yield.

E. Bombay, Development Policies, and Homelessness

Residents of Bombay may obtain affordable housing in a variety of ways. These include ownership, rental, tied housing, and unlawful squatting. In tied housing, rights of occupancy are included within an employment contract and revert to the employer when employment terminates. Some large-scale employers buy up a number of apartment units to use as negotiating incentives in hiring upper level employees. Trusted servants without a contract may similarly negotiate an arrangement by which they are permitted to sleep in the back of an employer's shop or on the verandah. Because Indian banks have no tradition of providing home mortgages, would-be purchasers must amass savings equivalent to the cost of the home.

In Bombay, old apartments fall under rent control. In one particular building, the same twenty-four families rent under agreements originating at the turn of the century. Monthly rents cost less than a good dinner out. That the current residents have lived as neighbors for decades is hardly surprising. Forced by the building design to share lavatory facilities, they also share newspapers, telephones, and holiday feasts. They coordinate their vacations, help each other produce the lavish weddings typical of Bombay. The landlord can only get out of the government's regulation of rent if the building is condemned, so the residents pool their money to keep the entire building in good repair. They know that the landlord's main interest lies in making a fortune by selling the land for upscale development.

Land within commuting distance of Bombay city center is scarce and commensurately valuable. Even usable airspace in the center of the city can be sold at a profit. Where a one- or two-story building is tenant occupied, another built on stilts converts airspace into residential units. New apartment units are generally costly, reflecting the value of land and what the market will bear. The market will obviously bear a great deal.

Along with the visibly poor who live in rag-covered hutments or simply sleep on the streets, some residents of Bombay are rich by any standard of wealth. Old money jostles new. Bombay is home to India's thriving movie industry. In a manner reminiscent of American movie stars of the 1940s, Bombay's movie stars live extravagantly. But those selling expensive new apartments also rely on purchasers with more mundane careers. For example, highly skilled computer engineers are sometimes sent to the United States to act as consultants. Their salaries, skimpy by American standards, are generally sufficient, given the favorable exchange rate between the rupee and the dollar, to obtain a reasonably nice apartment in Bombay. The Indian government, eager to obtain foreign exchange credits, passed legislation providing tax incentives and other forms of encouragement for Indians who have taken up permanent residence abroad to purchase dwelling units in India. Apartment prices reflect the availability of buyers who no longer need to count the cost in rupees.

At the same time, tenant protections are so strong that those who come to own their apartment-home believe that if ever they should lease to tenants, they will never again find themselves in a position to claim their home for themselves. Whether or not it is true, owners generally believe that an owner can never hope to succeed in evicting a tenant if all the owner has against the tenant is that the owner now wants to live in the apartment. Owners therefore frequently rent only to institutions, like banks, which cannot call upon tenant protection laws to prevent eviction. Alternatively, owners lock up an empty apartment to keep it ready for personal occupancy at some future time.

Meanwhile, land within commuting distance of the city grows scarce. The police are housed in government-constructed units built over an area that smells like an uncleaned cesspool. The commuter trains run every five minutes, filled to overflowing. Middle-class commuters think it no hardship to begin their working day by boarding a commuter train from the suburbs at 6 a.m. in order to reach jobs at 8 a.m.

Well-intentioned policies premised on development paradigms underlie some of the mutually reinforcing factors constricting the Bombay housing market. In line with an early assumption that every country develops through industrialization, experts at all levels promoted policies of intensive industrial growth. They depreciated the role of small, independent farms in employment. With hindsight, these policies obviously disadvantaged the poor and deepened rural poverty. The unforeseen effects of development policies adopted and forwarded over the past forty years especially harmed poor women (Shiva, 1988; Wignaraja, 1990; Dandekar, 1993). Faced with rural poverty and a dearth of non-farm employment opportunities in the rural areas, populations sought work in already crowded urban areas (Jazairy, 1992).

A rural employment scheme established in the countryside round Bombay early in the 1970s was considered the most successful in Asia. Financed by urban taxes, the Employment Guarantee Scheme of Maharashtra provides employment to the rural unemployed upon request. The World Bank found that, "In 1984-85, 180 million person/days of employment were provided, representing 3 percent of total rural employment in Maharashtra" (World Bank, 1990). But this level of employment support was never enough to stop the influx of employment seekers willing to accept the low "entry level" wages in Bombay.

Incidentally, at roughly the same time, new technologies reinforced banking policies that privileged large borrowers. It is far more costly for a large bank to provide very small short-term loans than very large longer-term loans. Until recently, limited credit opportunities forced a vegetable vendor who needed to borrow five dollars to rely on money lenders whose terms would require repayment at a manageable 20 cents per day for thirty days. Although the sums are small, the rate is a usurious 120 percent per annum on short-term loans (Chen, 1989).

Twenty percent of the fully employed live on the streets. They are better off than the rest of Bombay's homeless. First, because India is a poor country, no government safety net provides guaranteed income for the old or the sick. Development policies known as "structural adjustment" require that poor countries limit investments in what is called welfare and concentrate instead on investments in industrialization. Thus, Bombay's homeless population includes those unable to obtain full employment for reasons that include age or illness, physical or mental. Drug and alcohol addiction accounts for other street dwellers. In addition there is the Indian equivalent of what in the United States are called throw-away and runaway children. Children from abusive homes run away to the perils of street life, while other children, for one reason or another, have been tossed out by parents who will not permit them to return. Aid workers foresee that the policies which permitted AIDS to spread through such vulnerable populations as the truck drivers who ply the roads of India will very soon produce a new group of homeless children, AIDS orphans.

Some of the policies which entrench homelessness in the Bombay area grow out of well-intentioned efforts to promote "development." Other forces promote gentrification while ignoring the fact that many jobs pay such low wages that even full-time work cannot purchase access to decent housing. Frustrated households lead to throw-away and runaway children.

In light of these complex interactions, the lesson of Perrow's analysis is pertinent. We would be wrong to rely on social engineers to solve these problems both because they most likely cannot and because the effort to do so objectifies those who for various reasons are homeless in ways that are incompatible with participatory democratic theory.

3. Democracy Requires Participating Citizens

In theory, democratic forms of decision-making distinguish themselves according to citizens' equal rights of participation in decision making, with the assumption that they have the freedom to choose the purpose or direction of their actions (Ackerman, 1980; Rawls, 1982; Gould, 1988; Nino, 1991). By contrast, the social-engineering model enhances reliance on paternalistic interventions which remove the element of choice and conceal the lack of opportunity with an air of benevolence. As was attested in the 1949 I.Q. question, charity providers presumably understand how to use resources to solve homelessness better than someone who suffers the misfortune of becoming homeless. Moreover, as Perrow pointed out, reliance upon numerical manipulations promotes ignoring or overlooking the importance of values, and in this too it is inconsistent with the principles of participatory democracy.

Ladd (1991) argues that an answer to the challenge of Perrow's insights lies in finding ways to assume positive responsibility for resolution of social problems by recourse to participatory practices. Because complex technologies are statistically bound to produce catastrophic accidents, such catastrophes as Bhopal and other similar accidents challenge our traditional legalistic concepts of responsibility. To meet the challenge, Ladd formulates a positive conception of responsibility.

Unlike the negative and legalistic conceptions of responsibility, Ladd's conception specifically includes negative causes (omissions) as well as positive causes (actions). Thus, on Ladd's formulation, a causal relation between the agent's conduct and the outcome may be established as the failure of a piece of machinery to operate properly or the failure of personnel to do something like warn others about a danger. However, this causal relationship is insufficient basis for blame, as Perrow's analysis has established.

Ladd holds that we are drawn to place blame as part of the American fondness for turning moral problems into legal ones. But this, in the end, only reduces questions of moral responsibility to questions of fiscal responsibility. Ladd instead wants to establish a concept of responsibility which promotes solicitude on the part of the chief actors for the health and safety of the victims of disaster. Perhaps most importantly, Ladd constructs responsibility as a virtue

> to be contrasted with irresponsibility rather than with non-responsibility . . . people ought to order their actions taking into consideration their possible effects on the welfare of others. Responsible action, as such, aims caringly at the prevention of harm to others with whom one has a relationship of one sort or another. (Ladd, 1991, p. 89)

In an earlier publication, Ladd argues for a concept of responsibility specifically linked with participation: "In demanding participation, the individual claims that he needs or ought to have responsibility" (Ladd, 1975, p.103). He adds, ". . . if an individual has responsibilities . . . but lacks the power or competence that they imply, then others who do have the power or competence have a duty to help him obtain the power and competence necessary to fulfill his responsibilities" (p. 121).

When Ladd's conception of positive responsibility is used as a criterion for evaluating alternative approaches to homelessness, the requirement of caring becomes concrete. Consider just this one example: As Brad Kessler (1989) wrote somewhat bemusedly, Westchester, the place real-estate developers like to call "Country Club County," leads the nation in homeless people per capita. In 1989, 4,200 homeless people, including 1,710 children either couldn't pay rising rents or were forced out because of co-op conversion or gentrification. As Kessler puts it, "Homelessness exists here *because* Westchester is one of the wealthiest counties in the country. Professionals ... have been displacing poorer ... residents for decades. ... There is no central authority ... responsibility is dissipated among village, town, county and state governments" (Kessler, 1989, p. 62). In Westchester, the homeless stay in motels, many of which violate basic health, fire, and safety regulations.

> You may be placed as far as eighty miles from your former home. ... [C]hildren may be shipped back and forth from their school to the motel ... (though cab fare can run as much as $220 round trip). To put a homeless family up in a one-bedroom motel unit, Westchester county pays an average rent of $3000 a month. (p. 63)

Kessler quotes a county legislator who tried to fund low-income housing to exemplify a hard lesson in local politics: "Everybody wants to fund the soup kitchens. ... Nobody talks about ... building housing—because nobody wants it built" (p. 63).

Even a "transitional" housing facility, six two-story buildings that would house 108 families in the middle of a thirty-acre wooded site, aroused outrage among property owners. Though they knew that the county would donate the land and a charitable organization would build the site; though they knew that it would provide housing to the indigent for only ten years, after which the town would acquire it at no cost for use in housing the elderly or its municipal employees; though they knew that it meant the taxpayers would save money and the homeless would have better housing, still taxpayers protested. Objections ranged from fears about the effect on property values to fears about the loss of precious trees to fears about crime. As of 1990, the project remains bottled up in the courts.

Ladd reminds us that if we are to prevent catastrophes, we need to replace the ideology that teaches that commitment and concern for others is a matter of individual preference with an ideology that stresses an orientation toward a care for the common good (Ladd, 1991, pp. 89-90). We clearly need a reorientation of ideology when it comes to the way too many of us regard the phenomenon of homelessness. Can examples like Westchester county be transformed? Can this deeply needed virtue be developed?

4. Removing Barriers to Community

Judge Coates (1990) provides an introduction to various programs functioning in American cities. Coates chronicles the best solutions to the problems of the homeless and the process by which they have been put in place. He examines the socially constructed barriers placed before homeless people and shows how these barriers could be torn down.

Interestingly, Coates suggests that local efforts begin with planning. The language in this work draws upon the engineering model: "a city or community might assess its homeless situation, and . . . go about creating a blueprint for action that is something more than a gut response to somebody else's distress" (p. 28). These planners do not play the role of the social engineer who formulates the solution the rest of us accept, but instead assist in the creation of a value-oriented democratic forum. Coates's suggestions include joining the homeless, dressing and living homeless for a weekend. Another suggestion involves our finding ways of distinguishing and remanding chronic alcoholics (1.5 percent of San Diego's known homeless population) to a detox center. One of the activists who developed this approach describes the importance of involving as many citizens as will be consistent with community: involve the police chief, create a task force, and reinforce public commitment with appropriate dignified media coverage of the task force. His assessment is that the San Diego task force could have had greater success if they had known then what he has learned.

Throughout the book, Coates discusses ways of involving community members, clubs and homeless activists in mutually reinforcing patterns of problem solution and brainstorming. Pragmatically, Judge Coates warns, some people "perceive their own economic interests to be served best by the persistence of homelessness and they quietly act to assure that persistence" (p. 266). Coates maintains on the basis of experience what I have suggested on the basis of theory: "No battalion of experts can solve homelessness" (p. 269). His work suggests, however, that by doing, one develops the virtue of responsibility. Politically viable coalitions, with the help of expertise, can work locally, caringly, to undo homelessness.

Blau (1992) advocates a coalition organized around a web of unaddressed human needs which would include a system of social ownership for publicly financed housing. "The key here is the establishment of a social housing sector," he writes, "where housing could not be resold at a profit. . . . [R]esidents would not only acquire rights to their housing; they would also actively participate in its management" (p. 134). As in the Bombay apartment building, self-interest in retaining low-rent housing and mutual responsibility have woven long-term neighbors into a community. Practicing the virtue of positive responsibility may serve as a model for removing other important barriers to community as well.

Works Cited

Ackerman, Bruce A. 1980. *Social Justice in the Liberal State*. New Haven: Yale University Press.

Bellah, Robert N. 1985. *Habits of the Heart: Individualism and Commitment in American Life*. Berkeley: University of California Press.

Blackmun, Justice Harry A. 1971. "Majority Opinion in Wyman v. James," United States Supreme Court. 400 U.S. 309. Reprinted in *Social Ethics*, edited by Thomas A. Mappes and Jane S. Zembaty (New York: McGraw Hill), pp. 357-360.

Blau, Joel. 1992. *The Visible Poor: Homelessness in the United States*. New York: Oxford University Press.

Chen, Marty. 1989. "The Working Women's Forum: Organizing for Credit and Change in Madras, India." In *Seeds, Supporting Women's Work in the Third World*, edited by Ann Leonard. New York: The Feminist Press at the City University of New York.

Coates, Judge Robert C. 1990. *A Street Is Not a Home*. Buffalo, N.Y.: Prometheus Books.

Cohen, Carl I., and Jay Sokolovsky. 1990. "Alcoholism Contributes to Homelessness." In *The Homeless: Opposing Viewpoints*, edited by Lisa Orr. San Diego: Greenhaven Press, pp. 75-81.

Gould, Carol. 1988. *Rethinking Democracy: Freedom, and Social Cooperation in Politics, Economy, and Society*. Cambridge, U.K.: Cambridge University Press.

Jazairy, Idriss, Mohiuddin Alamgir, and Theresa Panuccio. 1992. *The State of World Rural Poverty: An Inquiry into Its Causes and Consequences*. International Fund for Agricultural Development. New York: New York University Press.

Kessler, Brad. 1989. "The Hidden Homeless: Down and Out in Suburbia." Abstracted from *The Nation*, 249:306 (25 September). Reprinted in *The Homeless Problem*, edited by Matthew A. Kraljic (New York: The H. W. Wilson Company, 1992), pp. 60-68.

Kourany, Janet A., James P. Sterba, and Rosemarie Tong. 1992. *Feminist Philosophies*. Englewood Cliffs, N.J.: Prentice Hall.

Kraljic, Matthew A., ed. 1992. *The Homeless Problem*. New York: The H. W. Wilson Company.

Krauthammer, Charles. 1990. "The Homeless Mentally Ill Should Be Institutionalized." In *The Homeless: Opposing Viewpoints*, edited by Lisa Orr. San Diego: Greenhaven Press.

Ladd, John. 1975. "Participation in Politics." In *Voluntary Associations*, edited by J. Roland Pennock and John W. Chapman. New York: Atherton-Lieber, pp. 98-125.

———. 1991. "Bhopal: An Essay on Moral Responsibility and Civic Virtue." *Journal of Social Philosophy*, 22:1 (Spring), pp. 73-91.

Levitas, Mitchel. 1990. "Homeless in America." *The New York Times Magazine* 140:45 (10 June). Reprinted in *The Homeless Problem*, edited by Matthew A. Kraljic (New York: The H. W. Wilson Company, 1992), pp. 11-24.

Marcuse, Peter. 1992. "Economic Factors Cause Homelessness." In *The Homeless: Opposing Viewpoints*, edited by Lisa Orr. San Diego: Greenhaven Press, pp. 81-87.

McMurry, Dan. 1990. "Family Breakdown Causes Homelessness." In *The Homeless: Opposing Viewpoints*, edited by Lisa Orr. San Diego: Greenhaven Press, pp. 71-75.

Nino, Carlos Santiago. 1991. *The Ethics of Human Rights*. New York: Oxford University Press.

Orr, Lisa, ed. 1990. *The Homeless: Opposing Viewpoints*. San Diego: Greenhaven Press.

Perrow, Charles. 1984. *Normal Accidents: Living with High-Risk Technologies*. New York: Basic Books.

Rawls, John. 1982. "Social Unity and Primary Goods." In *Utilitarianism and Beyond*, edited by Amartya Sen and Bernard Williams. Cambridge, U.K.: Cambridge University Press.

Rossi, Peter. 1990. "Increasing Welfare Benefits Would Reduce Homelessness." In *The Homeless: Opposing Viewpoints*, edited by Lisa Orr. San Diego: Greenhaven Press, pp. 106-112.

Shiva, Vandana. 1988. *Staying Alive: Women Ecology and Survival in India*. Delhi: Kali for Women.

Spelman, Elizabeth and Maria Lugones. 1992. "Have We Got a Theory for You! Feminist Theory, Cultural Imperialism, and the Demand for The Woman's Voice." In *Feminist Philosophies*, edited by Janet A. Kourany, James P. Sterba, and Rosemarie Tong. Englewood Cliffs: Prentice Hall, pp. 378-390. Originally published in *Women's Studies* (1983).

Tucker, William. 1990. "Abolishing Rent Control Would Reduce Homelessness." In *The Homeless: Opposing Viewpoints*, edited by Lisa Orr. San Diego: Greenhaven Press, pp. 161-168.

Wignaraja, Ponna. 1990. *Women, Poverty, and Resources*. New Delhi: Sage Publications.

World Bank. 1990. *World Development Report 1990*. New York: Oxford University Press, for the World Bank.

Young, Kate. 1993. *Planning Development with Women: Making a World of Difference*. New York: St. Martin's Press.

Zolo, Danilo. 1992. *Democracy and Complexity: A Realist Approach*, trans. from Italian by David McKie. University Park, Pennsylvania: Pennsylvania State University Press.

Thirteen

FAILED RIGHTS: THE MORAL PLIGHT OF THE MENTALLY ILL HOMELESS

G. John M. Abbarno

1. Introduction

In Robert Frost's poem "The Death of the Hired Man," speakers Warren and Mary richly capture the meaning of being homeless. Beneath their disagreement, we can sense a familiar sense of sympathy for and bewilderment at the homeless hired man who, as Mary tells Warren, "has come home to die":

> "Home," he mocked gently.
> "Yes, what else but home?
> It all depends upon what you mean by home.
> Of course he's nothing to us, any more
> Than was the hound that came a stranger to us
> Out of the woods, worn out upon the trail."
> "Home is a place where, when you have to go there,
> They have to take you in."
> "I should have called it
> Something you haven't to deserve."[1]

Frost echoes the general belief that having a home is not an award received on merit but a basic right.

Recent studies report that there are as many as 700,000 to 1,000,000 homeless in America, of which 200,000 to 400,000 are mentally ill. Researchers have discovered that some mentally ill persons only develop mental illness after an extended period of homelessness. The lack of a "home" undermines the conditions for stable personal interactions. The feelings of being unconnected and estranged over time begin to unravel the human spirit. Hopes of being contributing members of the community appear less likely; personal integrity erodes.

Peter Rossi provides an official definition of homelessness: "According to social workers, a person is homeless if he or she does not rent or own a dwelling place and is not a regular member of a household that does so."[2] Having a "home" in this sense is what, minimally, society ought to provide. For the mentally ill, "home" requires community supports as well. I argue that this involves an expanded notion of home due to special needs that provide its basis of rights claims. Part of this new sense involves a self that is community-reliant for its autonomy and dignity, two central values of libertarianism that failed in the entitlements to the mentally ill homeless. In this chapter these unfulfilled values will be seen as results of formal inconsistencies in the libertarian principle. City streets witness the fall-out of this principle's social impact.

2. Libertarianism and Basic Rights

In its strongest sense, libertarianism asserts the value of non-interference as the *sine qua non* of a fulfilled person. When applied to the mentally ill homeless population, libertarianism's focus on fulfillment seems absurd. Moreover, its principle justifies violating their rights while supporting the rights of others. This is, in large part, due to how libertarians stress certain select needs and the requirements for their satisfaction.

Not all members of society are in a position to satisfy their basic needs of food, shelter, and security. Yet, unless such basic needs are met, the poor among us will become more distant from attaining the goods that enhance their humanity. More importantly, without the satisfaction of these needs, we allow these people to live lives that are less than human. These needs, after all, are instrumental to other choices people make to exercise their capabilities and provide the foundation of rights they claim against society, without which only certain select people will flourish. Borrowing from Henry Shue's notion of basic rights, we can identify security and subsistence as needs that should be considered rights. Shue emphasizes that society is obligated to fulfill the rights of security and subsistence, for unless it does, it "paralyzes a person, preventing her or him from exercising any other right—as surely as actual beatings and actual protein/calorie deficiencies can. Social arrangements must be established that will bring assistance to those confronted by forces that they themselves cannot handle."[3] The right to security protects people from assaults which would interrupt their plans or force them to act in ways unbecoming themselves. Without security, choices of what to do, where to live, how to live, become drastically curtailed. Subsistence rights are a step beyond physical security, insofar as they provide the right to the minimal economic security. Most especially, it provides the right to a "home." The failure to fulfill this right renders millions of people hungry, chronically ill, unemployed, and exposed to random violence. Failure to honor this right creates a class of people for whom non-interference is an assault rather than a support for their well-being.

In the abstract, libertarians may acknowledge the rights to subsistence and security, yet they err in assuming that everyone has equal needs and is in comparable positions to act and satisfy them is false. In a larger class of the homeless, the need is for a subsistent level of care and privacy. The want of privacy is a deprivation of security where affections, interests, and self-doubts can be expressed along with the hope for survival. The smaller class of the homeless mentally ill need aftercare staffed in a community space to whose maintenance they themselves can contribute. Inasmuch as these needs are special, that is, felt more severely by some than others, they are not equal and so require a non-standardized formula for their satisfaction. Libertarian policy is blind to such differences.

The libertarian's principle imperils the mentally ill. It justifies releasing them from institutional care by appealing to autonomy per se as the primary value of individual rights. However, as many psychiatrists have noted, libertarians have created a situation in which the homeless mentally ill have become, in the sardonic words of two psychiatrists, "too entitled and protected by stringent commitment laws that allow their own wishes, and, as a result, permit them to perish in the streets with their rights on."[4]

A. Dilemma of Autonomy

The failed basic rights of the mentally ill homeless, whose condition I shall explain, reflects the moral inadequacy of libertarian social policy. In general terms, libertarians argues that all people fundamentally choose the course that will best express the desires and goals central to their lives; this autonomy gives rise to dignity, respect, and happiness. The strongest acknowledgment of another's moral personhood consists of the refusal to interfere with the goals, desires, and resources that are essential to the attainment of their good life. The justification for this autonomy is the natural right of being human, and the specific fulfillment of this right is nothing less than another individual's duty to respect it. It is on these terms that individual abilities develop, by mutually honoring the other's freedom to pursue his way of life unimpeded. This right to be left alone is what moves one to choose optimum goods commensurate with what he or she has been capable to develop. Every human being has the right to act in accordance with his or her own choices, unless those actions infringe on the equal liberty of other human beings to act on their own choices. I will refer to this sense of autonomy as "natural."

There are three difficulties with this libertarian sense of natural autonomy:

1.   It operates on the assumption that an individual's free choice is separate from and enhanced independently of social needs.

2.   It assumes that individuals have a fixed and healthy motivation to obtain goods.

3.   Insofar as it assumes that rights equalize status among individuals in society, it would overlook the value of collective rights as forces which equalize groups and individuals in the community.

As for the first difficulty, welfare rights theorists argue that there is a wider relationship between the goods sought and the individual choosing them. Some individuals require special nutrition or medical treatments simply in order to make a competent decision regarding subordinate goods. Physical disabilities require a different means of transportation, education, access to buildings, and so on. Unless a society provides social policies that value the choices made by select groups to satisfy their needs, the members of those groups will be excluded from the common good enjoyed by others.

Perhaps an example of allocating a natural resource will clarify how to attend to different needs related to a common good. Consider what individual value is operative when a natural resource is limited in one area of the United States, for example, and plentiful in another. Ongoing discussion has taken place about devising ways to take water from the Great Lake Region (North and Central United States) and reroute it to the southwest. On the face of it, this proposal has obvious value, since these bodies of water are part of the national domain. However, the only attraction to business and industry remaining in the Great Lake Region is the water that can be used to supply the continued growth rate of the southwest. This is not a selection justified by local benefit, whether it be employment, less expensive electric power, or revenue from prospective tourism. Choosing to reroute water supply is not an inherent value, but, rather a value that derives from policy-making. It is a relational good that can be meted out so that individuals of greater needs and modest abilities are considered in this choice, since the result can yield ill or good for the nation in general. Stressing the personal needs against the public benefit and the network of subordinate values is not simply good or bad. The social good such intervention would procure justifies the interference with individual life-plans of persons in one region.

The libertarian belief in natural autonomy renders abstract all the complexities, peculiarities, and personalities involved when describing actions as self-directed projects pursued with fixed motivation. As for this second problem with natural autonomy, welfare rights proponents remind us that actions take shape in a chaos of material goods and values, and if the actions are take on enough value, they become rights. D. D. Raphael writes that "needs may be called rights only when it is generally recognized to be of paramount importance and when the meeting of these are practicable."[5] The individuals and groups change among those in need and competing for rights. Abused children, starving populations, the newborn drug addicts, women, and African-Americans each requires study of the weight of need to be considered a right. The appropriate needs must be met in order to assess the motivation of those persons to pursue goods that contribute to the general well being; or whose need, if not a right, may diminish the worth of themselves and society. Welfare rights acknowledges the diversity of capabilities among individuals. It encourages individuals to expend the levels of effort necessary to make their own proper contribution the common good. It is a guide toward communal or relational free expression. Motivations to attain this good are not equal but complement each other.

On the libertarian account, competition will result in success of the more qualified candidate for any position. Upon closer examination, this is not the case. Should two persons, A and B, arise from very different environments and parentage where A is unfavorably regarded because of his or her sex or race and whose goals are continually daunted, a motivation of greater power than allowed by libertarian autonomy would be necessary in order to give him or her a comparable candidacy with B; whereas B's genuine (natural) incentive for success is groomed with confidence and a strong social network. The intensity of motivation is expected to be higher for some goods and some individuals than for others. It is not, however, something a libertarian would acknowledge when evaluating the need of competing groups. One of the applicants may have experienced great sacrifice simply in order to attain the status of candidate. The selection would be arbitrary on libertarian grounds since they were both free to choose this goal as individuals, but the gain or loss is morally significant for society.

The value of noninterference is loaded. Being "allowed" to be homeless is the opposite side of a coin. The other side is condemning them to be homeless. In either case, the homeless cannot help but leave us in "homes" with security and plans with flourishing lives. Such a principle contributes to the expansion of the gap between rich and poor. In contrast to the narrow notion of human goods allowed by libertarians, believers in welfare rights strongly value satisfactions of human needs even at the risk of denying a proportion of goods to some other person. The inequality of individual circumstances exacerbates problems caused by natural differences in abilities to achieve. The natural sense of autonomy with its formal criteria omits the substance from which choices emerge. When individuals satisfy their own desires regardless of (and perhaps in denial of) potential conflicts with another's freedom, they perpetuate the "blame the victim" syndrome. This has been the attitude that has comforted people's discrimination toward the homeless and the mentally ill in particular, echoed in the remark: "They choose to be out there!"

3. Welfare Rights and Autonomy

There is a cluster of values for welfare rights theorists. The securing of certain needs for people in order that a minimum of social goods could be attained demonstrates the important relationship between "forbearance and personal freedom in collective action." Such benefits transform recipients into autonomous people as the needs emerge and resources collectively satisfied. Basic needs indicate the kind of aims, projects, opportunities, and goods that cannot

be realized by individual abilities alone. They require support and encouragement in conjunction with others without sacrificing self-respect and the ability
to make choices.

The sense of autonomy implied in welfare rights I refer to as "conventional." Conventional autonomy asserts that a person's self-respect, freedom,
and dignity are central to being a person. These are not possible without the
interdependence of individuals in the community. Conventional autonomy
possesses the following characteristics:

1. It recognizes that a person's self-worth is through discovery among
    the members of society.

2. It asserts that any one individual or group's attained goods are
    realized by cooperative effort among people of different needs and
    abilities.

3. It seeks a common good which is open to alterations based upon
    what considered most valued for the collective without demeaning
    the life of any one individual or group of individuals.[6]

This sense responds to the salient needs that at different times will enhance
the value of society and will narrow or be broadened upon agreement. It is not
an arbitrary choice but is arrived at through reflection on what will be a
comprehensive state, including levels of agency. The national health-care plan
currently proposed in the United States typifies this kind of conventional
autonomy. There undoubtedly will be personal interests curtailed so that the
common good (35 million people without health insurance) may be realized. The
claim rights of the "forgotten" or disenfranchised and voiceless can make
substantive choices when welfare rights are met. Unlike the homogenous and
abstract autonomy of libertarianism, whose formal criteria promoted deinstitutionalization of the mentally ill, the conventional sense captures the collective
rights of these unequal agents whose rights could only be morally answered in
the good of the whole.

4. The Homeless and Conventional Autonomy

In the last portions of this chapter, I argue that this revised meaning of
"autonomy" as conventional refocuses society's duty to "home" a people whose
rights are shaped by their special subsistence needs. To begin with, this concept
allows greater weight to the perception of the victim. How people internalize the
varied encounters (the cold, hunger, exhaustion, and hatred) as conditions that
express their lives also expresses our own as witnesses to what society permits.

A veil conceals our obligation to them. It is unlike the duties that address the rights of individuals, for example, clearly formulated contracts between two parties. When someone legitimately claims a right, the individual against whom the claim is raised is morally obligated to fulfill it. Respect for human trust demands it. This is precisely why there is an option to view the mentally ill homeless position as a nonvalid claim: it is not against any one individual. The plight of this group is their silent claim against no one in particular. Yet society's failure to recognize their needs as rights is a failure to be facilitators of their agency to live as humans with dignity by creating roles for them in community centers designed for their care. Recipience alone will not move them to act beyond satisfied needs.

For this special group, the meaning of "home" must be expanded to include the community care providers that were merely expected to be established under deinstitutionalization. As members of this community, they can become more aware how their security and belonging is necessary to their autonomy. Expression of this autonomy can be found in roles in libraries, parks, or business districts, all of which have been targets of their manifest need that registers embarrassment. Here they can find some reception instead of the usual cruelty from spectators. This environment, viewed by us as "outside," disheveled and insecure, is what the homeless view "inside" as "home." Understanding this perspective is critical to taking on their claim for membership. Perhaps seeing them as embodiments of family members' love, hope, and dreams of a life interrupted by this twist of events will elicit a moral intervention required to complement their deficit with a home. For unless these persons are provided home in this sense, there will be no home for the moral community. Failing to honor this right diminishes our human aspirations and moral sensitivities. It is one of the more serious issues in morals, as A. I. Melden succinctly puts it: "The violation of a person's human right is . . . in effect to deal with him as if he did not count morally in our traffic with him."[7]

A few of the weaknesses in the libertarian's theory, earlier cited, are underscored with the mentally ill homeless; the principle separates rights from needs. This delineation insulates members from one another, in this case with grave results of deinstitutionalization. I am not arguing for a blind reinstitutionalization (although in some cases this might be the humane thing to do); I am arguing that the kind of rights claim of non-interference will not work as the needs and groups have outdistanced any one individual's duty to satisfy these rights. As these rights expand and change, our institutions, our collective bodies in community become better equipped to provide the support, these people need to achieve, in some measure, the good life. These institutions can also be instrumental in formulating the goods individuals will agree to pursue. Some such alternative to libertarianism will offer more interpersonal planning than what transpired: the release of mental patients.

A. Deinstitutionalization

Anyone even vaguely familiar with the deinstitutionalization program (which was initiated more than 30 years ago by President Kennedy) would know about the network which serves as a rehabilitation into the community life. These were Community Mental Health Centers (CMHCs). Although they were designed to serve the chronically severe patients, they did not. As these centers were set up, recent studies indicated that many of the people diagnosed with mental illness very often ranked as well among those in poverty. The CMHCs began focusing on preventative measures addressing the most afflicted groups. Their efforts went into rehabilitating group attitudes among the different races, genders, and income earners. Instead of concentrating on the chronically severe mentally ill, they became preventative in their strategy, caring only for the "worried well." For the most part, when psychiatrists did not seek positions in these centers, they were staffed by social workers, rehabilitation counselors, and nurses, none of whom could prescribe medication when needed. The state hospitals gradually stopped referring the released patients to centers. They had nowhere to go! Many of these people were on powerful psychotropic drugs (part of the reason mental health professionals and officials argued for release) that needed monitoring when decompensation began and the world was a threat. In those severe cases where patients are maintained on certain drugs, they are likely to experience akinesia. This leaves them unable to develop skills for employment and disfigures them. As Patricia H. Garman has explained to me in personal communication, drugs can debilitate learning social skills but the dosages still must be maintained in order to sustain a harmonizing of thoughts in general.

This set of circumstances was only compounded by the lack of what was called "skid row" housing. The gentrification of urban areas made it impossible for the poor and the mentally ill to afford the apartments. The once available places have become condominiums for professionals. The responsibility for this displacement is often ascribed to attorneys and psychiatrists who have promoted and defended mainstreaming of the mentally ill upon the libertarian principle. A closer look at deinstitutionalization reveals that it is not the only cause for the plight of the mentally ill homeless. In addition to deinstitutionalization, society was unprepared in constructing the entire bridge back into social life. Educating the communities where the CMHCs were established would have made for more positive attitudes and presumably better informed judgments about their neighbors. The extensive "after care" was greatly underestimated, and, as a result, the needs of the most vulnerable among the vulnerable groups in our society go unmet. Out of a relatively safe harbor they were set in uncharted waters. E. Fuller Torrey, a prominent psychiatrist, describes this failed plan rather tersely: "[R]ather than deinstitutionalization which implied that alternative community facilities would be provided, what took place was simply depopulation of the state hospitals. It was as if a policy of resettlement had been agreed upon but only eviction took place."[8]

5. Impact of Judicial Decisions

The aftermath in judicial decisions continued in the direction of viewing the mentally ill homeless as a public embarrassment. Cities throughout the United States enacted ordinances that made their low levels of raw comfort illegal. Conduct ranging from panhandling to sleeping on a park bench was judged as a violation and arrests were made. This is an indictment against a group of people whose status as mentally ill homeless does not warrant punishment, most especially the ad hoc variety. Shelters and homes are not met by incarceration! The Eighth Amendment (against cruel and unusual punishment) would suffice to prohibit this but it has not been enforced. Involuntary conditions such as mental illness and homelessness are not deterred by demeaning acts of the law.[9] Instead, the law exacerbates the feelings of denigration and profound loss of rights through illness. It is indecent to invoke a punishment for the condition a person is in. We do not punish Tourette's Syndrome victims or epileptics for accosting passersby or inadvertently damaging goods. The mentally ill homeless are paradoxically free, released from confinement and rigorously scheduled activities to an open and "free" yet unwelcomed space in the community. They are victims of an ill-conceived libertarian policy that essentially requires the enactment of welfare rights (admitting its own inconsistency) in the name of esteemed autonomy. Lon Fuller presents this tragic dilemma as an antithetical account of freedom implied by the libertarian position:

> Freedom can be thought as a capacity to choose from a large number of possibilities. However, if the number is bewildering or without priority, or the possibilities are beyond reach, the condition becomes chaos. A psychological manifestation of this phenomenon is schizophrenia. Acute schizophrenics must be helped to systemize some of the smallest tasks; or freedom can be regarded as order and regularity, the freedom that comes from functioning within known limits or internalized structure; taken to extreme, this freedom can lead to rigidity, confinement and loss of autonomy.[10]

Ironically, the libertarian position reckons an unwise choice for oneself a misfortune for the person involved; but, in this case, they have imposed an unwise choice on someone else, and by their own principle violated human rights. In one well-known incident, a mentally ill person brought a law suit against a public library when his rights were violated. Richard Kreimer of Morristown, New Jersey, spent every day in the Morristown library.[11] For several years he used the library as a reading place, as did some other homeless. None were as steady a visitor as he. Library patrons complained that he stared at them and had an unbearable odor. A new set of library rules was published and on the list was one which prohibited staring and low "hygiene." These were classified as a nuisance. Anyone violating this rule would be asked to leave the library. Mr. Kreimer brought suit charging that his Fourteenth Amendment rights were violated when he was barred from the library. Mr. Kreimer won a settlement for $230,000. Had the Morristown community found ways to embrace the skills and research interests Richard Kreimer had, he could have been a contributing member of the library staff rather than one scourged for his condition.

Conventional autonomy provides a flexible framework within which a person either widens or narrows choices of human welfare. One cannot both respect a person and be indifferent to whether he or she has the means to realize his or her abilities, and the goods achieved by Kreimer's case would not have been achieved without this positive intervention. To use another example, one that prompted a Supreme Court decision in New York State in February 1993, some New York City residents proposed that homeless people live on a barge that would be available should the neighborhoods become deteriorated by their presence. The court ruled that New York State should "develop a comprehensive, integrated system of treatment and rehabilitative services for the mentally ill" which would include "assuring the adequacy and appropriateness of residential arrangements for people in need of service."[12] The opportunity for selecting other goods for the mentally ill homeless is far more limited than the selection of means to house and provide rehabilitative care for them. According to the notion of conventional autonomy, the homeless must first have a home that can assist them in becoming both accepted and self-accepting. But everything depends on the willingness on the part of the non-mentally-ill community to recognize our moral duty to protect and encourage the value of human flourishing in people whose opportunities—whose humanity—is at risk. This end is not defined by any one individual's sense of the common good, but we are obligated to include the marginalized populations in this pursuit. Past failure to accept mentally ill people into public society helped create "sanism," an attitude characterized as "irrational" thinking, feeling, and behavior patterns of response by an individual or by a society toward the mentally ill individuals; "zoning out," group homes, and congregates for residences of mentally ill are paradigms of "sanism" attitudes.[13]

6. Conclusion

Only in an environment of satisfied needs can anyone exercise the right of conventional autonomy. The relative appreciation of the centrality of such needs distinguishes libertarian (natural) autonomy from welfare rights (conventional) autonomy. I discussed how the first sense of autonomy can be divisive. The second, conventional sense is cooperative and offers us a collective responsibility for generations to follow. To this end we come to realize other values than meeting individual rights. Instead, we come to realize how collective bodies may be the appropriate respondents to bring about human flourishing. We can obtain a measure of human development among the population of mentally ill homeless; the feeling of security, care, renewed hope in ill homeless, and friendship could underwrite what is meaningful in life, however challenged it is. The diverse needs and rights of groups in the community reminds us of its human frailty and the anonymity of its responsibility. In F. H. Bradley's organismic sense of society, when people abandon strictly personal views of their own places, they regain a more inclusive place shared with others. To this extent, individual liberties find their fullness in conventional autonomy where the oscillating needs strengthen our communal and individual well being. As members in society, we participate in each other's nature, and this common end is most ennobled upon satisfying the right to "home" the mentally ill.

Notes

1. From *The Poetry of Robert Frost*, edited by Edward Connery Lathem. Copyright 1930, 1939, © 1969 by Henry Holt and Co., Inc.
2. Peter Rossi, *Down and Out in America* (Chicago: University of Chicago Press, 1989), p. 12.
3. Henry Shue, *Basic Rights* (Princeton: Princeton University Press, 1980), p. 26.
4. Carl I. Cohen and Kenneth S. Thompson, "Homeless Mentally Ill or Mentally Ill Homeless," *American Journal of Psychiatry*, 149:6 (June 1992), pp. 812-823, p. 819.
5. D. D. Raphael (ed.), *Political Theory and Rights of Man* (Bloomington: Indiana University Press, 1967), p. 64.
6. G. John M. Abbarno, "Moral Aspects of Life Without Privacy," in *Ethics for Today and Tomorrow*, ed. Joram Graf Haber (Boston: Jones and Bartlett, 1997), p. 560.
7. A. I. Melden, *Rights and Persons* (Berkeley: University of California Press, 1977), p. 172.
8. E. Fuller Torrey, *Nowhere to Go* (New York: Harper & Row Publishers, 1988), p. 4.
9. Edmund V. Ludwig, "The Mentally Ill Homeless: Evolving Involuntary Commitment Issues," *Villanova Law Review*, 36 (1991), 1085-1111, p. 4.
10. Loren E. Lomasky, *Persons, Rights, and the Moral Community* (New York: Oxford University Press, 1987), p. 210.
11. "Richard Kreimer," *Washington Post* (14 October 1992), p. C9.
12. *New York State Mental Hygiene Law*, Section 7.01 (McKinney, 1996), p. 27.
13. See Michael Perlin, "Competency, Deinstitutionalization and Homelessness: A Story of Marginalization," *Houston Law Review*, 28 (1991), p. 89.

Fourteen

HOMELESSNESS, THE RIGHT TO PRIVACY, AND THE OBLIGATION TO PROVIDE A HOME

Shyli Karin-Frank

1. Introduction

In this chapter, I offer an interpretation of some primary concepts of liberalism that are compatible with rights of the homeless. For this purpose, I discuss the issue of homelessness within the liberal context of the definition of domains of privacy.

The extent of application of the right to privacy incites controversy. I examine "home" both as a physical component of and as a necessary condition for achieving a state of privacy, as well as an adequate place for exercising other forms of the right to privacy.

The right to privacy itself is too general and abstract to imply the right to privacy of home. This can be considered only on the basis of several constituents of the requirement of privacy. I do not mean to establish that the privacy of home is required universally and absolutely. Instead, I will explicate the meaning of privacy and its application in concrete areas in order to consider home as a local yet fundamental element of human existence, as conceived within the liberal context.

Whether homelessness is always a social disease that ought to be cured, or whether it may sometimes be chosen voluntarily by the individual and thus ought to be tolerated by society, is a crucial question for liberalism, since it has important implications for the morality of the measures taken by society. I advance the view that homelessness is usually a negative social phenomenon, and I attempt to arrive at the adequate means of fighting such a disease. However, this does not exclude the possibility of voluntary homelessness, which is a life-style that ought to be tolerated by society, despite its inhuman nature. Voluntary homelessness can be defended, for example, along the lines of justifying suicide: assuming that we can relinquish our rights, including our basic rights, and given evidence that by doing so we do not simply shift an unjustifiable burden on others, homelessness is acceptable.

Although the line of argument which I offer here does not firmly establish human beings' moral or legal right to have a home, it does found the first step for fighting socially and legally against homelessness. Homelessness can be shown to be a substantive violation of the constituents of the requirement of privacy, especially the right to self-defense and the right to equality. The violation of the right to self-defense involves a real danger of destruction to the individual's autonomous personality. Autonomy and individuality are considered to be basic moral concepts of liberalism, and their actualization is a primary goal of moral activity. Homelessness involves a risk of an unacceptable damage to the individual and thereby creates a moral burden on society.

I argue that, assuming political and moral grounds of liberalism, the ultimate obligation of the democratic state to protect the lives of its citizens can be interpreted to include protection from homelessness. Such protection cannot be provided by institutions, since they involve deprivation of privacy and control over persons. Instead, protection requires the provision of a private home, at least in the minimal sense of a physical territory. Arguing in terms of responsibility, care, or empathy, as alternative ways of fighting against homelessness, seems too thin and vague. These may be proper ways of taking care of the poor, less fortunate members of society, but only when they are accompanied by legal measures. Regarding homelessness, however, I argue that providing a home is not optional, nor an act of grace, but obligatory.

2. What Is Privacy?

The concept of privacy consists of factual and normative components. Privacy is both a state of existence and a value requirement (the state is implied by the value). Privacy is a state of being in private or withdrawn from the public: seclusion, secrecy, solitude. "Private" means, according to a popular dictionary, "peculiar to one's self; belonging to or concerning an individual only, personal, opposed to public or national, not known, open or accessible to people in general; secret, unconnected with others."[1]

Does a universal concept of privacy exist? Did the Greeks, for example, make a modern distinction between the private and the public spheres? The Greeks considered the difference between necessity and freedom fundamental; they considered individuality, self-perfection, and freedom part of the political sphere, whereas necessity of survival and continuity of the species belonged to the private sphere. Do such Greek notions have no connection to the modern concept of privacy or has the public-private dichotomy shifted in ways the necessity-freedom divide has not?[2] In either case, I will adopt the view that modern norms may be different in content from classical norms of privacy; yet the very need for privacy is essential to all creatures, including human beings, and is manifest in all cultures.[3]

In the modern world, privacy and secrecy are closely linked.[4] Secrecy can involve a range of related concepts, including sacredness, intimacy, privacy, silence, prohibition, furtiveness, and deception. The core of secrecy, however, is intentional concealment. What is private is not always secret. We do not conceal the ordinary events and experiences of everyday life but simply maintain them within the personal domain, not offered to the gaze and scrutiny of the public. Secrecy can be a means to or a form of privacy, if privacy is the condition of being protected from unwanted access by others.[5] Secrecy requires a specific object: that which is concealed. Privacy is more general; it is more like a way of life, a condition that is necessary (as we shall see later) for a satisfactory life. Like a secret, privacy can be shared between individuals, as in the case of intimacy of lovers.

Privacy is not only a state of being; it is also an institutional fact that is constituted through volition and choice. From the moral point of view, privacy is primarily a value requirement to respect certain domains of the individual as being immune from public intrusion. It is recognized to be a moral good, though not absolute, because the need for privacy presupposes the need for social interactions. The demand for privacy and immunity can be overridden by other valuable social interests, such as the sanctity of life, in the name of which the prohibition on murder overrides the privacy of one's bedroom.

In the modern world, privacy is the most institutionalized, controlled, and therefore legitimate form of withdrawal from public life.[6] We see this in the preponderance of social rules—expressed in law, language, habits, and architecture—preserving or enforcing the separation between the public and the private. Privacy is one of the social expressions of freedom as license; it involves a requirement of self-determination regarding participation in social interactions, exposure, and transfer of information.

The right to privacy has its origin in the concern for protecting the liberties of individuals against a political majority or against the government, which might abuse its political power.[7] Since privacy is a limited moral good, the right to privacy cannot be absolute, and it must be weighed against other rights and obligations.[8]

Even if definitions of the right to privacy are not satisfactory, the existing formulations of the right to privacy will suffice to support the claim of a necessary connection between valuable human existence and privacy in the form of home. Traditional formulations of the right to privacy are: "the right to be let alone," or "the very basic right to be free from sights, sounds, and tangible matter we do not want." The stricter definition of the Nordic Conference on the Right to Privacy is the right to be let alone to live one's own life with the minimum of interference. In expanded form, this means the right of the individual to lead his or her life protected against (1) interference with his private, family, and home lives; (2) interference with mental integrity or moral and intellectual freedom; (3) attacks on honor and reputation; (4) being placed in a false light; (5) the disclosure of irrelevant embarrassing facts relating to private life; (6) the use of name, identity, and likeness; (7) spying, prying, watching, and stalking; (8) interference with correspondence; (9) misuse of private communications, written or oral; (10) disclosure of information given or received in circumstances of professional confidence.[9]

In the American legal system, unlike the English system, a general legal right to privacy is recognized. Yet in both systems the moral right to privacy is recognized as a basic liberty, and this right is cited in the attempt to protect the individual from unjustified intrusions.

Within the context of modern liberalism, some behaviors, relations, and domains have been recognized as entitled to privacy, or at least, as candidates for such application. The reason is that they are believed to express or symbolize the individual's identity. For example, one's face, body, name, belongings, thoughts, or relationships have been considered in legal and moral terms as candidates for protection under the right to privacy. The protection of privacy might be sought in three overlapping areas, corresponding to three types of privacy. First, mental or communicational privacy allows a person to be alone with his or her thoughts and other mental processes. Second, informational privacy provides protection for personal information which is legitimately held in the files of public and private organizations, and prevents the disclosure of such information to third parties. Third, bodily or physical privacy provides space in which the body can exist, function, move, and be free from physical intrusions. This restricts unwanted proximity of other people or bodily contact and touching, as well as observational intrusions of onlookers, cameras, as well as other senses and sensors.

3. Why Is Home Morally Required?

Most human activities require access to privacy at some level, whether intellectual, emotional, or physical. Responsibility and autonomy, both attributes of a mature personality, require the moral significance of privacy. Certain conditions for a human and moral person must move from the status of possibility to actuality. Privacy, in general, and home, in particular, are among the conditions without which responsibility, autonomy, and individuality are mere postulates or abstract ideas.

The self is vulnerable, since it is always in the process of growing, and it needs to be protected from the pressures of the external world. Intrusion of privacy destroys defense mechanisms that are indispensable for the development of human personality. Privacy is a necessary condition for integrating personality, for it protects free action against external pressures. An important datum is revealed through psychological analysis of exposure and shame: the genetic core of shame is the need to cover that which is exposed.[10] Shame arises as a result of intrusion in privacy, and it underlines human vulnerability.[11]

The attainment and preservation of personal identity require that the individual draws a line between himself or herself and others, not only cognitively, but also psychologically and physically. This implies that the private dimension of life is regarded as ontologically and psychologically independent of the social realm, although the two are interrelated.

Biological research supports the psychological findings, presenting privacy as necessary not only for the welfare of the individual but also for the survival of the group. There is evidence of irreversible damage caused by invasion or denial of privacy: physiological changes, pathological behaviors, loss of ability to take care of children, mate, and smell. Social hierarchy is destroyed, aggression increases, sexual behavior becomes sadistic, natural selection takes the form of massive killings or suicides or bio-chemical deaths. In a loss of privacy, negative feelings erupt, and tension destructively increases, causing high blood pressure, heart diseases and diseases of the circulatory system.

Privacy in the biological form of territoriality has been shown to protect the ability to procreate the species, to improve selection of feeling males, to create a suitable environment for raising offspring, and to provide a context of physical reference for group activities, such as playing or learning.[12]

According to Erving Goffman's distinctions between "stage" and "off stage,"[13] the public dimension of life consists of series of behaviors, ways of speech, personal relations, styles of dressing, and so forth, through which interaction occurs between certain social roles that are adopted by the individual and are normally expected by others. Behind the stage lies the private dimension of life, which includes, among other things, the choice, control, and management of social roles. Withdrawing from the public to privacy, the self is disconnected from the roles and identities which playing such roles forces on it. In this way, the individual defines and preserves his or her individuality.[14]

Following Goffman's terms, home seems to be the most permanent and well-defined off stage. Its borders are clearly seen and recognized, as are the human behaviors that are expected with respect to home. Home provides privacy as solitude, which is a voluntary withdrawal from society. Although one can obtain a sense of privacy in a crowd, home is both a means for and a symbol of privacy in Western culture.

The basic human need for both social interaction and solitude has been expressed by Western institutions and manners as well as by architecture. Consider how walls, fences, doors, veils, and closets are used. Certain functions of privacy require the creation of secluded spaces, which are literally "off stage." These function to relatively separate the self from others: doors shut out, walls enclose,[15] and windows are primarily designed to afford a glance through to the outside, rather than a peep within.

Home also provides intimacy in order to achieve maximal personal relations. Inside the home, the bedroom is more private than the living room. Bedrooms serve the function of preventing other members of the family, such as children, from intruding on the intimacy of parents. Intimacy implies withdrawal from other persons as well as from sights, smells, noises. Even in the home, it is both possible and required that the individual maintain privacy against members of family, by closing a door or a drawer. Western custom regards intrusion as harmful to the self. It is morally or legally justified only if there exists an overriding consideration, such as in case of a husband abusing his wife in the privacy of their bedroom.

Only on the basis of accepted norms regarding home can we construct analogous off stage areas, permanent or semi-permanent, such as libraries or offices. In order to intrude or trespass borders such as walls, doors, and fences, special permission is required, according to which a map of social relations and hierarchy can be drawn.

The realization of personal ideals regarding human relations requires privacy, assuming that personal relations are crucial for the development of individuality.[16] Home is believed to be the adequate domain for exercising deep commitments as well as the elementary means for selectivity and isolation of critical aspects of the most cherished human relations.[17] Love, friendship, and family life are considered to be human goods and basic human needs of which the sexual expression is both common and essential.[18] Sexual relations are restricted to the privacy of home, not only on grounds of chastity, but also because home is considered to be the proper place for realizing decisions regarding family matters, marriage, and birth. Home is the physical center in which private affairs can flourish, with family as their context. Privacy in marriage is a fundamental right of the American constitution, and the court has determined that if the right to privacy has any meaning at all, then it is the right of the individual to be free from unauthorized governmental interference in matters that affect the individual, as much as matters of family and marriage. Throughout history, the court has granted legislative protection to the sanctity of home and family life.

If we consider the current controversy regarding the immunity of homo-sexual relations,[19] we see that on both sides of the debate home is unquestion-ably regarded as an indispensable condition for human existence. This is one reason why home is not merely a physical territory but also a fundamental social and political institution. The sanctity of home forms the basis on which concrete human activities are evaluated. The debate concerns the proper extension of application of the right to privacy.[20] In other words, the controversy has focused on the types of behaviors and activities which take place inside home and which should be considered immune against public intrusion.

For example, the debate is about whether or not homosexual relations practiced at home exhibit similarity in structure or content to cases of hiding weapons, drugs, or stolen goods. Unlike the cases of consenting homosexual adults, weapons, drugs, and stolen goods involve victims. These latter justify legal intrusion in one's home.[21] The implied norm is that physical intrusion in one's home is permitted only in extreme circumstances and under restricting conditions. This demonstrates the importance ascribed to private territories.

The question remains whether conduct considered immoral by the majority justifies intrusion in the privacy of home in order to regulate conduct. It is not clear whether the fundamental right to equality that protects heterosexual relations from interference in one's home extends to homosexual relations under similar conditions.[22] Regardless of the similarities and dissimilarities between traditional family life and homosexual relations, privacy of the family within the home is the accepted norm.

The same conviction underlines the debate regarding freedom of the press versus the right to privacy of the individual. Arguments which present the public interest to know as overriding the right to privacy regard home as a protected territory. Even when the press is entitled to disclose personal matters and identifying photos and stories, the methods of intrusion are restricted: physical harassment and trespassing inside the home are forbidden. This applies even more so in arguments that favor privacy over the public interest to know. Here, home is a protected territory against the anti-privacy nature of the press, and against the element of intrusion which is inseparable from the concept of investigative journalism, a genre which is generally held in high esteem by liberals.[23]

Privacy is needed for the development of awareness of free choice in life.[24] A crucial part of the practical social or moral meaning of autonomy is the decision when and how to appear in public. The proper functioning of social interactions requires that we respect the domain of control as a private domain. Without the establishment of real domains of privacy, people's human and moral attributes cannot be realized; they can be destroyed. From this perspective, human relations can be described in terms of series of private domains, circles within circles, which include the various secrets of the individual. The inner circle is the most guarded one, containing the individual's fears and hopes.

The right to privacy is ascribed to the human being as a moral agent. The principle of privacy is based on the principle of respect for personality, which regards human individuality as a self-conscious subject, a choosing and evaluating agent.[25] The idea is that privacy is required for the realization of political liberty and moral autonomy. The right to privacy is violated whenever there is interference into one's moral decisions, making it impossible for the individual cannot function as the captain of his or her soul. However, intrusion in the most private domains, such as home or intimate relations or fears and hopes, is morally wrong not only because it violates a moral right (which could still be justified on the basis of overriding considerations), and not only wrong because it abstractly treats the individual as a means and not as an end. It is wrong because it threatens the individual's actual autonomy; the exposure of one's fears and hopes will cause one, according to psychological research, shame and embarrassment that puts one under the control of others. Being subjected to constant intrusion has been shown to be destructive for the individual's dignity and autonomy. It diminishes his or her capability of functioning as a fully moral human being.[26]

Home is necessary for the possibility of choice. It provides privacy the choice of solitude, unlike isolation or loneliness, which do not involve choice. Sensations or feelings of personal autonomy are strengthened when we have our own personal space, such as a home or a room or a closet.[27] In a Supreme Court decision that denies the right of government to regulate homosexual relations which take place inside the home, as well as in the criticism of this decision,[28] home is considered a necessary place for exercising certain political liberties and free decisions.

The adaptation required by moral and social life is emotionally exhausting; being constantly on the alert can lead to the destruction of any organism. The tensions that are created through the burden of social adaptation[29] must be relieved if the individual is expected to successfully fulfill his or her duties and play expected roles.[30] Privacy of home makes emotional relief possible by enabling certain behaviors that are morally or socially unacceptable yet psychologically necessary for the individual. For example, the individual sometimes needs to be aggressively angry, irritating, lustful, or vulgar, without fear of the consequences of social reaction. Privacy of home affords one the opportunity to take off one's moral dress and rest for a while, so that moral and social life can continue safely.

The privacy of home also functions as an escape valve for social ills. Without legitimizing and requiring privacy, and without supplying an actual place in which it can take place, each withdrawal from the public would be regarded as obscenity, deception, spying, or subversion. Since every individual and every society present deviations from the norms, their mere constant exposure without being able to eradicate them could harm the fabric of society. This is why some activities which are generally unacceptable in public are protected in the privacy of home. Consider making racial remarks, or rebellious speeches, watching pornographic films, reading obscene literature, or strolling in the nude.

We have seen that home and privacy in general are not values in themselves, for they are necessary means for realizing other valuable human interests and goals. In addition, home and privacy in general cannot be regarded as mere means, for they are essential components of basic, valuable behaviors and relations.[31] Home has a triple meaning: first, it is a necessary condition for the autonomous self and other valuable aspects of human existence; second, it is a symbol of autonomous self; and third, it is its external expression that can be viewed as the extension of self. Being an extension of the self, home is analogous to private property. Private property is regarded in legal terms as an extension of the individual and therefore subject to the legal right to self-defense. The analogy also exists with historical and legal tendency to apply both the right to privacy and the right to self-defense in an extended manner. The right to self-defense has been extended to the lives and property of others, and the right to privacy has been extended to personal relations, abortions, and other matters.[32]

4. The Obligation to Provide a Home

In most of its forms, homelessness is unquestionably a social disease which can harm not only individuals, but also the fabric of society. Though the various and complex causes of homelessness might remain a subject of debate, the need to fight against such a negative phenomenon cannot be denied. Yet, remaining on liberal grounds, no morally and legally adequate way to combat this problem presents itself unequivocally.

In order to understand the kind of protection that can be justifiably expected in the case of homelessness, we must first understand in what sense homelessness is a violation of the right to privacy. Is it in the same sense that, for example, torture violates the rights of prisoners of war and racial segregation violates the right to equality? In other words, does the right to privacy specifically include home in the same way that the right to equality excludes racial discrimination?

A right to home is not recognized in any liberal system; were it recognized, its violation would automatically call for legal protection, which means, in this case, providing a home or a legally suitable substitute. Furthermore, demonstrating that homelessness is a severe violation of the right to privacy does not necessarily imply a legal or moral right to home.

Homelessness is not a clear and a direct violation of the right to privacy, because the right to privacy is too general and abstract, and it does not indicate its possible candidates for application. "Arguing from privacy" regarding moral or legal issues means no more than designating our intentional frame of reference and our requirements when considering a concrete case of intrusion in personal affairs. Either we look for criteria for applying the general right to privacy in concrete cases, or we look for specific means for solving particular problems of immunity. In any case, we cannot argue from privacy alone, if privacy is what we seek to arrive at. We can, though, establish privacy, by defining its moral context in terms of rights or obligations or utility considerations. Within this context, immunity is ascribed to actions and relations with the result of obligating protection by the law.

For example, regarding the confidentiality of the lawyer-client relationship, we do not argue from privacy but from self-defense through duty and privilege. This constitutes an area of privacy in the sense of confidentiality and entitles a person to immunity. The protection of privacy or confidentiality of the lawyer-client relationship is conceptually and practically built into the legal system. It becomes an institutional fact, without which all other elements of the system are not valid or obligatory.

A different example is homosexual relations, where privacy is not a constituent of a system but the result of accumulating considerations which belong to different contexts. In homosexual relations, "arguing from privacy" has a meaning only in historical terms which point at the gradual extension of already recognized types of privacy to analogous activities. On philosophical grounds, however, what we actually do in the case of homosexual relations is similar to our tactic regarding lawyer-client relationship: we argue from equality, self-defense, or self-identity, in order to constitute privacy and immunity.[33]

If home is not guaranteed a priori in any liberal system, nor included in the general right to privacy, its importance is still widely recognized in liberal discussions about privacy and immunity, where it is implied as a necessary condition for human life. We need not make a special philosophical or legal effort analogous to our tactic regarding homosexual relations in order to establish home as a private territory, entitled to immunity. Such an undertaking has been done on liberal grounds. Wherever the right to privacy has become fundamental, home has been recognized to be an indispensable element of privacy, and therefore valuable for human existence. Given the applications of the right to privacy, and regardless of the controversy about the extension of its application, homelessness is a deep deprivation of privacy. It is a substantial violation of the right to privacy, even if only indirectly, through violating the constituents of the requirement of privacy, as given in traditional liberal discussions.

What kind of protection, then, is adequate in cases of homelessness? Does homelessness dictate a concrete positive protection by the public or by the state, in the sense of providing a home or an acceptable substitute? At first glance, it appears that even under the notion that rights create obligations (which is controversial), the existence of the right to privacy is not sufficient to create any perfect social obligation, that is, an obligation that will guarantee adequate protection for the homeless. In addition to the abstract nature of the right to privacy, exercising this right is always relative to the contingent existence of other justifiable social interests, and can be overridden by them. Any appeal to social responsibility, as a justification, is too general and vague since it does not specify protection for the homeless.

However, on further analysis, the real danger of destruction of the individual's personality can serve as a starting point for creating public protection. Autonomy and ability to exercise responsibility, requires protection for the homeless in the name of the rights to self-defense and equality. Although the right to self-defense is usually reserved strictly for cases of physical harm, it can be applied to cases of ill psychological effects or damage to personal integrity or autonomy. Such consequences might be irreversible in the sense that they might prevent the individual from leading a morally acceptable life.

Earlier we saw that there is an analogy between the right to privacy and the right to self-defense. However, we should remember that the right to self-defense is also a traditional constituent of the requirement of privacy as demonstrated in the privacy of lawyer-client relationship or in the privacy of homosexual relations. The right to self-defense is combined with the general right to privacy, the right to equality, the right to political liberty, and together they constitute the requirement of privacy in various domains. Although it would be a mistake to replace the requirement of privacy by one of its constituents, that is, self-defense, it is through the component of self-defense that we can claim social protection for the homeless.

The right to self-defense is adequately applied to cases where there is a real and identifiable danger of harm to the individual. The minimal legal protection consists of "negative" steps, for it means that the individual is entitled to react to aggression and defend himself or herself by various means, including violence. Thus, the individual is not punished, despite the general prohibition on violence. However, a wider, "positive" meaning of protection also exists, one which consists of concrete actions and means which fall within the obligation of the state to defend its citizens against internal or external danger. Such an obligation is found in all versions of political liberalism, through the concept of self-defense. This is a stronger and a more fruitful concept than social responsibility. Assuming that all types of political liberal theories presuppose the concept of the ultimate obligation of the state to protect its citizens, what status, meaning, scope, and implications pertain to that obligation? Such an obligation of the state is distinguished from the political obligations of its citizens, the status of which is indeed controversial. My assumption, which requires a separate discussion, is that the obligation of the state to protect its citizens is presupposed by classical as well as by modern theories of the liberal state, whether in terms of justice, fairness, or consent.

A liberal state aspires to a moral justification for the imposition of specific duties on its citizens. Whether these duties are absolute or *prima facie* is controversial. But this controversy does not affect the nature of the obligation of protection imposed on the state. Whether the state is conceived as a minimal procedural context or whether it is assigned some further functions for realizing justice, the government is held responsible for the protection of its citizens, under different interpretations of such responsibility. Responsibility can be limited to cases of external or internal violence, or extended to other areas, such as health care, education, and the prevention of homelessness.

Given the variety of democracies, it is possible that not every state assumes an obligation to protect its citizens, just as it may be possible that not every state imposes duties on its individual members. But the core of political liberalism involves a fundamental obligation to protect, and in most cases, the obligation of the state to protect its citizens is a basic rationale for the liberal state. This obligation embodies moral content and is constituted on moral grounds. Yet, it is primarily a political obligation, not a morally universal one. It is dependent on a certain political order, which may be considered morally good, perhaps even the best; still, it is a concrete political order. The restricted scope of the application of the obligation of protection, therefore, does not concern all human beings but only citizens or residents of the state.

Whether or not the state is an indispensable means for the welfare of individuals, and whether or not the individual's right to self-defense can be protected by means other than institutional, are crucial questions. However, they are insignificant regarding the nature of the obligation of the state to protect its citizens. From the perspective of the government, this obligation ties the government to its duty. It does not permit the government to neglect efforts to defend citizens under any circumstances.

Rights of individuals, including the right to self-defense, do not entail a parallel unconditional obligation which is imposed on individuals. It is always possible to withdraw from rights voluntarily. In contrast, one can generally withdraw from obligations only if there exist other overriding obligations or the existence of a priority principle. The ultimate obligation to protect the citizens is a positive obligation that is presumably the government's sole obligation. By its very nature it is ultimate, and thus tautologically, it cannot be overridden by other obligations.

Individuals can perhaps violate their duties in a way that can be tolerated by the system, as long as everyone does not do the same. The reason is that individual violations of concrete obligations do not permanently harm the system or the meaning of these obligations. Unlike individuals, if a government withdraws from the obligation of protection it dissolves the state, conceptually and empirically, for the state is constituted on that obligation. Therefore, such an ultimate obligation is also absolute.

The obligation of protection, which emerges from the right to self-defense of individuals, concerns only citizens and residents. However, because of the right to equality, the obligation of protection applies equally to all citizens or residents. Usually, such an obligation is applied in times of war and in conjunction with a theory of just war. But it can be interpreted to apply also to other issues, such as health care, where physical and psychological integrity of individuals are involved. Such an application can be argued for, although the question of extension of application remains open. The same is true with respect to homelessness, which involves similar physical and psychological problems, and should be included in the group of issues which are within the government's obligation of protection and not merely within its responsibility.

From the moral point of view of a political theory, the restriction that is imposed on the government's obligation involves the efficiency and morality of the means of protection. The adequate means of protection against homelessness is the provision of a home, at least as a private physical territory. This only guarantees that the individual is not robbed of elementary conditions necessary for human life, although it cannot guarantee the achievement of this goal.

Houses for the mentally ill or shelters or institutes can be proper substitutes only in extreme cases and as a last resort: for example, when homelessness is accompanied or caused by diseases which leave the individual defenseless and requires professional care. However, regarding homelessness "proper," these institutes are unjustifiable substitutes, for they necessarily fail to protect the privacy of the individual. On the contrary, institutes do essentially deprive the individual of his or her privacy. The activity of institutes involves a significant moral evil, which shifts control of one's life from the autonomous self to representatives (authorized or unauthorized) of society. One's moral and existential "core" is being handed over to others. Perhaps such institutes do comply with the demand of providing physical protection; yet, they do so at the expense of losing autonomy and the integrity of one's personality. Again, moral evil of this kind can sometimes be justified from other, overriding considerations, but it requires severe restrictions.

Institutes can indeed be regarded as private persons for legal purposes, in the sense that intrusion in a clinic, for example, is forbidden, or that information held by a bank is considered confidential. Institutes cannot justifiably take control over private matters of individuals, unless authorized to do so. A paradigm case is that of prisoners, who are deliberately deprived of most forms of privacy, along with other rights enjoyed by citizens, as part of their justifiable punishment. However, with respect to institutes for the homeless, this paradigm is irrelevant. Deprivation of privacy by institutes is usually only dressed up in an appearance of legitimacy, through the professional work of doctors and social workers, without real moral justification.

The philosophical tactic of protecting the homeless through the conjunction of the right to privacy and the obligation of protection of the state, does not solve the problem of homelessness. On a theoretical level, it points in a fruitful direction. A host of problems still remains to be considered. For example, providing a home by the state is an economical burden, as are military means of protection or costs of health care. Standards of a theory of justice should be established for distributing resources to prevent homelessness as well. The difficulty of this task does not diminish the duty to provide a home to all.

Another problem which emerges for this line of argument is that of defining the legitimate expectations regarding "home." In this discussion, I have referred to "home" in a minimal sense only, that is, as a private physical territory. Standards should be established for defining an acceptable minimum.

Furthermore, by providing a minimal home for the homeless, who probably suffer from other social, economical, and mental ills, we may create new problems or aggravate existing problems, such as slums, diseases, drugs, and violence. Providing a minimal physical territory without treating all the psychological and social aspects of the homelessness problem might result, ironically, in too much privacy, and this can lead to a trap of loneliness. Loneliness consists of similar elements to privacy, yet is an involuntary state of mind, a sad result of neglect. But loneliness is not only sad, it is also dangerous: it, too, involves the risk of destruction of personality, in a similar manner to that caused by lack of privacy.[34]

Without underestimating the complexities of these difficulties and other expected problems, a person can argue from the right to privacy and other constituents, especially the right to self-defense, to the obligation of providing a home for the homeless. This line of argument does not require abandonment of the familiar grounds of liberalism and a radical switch to communism or socialism, where home is taken for granted as a basic human good. Liberalism might, in fact, learn something from the Marxist analysis of the inhuman feelings that are characteristic of a capitalist society because of its basic ideas about human interactions. For example, the element of competition stresses radical individualism, which in its turn requires privacy. Competition outlines the over-independence of human beings who are considered to be self-sufficient. This allegedly brings about suspicion in others and a need for being cautious of them, with the result of factual withdrawal and isolation. The exaggerated demand for privacy necessarily makes interpersonal relations instrumental, manipulative, and inhuman. Thus privacy is perceived as an essential product of the liberal ideology that, according to the Marxist beliefs, expresses escapism and selfishness. It is one mode of social alienation with loneliness as its symptom.[35]

Contrary to criticisms made by opponents of liberalism, indifference toward social ills and sterile solutions have been shown to be contingent qualities of current applications of liberal principles. The fundamentals of traditional liberalism have been reinterpreted to afford a direction toward a moral solution for homelessness.

Notes

1. *The New Webster Encyclopedic Dictionary of the English Language*, Virginia S. Thatcher, ed. in chief (Chicago: Consolidated Book Publishers, 1994), p. 661.

2. The two alternatives of interpretation, expressing the views of Arendt and Cranston, are presented in L. C. Veleky, "The Concept of Privacy," in *Privacy*, ed. John B. Young (Summerset, N.J.: John Wiley & Sons, 1978), p. 16.

3. Alan F. Westin, *Privacy and Freedom* (New York: Atheneum, 1967), p. 8.

4. Sissela Bok, *Secrets: On the Ethics of Concealment and Revelation* (London: Oxford University Press, 1984), pp. 5-6.

5. *Ibid.*, p. 10.

6. Christopher G. A. Bryant, "Privacy, Privatization, and Self-Determination," in *Privacy*, ed. Young, pp. 59-60.

7. M. J. Kappelhoff, "Bowers v. Hardwick: Is There a Right to Privacy?", *The American University Law Review*, 37 (1988), p. 490.

8. Gerald Dworkin, "Report of the Royal Commission on the Press," in *Privacy*, ed. Young, p. 115.

9. *Ibid.*, p. 114.

10. Carl D. Schneider, *Shame, Exposure, and Privacy* (Boston: Beacon Press, 1977), p. 37.

11. *Ibid.*, pp. 28-29.

12. Westin, *Privacy and Freedom*, p. 8; Barry Schwartz, "The Social Psychology of Privacy," *American Journal of Psychology*, 73 (1968), pp. 741-742.

13. Roger Ingham, "Privacy and Psychology," in *Privacy*, ed. Young, p. 41.

14. Schwartz, "The Social Psychology of Privacy," p. 752.

15. *Ibid.*, pp. 746-747; p. 749.

16. S. I. Benn, "Privacy, Freedom, and Respect for Persons," in *Today's Moral Problems*, ed. Richard Wasserstrom (New York: Macmillan Press, 1975), pp. 4-10.

17. D. J. Langin, "The Right of Privacy and the Question of Intimate Relations," *Iowa Law Review*, 72 (1987), pp. 1443-1460.

18. Kappelhoff, "Bowers v. Hardwick," p. 496.

19. Langin, "The Right of Privacy and the Question of Intimate Relations," p. 1445; C. W. Ferree, "Bowers v. Hardwick: The Supreme Court Closes the Door on the Right to Privacy and Opens the Door to the Bedroom," *Denver University Law Review*, 64:3 (1988), pp. 599-612.

20. *Ibid.*, p. 600.

21. Kappelhoff, "Bowers v. Hardwick," p. 511.

22. Ferree, "Bowers v. Hardwick: The Supreme Court Closes the Door on Right to Privacy," p. 607.

23. For example, Dworkin, "Report of the Royal Commission on the Press"; also in Velecky, "The Concept of Privacy," and in D. MacCuail, "The Mass Media and Privacy," in *Privacy*, ed. Young, p. 177.

24. Westin, *Privacy and Freedom*, p. 34.

25. Benn, "Privacy, Freedom, and Respect for Persons," pp. 4-10.

26. Schwartz, "The Social Psychology of Privacy," p. 749.

27. Ingham, "Privacy and Psychology," p. 50.

28. See for example, Kappelhoff, "Bowers v. Hardwick," pp. 503-504.

29. Paul Helmos, *Solitude and Privacy* (New York: Routledge & Kegan Paul, 1952), p. 117.

30. Westin, *Privacy and Freedom*, p. 35.

31. C. Fried, "Privacy: A Rational Context," in *Today's Moral Problems*, ed. Wasserstrom, p. 21.

32. Ferree, "Bowers v. Hardwick: The Supreme Court Closes the Door on the Right to Privacy," pp. 600-601.

33. As I have argued in my unpublished paper, "On Constituting Moral Contexts for Privacy."

34. In my forthcoming paper on "Moral Education, the Value of Privacy, and the Threat of Loneliness."

35. See Helmos, *Solitude and Privacy*, pp. 108-116.

Part Five

TO HAVE A HOME

What Difference Does It Make to Be Home?

Fifteen

THE HOMELESS HANNAH ARENDT

Joseph Betz

1. Introduction

Hannah Arendt was a German Jew who became homeless when she fled her homeland and Nazism in 1933. She was in Paris when the war began. The French government rendered her homeless again by placing her and other German nationals in an internment camp at Gurs. When France fell, she took advantage of the confusion and fled. She eventually arrived in the United States where she had a brilliant career as a writer and teacher.[1] I believe that the writings of the once homeless Hannah Arendt elucidate the human condition of homelessness. Home and homelessness are important sub-topics in what Arendt would call her "political thought."[2]

Most of us would call Arendt a social philosopher. She called her discipline "political thought."[3] But she did claim to "come . . . from the tradition of German philosophy."[4] She made it her life's mission to recover for her contemporaries what was distinctive about democratic political practice in Periclean Athens and Republican Rome. Her fundamental question was: What is authentic democracy and what are its presuppositions?

For one, democracy requires the possession of a stable home. Arendt uses the term "home" far less frequently than I do in interpreting her. It occurs neither in the table of contents nor in the index of her basic work in political thought, *The Human Condition*. Her term is more likely to be "household," though one does sometimes find her referring to a person's "private home."[5] These presuppositions of democracy are explained in *The Human Condition*.

The Human Condition is also foundational to Arendt in that she makes and explains the two basic distinctions of her political thought there. Arendt begins with the ancient division of the active life into labor, work, and action. The distinctions she makes in this first triad are interwoven with those she makes in a second triad—the private, the social, the public. These two triads frame her political thought and situate her reflections on having a home.

2. Labor and Work[6]

Labor is the human response to ever-changing nature. Nature's cycles and rhythms would soon obliterate humans unless we intervened in nature. An intervention is exemplified by earning our daily bread, with the "labor of our bodies," which provides us short-term satisfaction.

Arendt borrows from the phrase, "the labor of our body and the work of our hands," from section twenty-six of John Locke's *Second Treatise of Civil Government*. Labor yields a transient, consumable object like bread. "The work of our hands" yields more permanent shelter from nature's flux, like the house and its furnishings. Labor yields bread and cooked meals, and these processes must be repeated daily. Work yields beds and tables and dwellings, and these permanencies often endure for hundreds of years.

Christians might believe that nature is mortal and humans are immortal. But Arendt, along with the ancient Greeks, held the opposite belief: humans are mortal and nature is immortal. Nature is that all-encompassing, cyclical pattern of birth, death, and regeneration which consistently threatens individual human life. Humans are far from helpless in the face of this threat. Labor keeps death from the doorstep as we provide food for ourselves and repeatedly clean the house to keep away germs. Work not only expels immediate mortal dangers, like freezing to death, but provides the accommodations and furnishings that make us comfortable. Labor keeps hostile nature at bay, while work tames it. Artifacts made by a person's work complete the emergence from nature's threat to the artifice's safety.

Here are the first truths about having a home according to Arendt. Homes are permanencies we introduce into nature's flux as protection from it. Homes make us feel at home in an otherwise hostile nature. Homes represent the higher human capacity of fabricating durable and delightful goods. We build our homes with walls to keep out the cold, roofs to keep out the rain, doors to let in the neighbor and stop the wolf, and windows to let in the light. We build our homes to put into them couches, carpeting, color TVs, and computer games which make our homes comfortable. Art, in the sense of artifice, overcomes nature.

But nature also has its place in our homes. Nature enters only as domesticated or to be domesticated. Natural flour enters as bread; milk enters when pasteurized and homogenized; eggs are admitted in order to become omelettes. If nature enters as dirt, soil, germs or grime, we expel it again as we clean. We clean today and again a week from today, for labor can introduce relatively little permanency because of its close connection with ever-changing nature. We uproot the underbrush to establish a lawn bordered by a hedge. We treat the lawn with weedkillers to keep the grass dominant; the grass is cut weekly and the hedge monthly lest they dominate us. Work on artifacts achieves more permanency than labor on natural objects, for the house's windows need only be washed yearly and the stucco needs painting only every ten years.

If this describes our homes, then what is human homelessness like? Homelessness is the loss of protection against the threat of being caught up in the natural flux. We, then, are as nature is: too hot or too cold, too wet or too dry, in too much dark or in too much light, too close to wild predators and too far from gentle climes. Again, homelessness leaves us without the place in which daily labors of food preparation occur. We can cook no dinner, and we have no cabinets to store our canned food or refrigerators to store our perishable food. No home means no toilet or shower or bed, and no home means no security, no comfort, a relapse into a state of nature. Unlike in the Hobbesian state of nature, nature itself is the threat, not human nature. The comfort and security of civil society is provided more by a humble home than by an exalted Leviathan.

3. Property and Law[7]

Human beings are secure in their homes. Human labor puts the food in the cupboard and human work builds the cupboard, the wall it is on, the roof, the whole building. Homelessness means expulsion from one's house or dwelling, so the maximum security against homelessness comes from owning one's own home. This is the gist of Arendt's doctrine of property. Property allows for our maximum mastery of necessity; so everyone should have property. By "property" Arendt means a home. It is intimately connected with work and labor, for dwellings result from work and are kept and maintained by labor. In our homes our basic acts of labor occur: cleaning, food preparation, putting things in order. In a farming or manufacturing economy which was still pre-industrial, work also occurred at home.

Private property, according to Arendt, means the personal ownership of one's home. Property is proper to the person, the immediate extension of the self exhibited in clothing, food, household goods, and home. It enables the person to master necessity and overcome nature.

Property is more secure if walled, hedged, or fenced in. Arendt understands law as such a fence or wall, part of the hard permanencies which make this world habitable for us. The role of law is to protect property, the household and its contents. Law protects the property of each of us from the other and of all of us in our private homes from the public gaze and view. The wall protects us from nature and neighbor. The law protects us from neighbor.

If property and law are defenses of the home as Arendt claims, then Karl Marx's denunciation of bourgeois private property and law manifests something wrong. To Arendt, private property and law are not what the rich use to impoverish the poor and keep them miserable. Instead, private property and law, homes and their government-guaranteed security, protect the average person against ever becoming poor. Private property and the laws should be blocks against exploitation by the rich. They are guarantees that there will not be any poor, or, at least, anyone abjectly poor. Everyone's home should be secure as legally protected property.

But when Marx denounces private property, he does not mean to denounce the personal ownership of one's home. It is a denouncement of private ownership of the means of production. According to Marx, this allows the bourgeoisie to exploit the poor and to render so many of them homeless. How does Arendt stand on the private ownership of the means of production?

Arendt's model of the home comes from ancient Greece and Rome. In our society, the home results from work and labor. We must at least labor in the home and maintain it. But we usually think of labor and work as meaning our jobs, and our jobs are usually outside the home at an office, factory, shop, or store. Our economy is an away-from-home economy. In ancient Greece and Rome, work—fabrication, production, manufacturing—was the business of the household, not just the function of businesses. So the private ownership of the means of production was then part of the private ownership of the home. But this home was usually a large estate which was often maintained by slaves. So household production was made possible by slavery.

Arendt strongly favors the private ownership of production, for she believed that public and political control of production are the corruption of politics and the ruination of the public space proper to politics. Production can no longer be in the home and cannot be the work of slaves. But the labor-power of slaves is more than adequately replaced in modern times by technology. For this reason, Arendt favors the private ownership of production; public ownership leads to the corruption of politics by economics. Productivity by slaves is, then, unthinkable. Technology is a more than adequate replacement for slave production and promises greater abundance than any human labor could. The measure of productive success, to Arendt, is not private profit but the provision for all of those durable permanencies humans require for protection from ever-changing nature.

4. Action[8]

Labor and work, for Arendt, are explained by the home. But Arendt's triad was that of labor, work, and action. Action occurs outside the home. What is action?

Action has its own space, the *polis*, a space created by action as well as for action. All action is political; so the phrase "political action" is redundant. All action is conjoint; one cannot act alone. Action is the saying and doing of citizens who meet to plan and carry out the acts of their *polis*. It implies citizenship, an equal status in having responsibility for common interests. Action has two phases, proposal and acceptance. It involves distinctively human faculties. Labor is of our bodies; work is of our hands; action is of our reason and speech. In action we take our place in front of our equals to join in the debate about what we should do in our common interest. We try to persuade others; others try to persuade us. We negotiate, we concede, we win a concession, and we cooperate. We play a part in the beginning or carrying through of a joint enterprise.

The superiority of action to work and labor is enormous. It is the difference between the human and the animal, mind and body, speech or reason and digestion or procreation, life at its human highest and life at its animal basis. Arendt calls all of us to action, to democratic political participation at the grass-roots level. We are called to exercise the powers made possible by interaction with others enjoying the highest exercise of their powers. The reward of a life of action is the public happiness of a Benjamin Franklin, a John Adams, or a Thomas Jefferson when a human agent manifests wisdom, integrity, courage and patriotism in establishing and preserving our state or *polis*.

Arendt calls the goal of action "the foundation of freedom." But this can be achieved only if the "liberation from necessity"[9] through the enterprise of labor and work is first achieved. The best gauge of success in the liberation from necessity in the general population is contentedness with their homes and jobs. People feel secure about their homes and their ability to provide for their families. Contentment in the private happiness of the home leads to the glory of public action in the *polis*. The secure home is the precondition of confident political action.

If there is not private happiness at home, then a precondition for achieving public happiness in the *polis* is lacking. Homelessness is the ruination of participatory democratic politics. Homelessness means our pre-political needs are not met, and so we cannot get on to the fulfillment which should be ours in political participation. To flourish in political action, a human being must first achieve adequacy as an animal in the stable home which is the platform for reaching higher. The bird has its nest, the fox its den, and if humans lack their homes, they fail both as shelter-seeking animals and as politically participating humans. The higher builds on the lower; before the public glory must come the private satisfaction.

5. The Balance of Private and Public Happiness

Arendt has only praise for the person who learned to seek public happiness in the *polis*. The person who seeks private happiness only at home is not as highly regarded. The withdrawal from public life occurs because so many homeowners have entered the public sphere only to seek wealth, debasing this sphere and turning it into the counterfeit public. Arendt thus sometimes leaves one with the impression that real happiness is the public happiness of the *polis* and the private happiness of the home is only a weak counterfeit of it.[10]

This is true only if private happiness becomes the replacement of public happiness rather than its precondition. According to Arendt, we fulfil the human condition by satisfying and moving along a sequence of needs. We must be liberated from necessity before we dare attempt freedom. This can be done without the lower liberation from necessity usurping the role of the higher foundation of freedom. In *On Revolution*, Arendt praises the American Revolution for getting the order right while condemning the French and Russian Revolutions for getting the order wrong.

So happiness to Arendt is not private happiness excluding public happiness to the ruination of the public sphere and politics. Nor is it public happiness excluding private happiness, for our human potential can be achieved only after our animal needs are met. Therefore, it is both the achieving of private happiness in the home and public happiness in the forum, with private happiness achieved first, which constitutes complete happiness.

In his *Utilitarianism*, John Stuart Mill explains the matter in a way Arendt could accept and incorporate into her social thought. Defending his claim that happiness is the end of life, Mill writes:

> The main constituents of a satisfied life appear to be two, either of which by itself is often found sufficient for the purpose; tranquility and excitement.... There is assuredly no inherent impossibility in enabling even the mass of mankind to unite both; since the two are so far from being incompatible that they are in natural alliance, the prolongation of either being a preparation for, and exciting a wish for, the other.[11]

The key is balance, achieving the right rhythm between tranquility and excitement. If tranquility is the specific excellence of the home, and excitement the specific excellence of politics, then Mill helps explain Arendt. To be happy, first build a home life where biological satisfactions, rest and tranquility, are guaranteed. Then go forth to a public life where human faculties are extended in the excitement of challenge and agonistic striving.

In another way, this balance or rhythm of home and abroad, rest and activity, permanence and change, is important in contemporary human rights documents bearing on homelessness. The 1948 United Nations Universal Declaration of Human Rights expressed it in Article 13:

1.   Everyone has the right to freedom of movement and residence within the borders of each state.

2.   Everyone has the right to leave any country, including his own, and to return to his country.[12]

The home and the homeland being port, the sailors venture forth bravely because they already envision confidently their return and rest in their residences. It is as William James says, the rhythm of experience is like the flyings and perchings of the bird. We fly abroad to excitement: we return home to perch.

6. The Private and the Public[13]

This discussion of private and public happiness suggests another of Arendt's basic distinctions needed to understand homelessness: the private, the social, and the public.

Initially, Arendt thought of this distinction as a dyad, not a triad. It was the private/public distinction. This was the difference between that which should occur in darkness and that which should occur in light, between what is fit to be seen and what is not fit to be seen. The emphasis is on seeing, our main way of knowing.

What should be seen, what unseen? Arendt's answer to this employs the human/animal distinction. That which is most distinctively human, those manifestations of reason and speech of which we should be most proud, should be seen, heard, and judged by all. Our oration before our fellow citizens in the forum and the acts which result should be displayed in the public, the space of appearances. That which is most distinctively animal, the biological behaviors we normally perform out of sight, which evoke shame when observed, belong in private. Private means deprived of light, visibility, and publicity.

The space for action is the public. The private space is *par excellence* the home. So Arendt's private/public distinction displays a new aspect of what the home and homelessness are all about. I have been emphasizing the comfort and security and protection from nature which the home provides. But humans have another need, that of privacy. The home protects the individual from nature but is also the space where our natural needs are met, our animal and biological needs. As we satisfy these needs, the home protects us from the public gaze. We need homes for the privacy to dress and undress, bathe, stay in bed when sick, defecate and urinate.

Even in the privacy of our homes there are private and public spaces. The downstairs is more public; the upstairs is more private. Usually the public rooms in our home are the parlor, the living room, and the family room. Our guests are taken from the door to the family room immediately. If we know our guests well, they infiltrate our privacy more as they share a meal with us in our slightly more private dining rooms. If we really know our guests well, they join us for a meal in the still more private breakfast room or kitchen. The bedroom is even more private, and the bathroom most private. We reserve the bathroom for activities that are biological and animal-like activities. These are our most private ones. We share the bathroom with no one—not guests, not friends, not spouses. Having a home, we can admit others to different gradations of intimacy and privacy. Lacking a home, we have no such power.

In Arendt's doctrine of the private is thus another side of homelessness. With labor and work I had stressed that the home is a fabricated permanency to protect us from nature's transiency. It is where our labor and work earn us food, shelter, and comfort in a secure non-natural place. This we dearly need. But we also need a place to be natural outside of society's notice of us and expectations of us. We need a darkness outside the public glare. The homeless are unprotected from two threats, nature's rain and ice and society's observation and icy stare. Homes bring us light as protection against nature's darkness but also bring us darkness as protection against people's view. Homeless means too little light in the first sense and too much light in the second. The homeless are banished to public spaces where they must sleep and urinate and defecate where they can be seen. As they "go to the bathroom" in a park bush, or bathe naked in a public fountain, the homeless are guilty of the crime of public indecency, a crime they cannot help but commit. The homeless come close to an absolute deprivation of privacy.

The individual lacking a home has no privacy in which to take care of the necessities of nature. But the natural individual tends to mate and to found a family. This too is our animal nature and biology. Mating and raising a family are also activities demanding the privacy of the home. So homelessness not only mocks its victims in their need to be alone, but it mocks them, too, in their need to have a family.

For the individual who has a home, it is good to be home alone to escape the pressure of work, business, the public. If we have had enough of society, we go home to be alone. If there are unwanted others at home with us in the common areas, we go to our rooms to be alone. But being homeless and alone is an entirely different experience. Getting off alone to one's home is a pleasure and a reward; being left alone homeless is full of pain and punishment.

The same duality in aloneness offers even more extreme alternatives for the family. The family alone at home is blessed in its aloneness: husband and wife enjoying one another's sexuality and companionship, parents enjoying the cuteness of their toddlers, children enjoying the toys and instruction caringly provided by their parents. But the homeless family is cursed in its aloneness. Wife blames husband, children blame parents, parents are impatient with the children, the children's suffering becomes the parents' guilt. A homeless man and woman are tempted to loathe the fact that they ever mated or had children.

When Arendt emphasizes the private, she tends to have the sexual and the familial in mind. Arendt thinks of sexual appetite as part of the inescapable realm of biological necessity. We are properly ashamed to be seen naked or in sexual activity in public. Sex is for the bedroom, if not for the darkened bedroom. Love as the source of sex or marriage or family is a private emotion unfit for the public realm. So are the children who are the flowering of sex and *raison d'être* of the family; their proper place is the private home. They grow up well, Arendt believes, only when sheltered in the dark and away from the harsh gaze of the public. Since children without privacy as protection cannot develop normally, the homeless child can be corrupted or, at least, badly deprived. Homelessness is especially harmful to children.

What have we learned so far about homelessness from Arendt? From her labor, work, action distinction we have learned that labor and work are not yielding their proper results if they do not build secure homes. And we learn that the homeless lack the preconditions for political action. From her private/public distinction we learn that the home provides protection from publicity as well as from natural threats. We learn of the need for privacy that individuals and families require. Just as political action is wanting if labor and work do not yield its preconditions in secure homes, so public spaces are used inappropriately if private space in a home is lacking. The homeless sleeping in the streets, the parks, the porticos of public buildings are forced into a false public display, personal and not political, the displaying of what should be hidden.

7. The Social

Arendt eventually expanded her private/public distinction by adding the social between them. Chapter Two of *The Human Condition*, "The Public and the Private Realm," begins as if the private/public distinction is all that is needed. But Arendt soon, reluctantly, introduces the social between them and "social" is in the title of three of the seven sections of this chapter. The reason she did this also relates to our topic of homelessness. As we mentioned, in the ancient world, labor and work occurred in the household. Thus, economics means, etymologically, household management. The public participation in political action was made possible, Arendt believed, only when economic problems had been privately solved. Even when the means of production moved outside the home—and what we know as economy became separate from the *nomos*, the home—Arendt believed that it was still a pre-political matter and the provision of goods and services must be secured to all *before* anyone could be political actors. Arendt believed that the economic liberation from necessity had to precede the political foundation of freedom. Economics provides enough for all privately so that politics, though inviting participation by all, can bring public distinction to the few who excel at it. Arendt wants the private organization of labor and work so that all enjoy adequate incomes and homes.

Modern economics changed this. Material production had moved from the household to the factory, from the private to the public, from economics to political economy. In Arendt's vocabulary, the social had been created. She understood the social as "social science," "the demands of society," and, especially, "the socialization of the means of production" as in "socialism." Socialism, Arendt believed, had completed the harmful tendency begun in capitalism. *Animal laborans* and *homo faber* had triumphed over *zoon politikon*. Economics had moved from the private to the public where it had corrupted politics. The realm of those freed from economic necessity and satisfied in their individual interests so that they could discuss and pursue only common interests had become the realm of those fighting to deflect public resources to their private ends. Politics had been ruined. Arendt, then, loathed the social, society, the social sciences, and socialism. Householding should never have become a public chore; it should have remained private.

Arendt thinks political debate about homelessness, or providing governmentally built homes, is out of place. What is obviously true should not be debated. Appropriate topics for discussion in politics are limited to: (1) What is our common interest? (2) What matters appear differently to different observers? Debate about homelessness meets neither of these criteria. That people should have homes is in their individual interest and should be beyond dispute. It is not the subject of political discussion.

But Arendt would allow that providing homes for the homeless could be the work of government even if not of politics. What is the difference? Politics is the realm in which those equal in citizenship meet face to face to discuss what actions to initiate and to carry through. Government would be the servant and creature of political actors. It would be that permanent arm of the political actors which endured after they went home and which they instituted to carry through what they had begun. Government would collect taxes and, in a phrase Arendt liked, "administer things,"[14] which is different from a phrase like "initiate acts." It would be the realm of the bureaucrat, a person laboring rather than acting. In fact, the bureaucrat usually labors rather than works, for the bureaucrat tends to give his or her whole time to repeating the same processes over and over again, issuing driving licenses or passports or building permits. Bureaucracy or administration may serve the political, but God help us if it rules instead of serves, because in that case no one at all—only an impersonal set of rules— would be governing. One bureaucrat, deciding that a plea is outside his or her responsibility, passes the problem on to another. Arendt thinks bureaucracy entails the continual evasion of responsibility. The suppliant's plea is never granted, though it is also never refused.

So, to Arendt, bureaucracy must not control but it can administer. She allows that government bureaucrats can administer housing programs. Give administrators the standing charge to care for the homeless. They count the homeless and determine what sort of homes to build that will satisfy their needs. The administrators hire the contractors who build the homes and the people move in. The financial support is presumably from taxes and is already at hand; so there is little to dispute about either collecting or dispensing it. The alternative might be housing grants directly to the homeless. This would be more agreeable to Arendt if it allows the whole business of housing to remain more private and less public, more an issue of economics than of politics. In this manner, then, the administrative bureaucracy would have solved the social problem. The forum, or halls of congress, or, even better, the town hall would not have become excessively involved; it remains free for the discussion of political action.

In economics we behave in ways the social sciences might study to discover deterministic laws. We act in politics in ways which cannot be predicted and thereby manifest our freedom. For Arendt, government can get into the business of housing the homeless as long as it does so as an economic agent, not a political actor.

8. The Rightlessness of Non-Citizen Householders Expelled from Homeland

Thus far we have been discussing domestic homelessness (an ironic conjunction of words since "domestic" comes etymologically from the Latin *domus*, home), local homelessness. We might also discuss the homelessness of foreigners, the homelessness of refugees from war, and perhaps of the victims of religious or racial persecution as were German Jews like Arendt herself. In Arendt's experience, totalitarianism was a major cause of homelessness.

Arendt's *The Origins of Totalitarianism*[15] studied totalitarianism of two sorts. On the left, Bolshevism predicted the survival of the fittest social class, the working class. The refugees of Bolshevism belonged to the bourgeois class; they were economic refugees. On the right, Nazism predicted the survival of the fittest race, the Aryan race. Nazism produced ethnic refugees, members of the Jewish race or other minorities like Gypsies. Here were many more homeless people of an other than local sort for Arendt to think about.

Local homeless exist, Arendt would say, because of a failure of the pre-political. The activities of labor and work somehow did not do what they should have done, provide homes and jobs for the householders. The homelessness of refugees, I think Arendt would say, is a failure of the political rather than of the pre-political. The Jews of Western Europe before World War II had solved their pre-political problems of acquiring homes so well that they were seduced into the belief that politics was unnecessary for them. This was their downfall.

Part One of *The Origins of Totalitarianism*, entitled "Antisemitism," tells a story which makes Arendt sad, for it is the story of her own people, the Jews of Europe. In the Diaspora, Jews spread from the Middle East all over the known world, especially all over Europe. They were always a racial and religious minority settling in the sort of state inhospitable to them, the nation state. The nation-state accepts an ideology, the belief that the people are one race, one blood, rooted in the homeland's soil, sharing one culture, one religion, and one language. France for the French, Germany for the Germans. France or Germany might contain Jews and think of themselves as democracies of, by, and for the people, but these people were not Jewish. Citizenship in Germany was for the German-born descendent of many generations of Germans, with a German first and last name, and German blood, and practicing some variant of the German national religion, Christianity.

Why did some Jews stay for centuries in nation states in which they lacked citizenship and were barred from politics and its public space? In part, they thrived in the private space allowed them. They did well in business and economics and so could provide comfortable homes for themselves in prosperous Jewish neighborhoods centering around welcoming synagogues. They were supremely well-cared for at home, in private, and by themselves. They thought that they did not need politics.

They fell into what might be described as an economic trap. Having done so well in economics, they ignored politics. This apolitical behavior of the Jewish people was their downfall. When German politics turned against them, the Jews had no say in the political process. Though they had a chance at a politics of their own organized against the politics of the majority Christians, they did not mobilize their resources until it was too late. Arendt would like to have seen the Jewish Councils, which the Nazis used to facilitate rounding up Jews for deportation to death camps, become genuine political fora and centers of opposition to the Nazis, but this never happened. Arendt would have liked to have seen the Jews of Europe organize a Jewish army to fight Hitler, a supremely political act, but it never happened. These Jews paid for their tradition of political inactivity, first with the loss of their employment, then their homes, then their lives.

The genocide of the Jews, most of us would say, was in violation of their natural or human rights, the Rights of Man celebrated in the French Revolution.[16] The Nazis, consulting the natural light of reason, should have known it was wrong to violate the Jews' natural rights. But for Arendt, what happened to the Jews unmasks the doctrine of natural rights. She agrees with Edmund Burke, who would rather have had the rights of an Englishman than the Rights of Man of the French Revolution. The rights of English citizens were enforced and were guaranteed in a political process in which all could participate. The Rights of Man were invoked with no success by Jews excluded from the political process which provided no guarantees for Jews. Having no *polis* meant having no rights. The comfort of the homes, neighborhoods, businesses, and private concerns of the European Jews utterly vanished in the rightlessness of this apolitical people, and it soon became their statelessness.

Having been rightless because she was stateless, Arendt had little sympathy for a natural or human rights approach to homelessness, the claim that all possess a human right to a home. But surely this was part of the reaction to the Nazi treatment of the Jews that characterized the post–World War II climate. President Franklin Roosevelt's 1944 "Economic Bill of Rights" spoke of "the right of every family to a decent home."[17] Article 25 of the 1948 United Nations Universal Declaration of Human Rights reads:

> Everyone has the right to a standard of living adequate for the health and well being of himself and of his family, including food, clothing, housing and medical care and necessary social services, and the right to security in the event of unemployment, sickness, disability, widowhood, old age or other lack of livelihood in circumstances beyond his control.[18]

And we know that this guaranteed housing is to enjoy the full privacy which Arendt demands in a home because of Article 12: "No one shall be subjected to arbitrary interference with his privacy, family, home or correspondence, nor to attacks upon his honor or reputation."[19] Since the human rights approach to homelessness is so important a part of the probable solution today, it is a shame that Arendt distances herself from it.

Since losing their homeland led to such a catastrophic loss of life, the Jewish demand for a homeland gained force directly after World War II. At first, Arendt fully accepted this, working for Youth Aliyah, trying to organize the smuggling of European Jewish orphans into Palestine. But she came to believe that things were developing wrongly in Palestine. The trouble was that the Jews were trying to develop their nation there at just the time that World War II had proven the bankruptcy of the nation-state idea. Arendt was part of only a small minority of influential Jews who favored the development of a bi-national, Arab-Jewish, secular state in Palestine. Otherwise, solving the problem of homelessness for the Jews would give rise to a problem of homelessness for the Arabs. To her great dismay, that is what she saw happen.[20]

Failure in politics brought dire consequences: homelessness, rightlessness, and statelessness. The homelessness of the refugee was an experience which moved Arendt deeply. Homelandlessness or statelessness was especially a horror to her. She was influential in persuading the U.S. Supreme Court to judge similarly when the question came before it: Can we punish American citizens by stripping them of their citizenship, by rendering them stateless? The Supreme Court decided that this was an improper and unconstitutional punishment and quoted Arendt for support.[21] In *Trop v. Dulles*, 1958, Chief Justice Warren observed that the expatriate has lost "the right to have rights," a phrase which originated with Arendt. A part of the 1940 Nationality Act which prescribed expatriation as a punishment for certain crimes was unconstitutional since, as Warren concluded, citizenship is not "a license that expires upon misbehavior," which could be "lost every time a duty of the citizenship is shirked." Five years later, Justice Goldberg quoted Arendt even more directly to the same effect.[22]

9. Conclusion

The homeless Hannah Arendt suffered as does any homeless John Doe or Jane Doe. Arendt's distinctions between labor/work/action and private/social/public explain the suffering that is human homelessness and how it is a serious violation of the human condition.

A home is a durable, permanent artifact or fabrication, the result of work, which shelters us against ever-changing, all-consuming nature. In it we labor to meet our daily needs. From it we go forth to labor or work for others. The home comes first from work, then comes the buildings which are the glory of a civilization exhibited by the churches or temples, the large commercial build-ings, the monuments, the magnificent government buildings. Work gives us a human world in which we are comfortable and in which we labor to domesticate nature. If this is attained, we can and should go forth to politics. If this is not attained, life is insecure, uncomfortable, perilous, since we lack the benefits of work and the place maintained by the most common human labor. We do not go forth to politics. Politics lacks participants.

Home gives us privacy. If homelessness robs us of proper privacy, we are forced into a false public realm. It is false because it is not that glorious public where human excellence is proudly displayed, but instead the inappropriate public display of shameful necessity, due to our biology and fit only for dark-ness and secrecy. No home means no privacy and only a false publicity. No society either even if society appears to be improper public housekeeping, with no home or house, no housekeeping exists at all, public or private. Disaster follows.

Lastly, the home to Arendt is intimately connected with the pre-political, with labor, work, and the private. But the experience of the Jews shows a proper connection between the home and political action in the public sphere. Having a comfortable home, we should never think we have enough and so feel bribed to stay out of politics. When the Jews were denied political participation, and accepted the denial, they lost their homes, their rights, their states, and their lives. At the least, Arendt believes, the Jews of Europe would have been no worse off had they performed the political act of organizing to block Hitler's deportations and, though even more risky, to fight against his army.

How bad is it to lack a home and its protections from nature and from the gaze of the public, and to be deprived of the protection of a homeland? The Pragmatists help Arendt to answer this final question. When most of us encounter problems, we have the wherewithal on hand to solve them. Normally, only a part of our experience is problematic, and the unproblematic parts afford us the leverage to change the problematic parts more to our liking. This unproblematic part of our experience is normally in the home. Having a problem, we go home to think it over, to make phone calls, to consult the records and books we keep there, to get the tools we have there, to discuss it with our family, to let off steam, to sleep on it overnight. With a home our problems are soluble. No home tends to mean no solutions and our problems overwhelm us.

Notes

1. For Arendt's biography, see Elisabeth Young-Bruehl, *Hannah Arendt: For Love of the World* (New Haven: Yale University Press, 1982).

2. See Joseph Betz, "An Introduction to the Thought of Hannah Arendt," *Transactions of the Charles S. Peirce Society*, 28:3 (Summer 1992), pp. 379-422.

3. On the nature of political thought, see Hannah Arendt, "Preface: The Gap Between Past and Future," in *Between Past and Future: Eight Exercises in Political Thought* (New York: Penguin Books, 1980), pp. 3-15.

4. Young-Bruehl, *Hannah Arendt*, p. 104.

5. Hannah Arendt, *The Human Condition* (Garden City, N.Y.: Doubleday Anchor Books, 1959), p. 54.

6. Chapter 3 of Arendt's *The Human Condition* is "Labor," and ch. 4 is "Work."

7. Property and law are treated in section 8 of ch. 2 of Arendt, *The Human Condition*, "The Private Realm: Property."

8. "Action" is the title of ch. 5 of *The Human Condition*.

9. Arendt's phrases, "the liberation from necessity" and "the foundation of freedom," play an especially important role in Hannah Arendt, *On Revolution* (New York: Viking Press, 1965). See, for instance, p. 161.

10. Arendt, *On Revolution*, p. 124.

11. John Stuart Mill, *Utilitarianism* (Buffalo: Prometheus Books, 1987), p. 24.

12. "United Nations Universal Declaration of Human Rights (1948)," in *The Human Rights Reader*, eds. Walter Laqueur and Barry Rubin, rev. ed. (New York: Meridian, 1989), p. 199.

13. Chapter 2 of *The Human Condition* is titled "The Public and the Private Realm."

14. *Ibid.*, p. 41. See also Young-Bruehl, *Hannah Arendt*, p. 219.

15. Hannah Arendt, *The Origins of Totalitarianism* (New York: Harvest/Harcourt Brace Jovanovich, 1968). This edition is in three separate volumes: Part One, "Antisemitism"; Part Two, "Imperialism"; and Part Three, "Totalitarianism."

16. Arendt, "Antisemitism," p. 70.

17. *Human Rights Reader*, eds. Laqueur and Rubin, p. 313.

18. *Ibid.*, p. 20.

19. *Ibid.*, p. 199.

20. Hannah Arendt, *The Jew as Pariah: Jewish Identity and Politics in the Modern Age*, edited with an introduction by Ron H. Feldman (New York: Grove Press, 1978).

21. Young-Bruehl, *Hannah Arendt*, p. 293.

22. *Trop v. Dulles*, 356 U.S. 86 at 92,102 (1958) (Warren, C. J.); *Kennedy v. Mendoza-Martinez*, 372 U.S. 144 at 161 (1963) (Goldberg, J.). See also Stephen J. Whitfield, *Into the Dark: Hannah Arendt and Totalitarianism* (Philadelphia: Temple University Press, 1980), pp. 110-112.

Sixteen

TALKING ABOUT THOSE HOME IMPROVEMENT BLUES

Ron Scapp

1. Introduction

In 1986, I wrote about the way in which both the American right and left raised the issue of homelessness.[1] In that discussion of homelessness, I attempted to express some concern about the question of representation and the connection between contemporary public policy and past governmental intervention with regard to individuals and groups cast in the symbolic role of outsider. "Outsiders," here, are the individuals and groups who find themselves beyond the American desire (*eros*) to occupy one's own real and proper place[2] and as such are given an important symbolic function within the discourse of American responsibility and liberty as related to the ownership of property.

In "Lack and Violence,"[3] I pursued the perceived threat that an individual or group could represent to the myth of foundationalism, a myth I attribute to the American sense of well being. I have since continued to follow the development of the national debate concerning homelessness and the juridical dynamics of individual autonomy and self-expression.[4] In New York City, the street dynamic of this usually gets reduced to the subway chorus of, "Excuse me, I am not a drug addict or currently contemplating any immediate criminal activity but I am . . . ," or any of the other variations on this theme.

Many of us who have encountered such public self-expressions of want have witnessed a full range of emotional responses—from fear to laughter, from annoyance to generosity—emanating from ourselves and others. But we have also encountered the media's sustained move to universalize these numerous "street people" as the operational image of all homeless individuals. The message has remained the same: All homeless people are either emotionally or morally deficient. They are either crazy or scamming us, and the reaction to them has remained the same: Since they have nothing, no mind or scruples, we must protect ourselves and our future social security. Instead of revisiting that threat and the violence which has been used historically to squelch it, I want to briefly note some of the contemporary excesses which express a renewed struggle towards the improvement of status in various modes of (self) construction. I would like to examine another side of homelessness, the side that is about having and maintaining one's home, a side that attempts to reinvigorate the myth of foundationalism, a side that some may view as desperate as the acts of violence which remain part of the drama of American life.

2. Building the Future (of an Illusion)

In 1927, a year after Martin Heidegger had initiated his destruction of Western metaphysics, Sigmund Freud, in *The Future of an Illusion*, inaugurates an attack on the nature of human existence from a different front by claiming that people have to "reckon with the fact that there are present in all men destructive, and therefore anti-social and anti-cultural trends and that in a great number of people these are strong enough to determine their behaviour in human society."[5] Freud goes on to say:

> This psychological fact has a decisive importance for our judgement of human civilization. Whereas we might at first think that its essence lies in controlling nature for the purpose of acquiring wealth and that the danger which threatens it could be eliminated through a suitable distribution of wealth among men, it now seems that the emphasis has moved over *from the material to the mental.*[6] [Emphasis added]

Freud, once again, makes economics no less important than psychoanalysis but one step removed from his own analysis of the dynamics of social affairs. Oddly enough, many Americans—led by what Cornelius Castoriadis might be tempted to call simply *the economic,*[7] and in principle at odds with the tenets of psychoanalysis—are nevertheless embracing (unconsciously?) the psychoanalytic notion of a "destructive" presence in humankind to provide the bases of a narrative to explain so many other Americans' failure, out of inability or unwillingness, to build a future for themselves. Violence, as contradictory as it might sound, is one reaction to this destructive impulse. But since the issue of homelessness has become part of the American saga of success and failure, we know that building a future means more than just the systematic violation of the other; it also means the production and reproduction of that which is at stake, namely the image of America.

We find ourselves either part of the community of those building and rebuilding America or ex-centrics (those beyond the core of humanity) whose very existence poses a threat to the momentum of this ongoing patriotic process of construction. In other words, we are part of a history that lends metaphysical importance to the relationship between building and maintaining homes, and between civic duty and political (moral) identity.

The imperative to build and maintain homes can be traced to Aristotle's admonition in the *Politics* that "before speaking of the state we must speak of the management of the household."[8] We are told, in no uncertain terms, that the foundation of the state is the household. Aristotle connects the natural origin of the state with a community able to acquire and maintain homes. He goes on to stress that a person without a state is "either a bad man or above humanity; he is like the 'tribeless, lawless, hearthless one,' whom Homer denounces—the natural outcast . . . [and] he may be compared to an isolated piece of draughts."[9] As homes and households are necessary antecedents to statehood, any and all who threaten statehood are to be denounced. It must follow that those who are homeless, by definition, undermine the state, civic duty, and political identity.

In the attempt to reestablish its positive role in building a better tomorrow, (white) America has reactivated the icon of American stability: the home. With this move to reconstruct the (image of) home, back come the (television) households of the late fifties and early sixties, back comes the future of an illusion.

3. How One Philosophizes with a Hammer, or *This Old House*

Few would readily evoke Friedrich Nietzsche when thinking of remodeling a kitchen, though when his delicate stomach would allow, he did seek and enjoy the pleasures of a simple meal from the kitchen of more than one Turinese *pensione*. I will not, however, focus on Nietzsche's reveling in the Dionysian appetite as discussed, for example, by Allen S. Weiss in his *Aesthetics of Excess*,[10] other than to note the excessive appeal to the hammer itself as the metonymic implement of building. Together with the rest of the domestic paraphernalia presented to television viewers each week on shows such as *This Old House* and *Home Improvement*, many Americans are taught and guided to construct and reconstruct a home somewhere apparently far from the hustle and bustle and corruption of urban America. The indulgence of participating in (home) improvement programs indicates another instance of the current response to being (feeling) unrooted and illegitimate. These shows seem to share a common reference to a pristine place of unquestioned being and unchallenged purpose. It is what such a place has as a given that is represented as what all good places should evoke and what all good people should strive towards.[11]

In an earlier article about Italian-American culture, the issues of ethnicity, and the striving toward and the contradictions of assimilation,[12] I wrote:

> At a time when books and television shows on and about gardening have reached a new high, as is true with shows about home repair and renovation, it is interesting to note that there is a distinctly New England aesthetic (perhaps asceticism) that clearly characterizes the look and feel to the homes and gardens being viewed. This is the case not only for the prototypical home renovation show, "This Old House," but also for the many replicas of this show that seem to name no particular place other than somewhere in suburban America. What we as viewers see are the proverbial New England home and barn being restored, however modernized, to recall the "spirit" of the original. What we get is American

colonial, neo-classical, neo-colonial *simplicity* and *calm*, if not an outright
denial of excitement and pleasure. The moldings all are properly squared
and the colors match perfectly the sedate hues of homes evoking
American-pastoral, and the "victory" gardens that accompany such homes
are filled with perennials and vegetables that perhaps nostalgically remind
us of the growth/harvest cycle that was American agrarian society until the
explosion of urban life at the end of the nineteenth century.[13]

The appeal of "being-in-the-world" as connected to the beauty and glory
of America's past is one way that we get our answer to Heidegger's question
about *Dasein*, namely that ontic-ontological tension over the place (source) of
our being. "From whence we come?" We come from true value (put more
precisely these days, True Value Hardware Stores).

Filled with purpose, we reassert and rebuild ourselves, if only on the
weekends. One is forced to step back in amazement, confronted by the sheer
numbers of people who, though living in apartments (and rental units at that!),
nevertheless comport themselves in a home-improvement mode as if their
domestic voyeurism, their watching shows like *This Old House* or its less
cerebral but no less metaphysical counterparts like *Home Improvement* can
reconstruct the weakened site of their being in thirty minutes. How many of us
take delight at the chance to browse in a hardware store? It is there that we find
ourselves among "the nuts and bolts" of everyday existence. How many closets
are filled with unused tools, but "ready-at-hand," just in case? Eve Kosofsky
Sedgwick has given us the *Epistemology of the Closet*,[14] and now we must also
ask whether or not that closeted person in there is a handy-man just waiting to
come out.

4. A Few (Too Many) Good Men

In his keystone work *The Republic*, from which the rest of Western metaphysi-
cians continue to build systems of all sorts, Plato had Socrates say that "the
minimum state will consist of four or five men."[15] We know that this minimum
state is quickly passed over because the rest of the crowd participating in this
conversation protests that such a state would prove to be a bore, regardless of
size. Whatever Socrates' critique might have been concerning this minimum
state of affairs, it is quickly broken off and his attention is turned toward that
Greek evil: excess. Socrates, ever the attentive listener, notes:

> Ah, I see . . . we are to study the growth, not just of a state, but of a
> luxurious one. . . . The community I have described seems to me the ideal
> one, in sound health as it were: but if you want to see one suffering from
> inflammation, there is nothing to hinder us. So some people, it seems will

not be satisfied to live in the simple way; they must have . . . delicacies . . . all in plentiful variety. And besides, we must not limit ourselves.[16]

As a result, the discussion moves from the idyllic life of simplicity to that of war, what Paul Virilio and Sylvere Lotringer identify as pure war.[17] This shift is made necessary by virtue (if that is the right word here) of Socrates' comrades' desire to have more, more than the state of a few good men would allow.

Much can be made of the insistence upon having more than seems appropriate. In the name of saving America, a contract has been declared limiting everything. Yet, the frustrating point is the fact that this contract of limitation is offered to distract us from the maintenance of a state whose existence was predicated on excess, that is, expansion, growth, as many still like to call it. The call to rebuild America, to make it strong (again), has been the battle cry since long before the Reagan presidency; the stories we tell and hear about our current state, by necessity, focus on excess in one form or another. We have built too much already, gone too far, but this might be our fate. We are forever involved in acts of repeating those gestures to lay down a foundation (for democracy?), to reaffirm the ground we have built upon.

5. Why Derrida Is No Real Threat

When I was a teenager, Mercer Street in Greenwich Village was not considered "well kept" or part of a "desirable" residential area. Certainly it was nothing like the way the (new) New York University (NYU) has redesigned it and the whole NYU campus, which includes Mercer Street and other formerly "less-desirable" streets. NYU has rebuilt itself and in the process has become more visible, even making front page news, as it can now boast as a result of its efforts to reconstruct its image.[18] My friend and colleague, the sociologist Stephen Steinberg, who lives behind the Stern's Business School of NYU in one of the Washington Square Towers, can offer us a phenomenology of the sound of expansion: *Progress is noisy.* But more importantly for the current discussion, it was precisely during this accelerated period of building that Jacques Derrida moved downtown from the City University of New York Graduate Center to his new haunts at NYU. One might be tempted to suggest a possible conflict of interest: the world's premier deconstructor in the midst of all this construction? But in fact he was part of the expansion, part of the building up, part of the (evidently successful) attempt to reconstruct the image of NYU.

Perhaps the NYU administrator who approved Derrida's (limited) role in this construction project understood, that despite all his "deconstructing of Western metaphysics," things still stand (same as they ever were or even better, in other words, bigger). Different from the Christian Right's return from the

Cartesian epistemological destruction of (scholastic) theology, Derrida's work, though clearly important to contemporary social and political thought, has been overcome, that is to say, his criticism doesn't matter! Academics who were initially shaken by Derrida's deconstruction of foundationalism of all stripes and retreated into the security of their home disciplines have returned more convinced of the staying power of real foundations, roots and origins. Just as an institution such as NYU realized it could continue to build and reconstruct its image despite Derrida's formidable deconstructive presence, foundationalists and traditionalists of all sorts have come to realize their own ability to continue building and maintaining systems. Whatever damage Derrida's deconstruction may do, it leaves many of the monuments of Western thought and civilization still standing (at least as far as most administrators and security officers can see). Total deconstruction doesn't seem to harm any of the things that matter (or more to the point, things that are made of matter). So as long as such matters remain the same, Derrida can keep deconstructing and can simultaneously amuse and annoy, but only as long as his deconstruction does not damage anything of value, of (or from) true value. All his talking about *complicity* and *différance* is of little importance compared to those projects being planned and executed to help reconstruct the damaged image, the perverse icon we have yet to recognize as our own projection of grandeur and significance.

6. Coda

Writing about the New York Knicks' return to their home court at Madison Square Garden in his column "Sports of the Times," *New York Times* reporter George Vecsey exclaims,

> Home game. Home run. Home cooking. Homeward bound. *The pull of home makes us do desperate things*—wake up on little sleep in order to have the first good cup of coffee in midmorning in our own kitchen, to see loved ones on a Spring Saturday. Just get home.[19] [Emphasis added]

We are motivated viscerally to get home and are reminded of this "natural" urge everywhere, even in the sports pages of our hometown newspapers. The imperative to build (homes) remains strong, perhaps even overpowering, and as a result those unable and unwilling to participate successfully in the (excessive) attempts to lay down a foundation from which to build are to be forever a threat to the process and security of building itself: Building a career, building a home, building a family, in short, building a life, and maintaining all of it. That the numerous contradictions that manifest themselves throughout this dynamic ought not make us any less inclined to start *Talking About Those Home Improvement Blues.*

Notes

1. See Ron Scapp, "Lack and Violence: Towards a Speculative Sociology of the Homeless," *Practice*, 6:2 (1988), pp. 33-47. An earlier version of this article was presented at the 1986 Socialist Scholars Conference in New York.

2. See Scapp, "Lack and Violence," p. 36.

3. *Ibid.*

4. See Charles Hoch and Robert A. Slayton, *New Homeless and Old: Community and the Skid Row Hotel* (Philadelphia: Temple University Press, 1989).

5. Sigmund Freud, *The Future of an Illusion*, trans. W. D. Roberson-Scott (Garden City, N.Y.: Anchor Books, 1964), p. 5.

6. *Ibid.*

7. See Cornelius Castoriadis, *Philosophy, Politics, Autonomy* (Oxford: Odeon, 1991), pp. 186-194.

8. Aristotle, *Politics*, in *The Basic Works of Aristotle*, ed. Richard McKeon (New York: Random House, 1941), p. 1130.

9. *Ibid.*, p. 1129.

10. See Allen S. Weiss, *The Aesthetics of Excess* (Albany: State University of New York Press, 1989), pp. 3-11.

11. Here I have in mind the tradition that runs from Plato (for example, *Timaeus* and *Phaedrus*) through Heidegger (*Being and Time*). Also see Edward S. Casey, *Getting Back into Place* (Bloomington: Indiana University Press, 1993).

12. Ron Scapp, "Watermelons, Tee Shirts, and Giorgio Armani: Eight-and-a-Half Epigrams on Italian-American Culture," *Differentia*, 6 and 7 (double issue) (1994), pp. 33-44.

13. *Ibid.*, p. 38.

14. See Eve Kosofsky Sedgwick, *Epistemology of the Closet* (Berkeley: University of California Press, 1990), pp. 1-66.

15. Plato, *The Republic of Plato*, trans. and ed. F. M. Cornford (Oxford: Oxford University Press, 1941), p. 56.

16. *Ibid.*, pp. 60-61.

17. See Paul Virilio and Sylvere Lotringer, *Pure War*, trans. Mark Plizotti (New York: Semiotext(e), 1983), esp. pp. 103-134.

18. See William H. Honan, "A Decade and $1 Billion Put N.Y.U. with the Elite," *The New York Times* (20 March 1995), p. A1.

19. George Vecsey, "Sports of the Times," *The New York Times* (21 May 1995), Section 8, p. 1.

ABOUT THE CONTRIBUTORS

G. JOHN M. ABBARNO is Professor of Philosophy at D'Youville College in Buffalo, New York. His areas of specialization include ethical theory and applied ethics, particularly in business, nursing, and psychiatry. His several journal publications include "Value and Role Responsibility" in *The Journal of Value Inquiry* (1991), and he co-authored the book *The Corporation in the Moral Community* (Harcourt, Brace and Jovanovich, 1992). He is past President of the American Society for Value Inquiry (1991), President of the International Society for Value Inquiry (1998-2000), and Vice President of the Conference on Philosophical Societies (1997-1999). He remains active in several other philosophical societies.

JANICE AGATI-ABBARNO is Instructor of Fine Arts at D'Youville College and Holy Angels Academy in Buffalo, New York. A working artist, her work has been exhibited throughout the United States and is represented in several private collections.

NOAH S. BERGER is a community service worker and low-income advocate for the Champlain Valley Office of Economic Opportunity/Franklin Grand Isle Community Action in St. Albans, Vermont. He has worked with the homeless at the Parker Shelter and the Fort Point Shelter, both in Boston, Massachusetts, and is a doctoral candidate in Philosophy at the State University of New York at Stony Brook.

JOSEPH BETZ is Professor of Philosophy and Director of the Graduate Liberal Studies Program at Villanova University. For five years he was the editor of *The Journal of Social Philosophy*. He was President of the Society for the Advancement of American Philosophy (1994-1996) and is President of the North American Society for Social Philosophy (1998-2001). His present research interests are in human rights and the ethics of war. He is Vice-Chair of the board of an organization founded to house the homeless.

KEITH BURKUM is Assistant Professor of Philosophy at Felician College in Lodi, New Jersey. He did his graduate studies at Vanderbilt University. He resides in New York City with his wife, Sherah Stacy Burkum, and his daughter, Chana Burkum.

PIO COLONNELLO graduated with distinction in Philosophy, Law, and Humanities. He was awarded a scholarship by the Istituto Italiano per gli Studi Storici, founded in Naples by Benedetto Croce, and attended courses and seminars taught by Hans-Georg Gadamer and Paul Ricoeur at the Istituto Italiano per gli Studi Filosofici in Naples. He is currently a research fellow (ricercatore confermato) in the Dipartimento di Filosofia "A. Aliotta" of the Università degli Studi di Napoli "Federico II." His research interests include phenomenological existentialism and contemporary Italian philosophy. Along with a long list of essays and articles, he has published the books *Croce e i vociani* (1984), *Heidegger, The Interpreter of Kant* (1981), *Time and Necessity* (1987), and *The Philosophy of José Gaos* (Rodopi: Value Inquiry Book Series, 1997). His current research activities concern the phenomenological and existential reflections of Husserl, Jaspers, and Heidegger on the topic of temporality and historicity and the closely related question of hermeneutics.

NATALIE DANDEKAR has a Ph.D. from the University of Chicago. She has taught at Reed College, Bentley College, and the University of Rhode Island. She continues to work on the concept of altruism and the international assistance as part of a larger effort to understand the interconnections of justice, gender, and international development. She served as Vice President of the American Society for Value Inquiry and is on the board of the International Development Ethics Association.

ROBERT GINSBERG was born in Brooklyn, New York, and makes his home in Takoma Park, Maryland, a suburb of Washington, D.C. As philosopher and photographer, he works on human concerns, such as war and peace, injustice and joy, oppression and love. He studied at the University of Chicago (B.A., M.A.), University of Pennsylvania (Ph.D.), University of Paris, University of Vienna, Brandeis University, The John Hopkins University, University of California at Irvine, and at institutes in Rome, Yugoslavia, Stockholm, and The Hague. He has taught in France and Turkey, and for thirty-one years at The Pennsylvania State University, Delaware County, in the suburbs of Philadelphia.

RENÉ A. C. HOKSBERGEN is married and has two children. He studied Social Psychology and Social Pedagogics at the University of Amsterdam (1962-1967). He obtained his doctorate with a thesis on "Profile of the Evening Secondary School Student" (1972). At present, he is Professor in the field of Adoption of Dutch and Foreign Foster Children at Utrecht University, the Netherlands. He holds various posts in the fields of teaching (Policy Adviser of the Minister of Education and Science) and adoption. He is General Director of the Adoption Center of the Social Faculty of Utrecht University. His specialization is problems in adoption. He is often invited to lecture at home and abroad, as well as to advise adoptive parents with family problems.

SHYLI KARIN-FRANK is the author of *Uri Givon*—a philosophy book for children—and *Utopia Reconsidered*. Her papers concern moral issues of civil disobedience, revolution, war, terrorism, the right of privacy, and medical ethics.

At present, she is working on two books: *Resolution of Political Conflicts: A Moral Theory for Doing the Best Possible* and *The Quest for Privacy and the Fear of Loneliness*. She is an associate editor of *The Journal of Value Inquiry* and Director of International Affairs for the International Society for Value Inquiry.

PATRICIA ANNE MURPHY grew up in Arlington, Virginia. She received her B.A. degree from George Mason University in Fairfax, Virginia, in Philosophy and Religion. She received her Ph.D. in Philosophy from Temple University in 1988. She has worked continuously with the homeless since 1984 in a variety of capacities such as food-service worker (St. Vincent's Soup Kitchen, Philadelphia), tutor, tutor trainer, community educator (Carpenter's Shelter, Alexandria, Virginia), advocate, and barber (Hospitality House, Church of the Pilgrim, Washington, D.C.). Since 1982, she has taught at St. Joseph's University in Philadelphia, where she is currently Visiting Assistant Professor of Philosophy. She writes on many subjects involving peace, social justice, and applied ethics.

UMA NARAYAN received her B.A. in Philosophy from Bombay University and her M.A. in Philosophy from Poona University, India. She received her Ph.D. in Philosophy from Rutgers University in 1990 and has taught at Vassar College since then. Her areas of interest are social and political philosophy, philosophy of law, applied ethics, and feminist philosophy. Her publications include "What Do Rights Have to Do With It? Reflections on What Distinguishes 'Traditional Non-Western' Frameworks from Contemporary Rights-Based Systems," *Journal of Social Philosophy* (Fall 1993), "Eating Cultures: Identity, Incorporation, and Indian Food," *Social Identities* (January 1995), and "Affirmative Action and the Myth of Preferential Treatment: A Transformative Critique of the Terms of the Affirmative Action Debate," co-written with Luke Harris, *Harvard Blackletter Law Review* (December 1994). She edited a volume entitled *Reconstructing Political Theory: Feminist Perspectives*, with Mary Lyndon Shanley, for Polity Press, and is writing a book on feminist theory for Routledge Press.

MICHAEL PARKER is currently Lecturer in applied ethics at the Centre for Professional Ethics, University of Central Lancashire, Preston, England. He is working on a research project with the Children's Society on social justice and decision-making for children in care. He has worked with the young homeless in central London in a range of capacities for ten years. This includes a period when he managed one of Centrepoint's supportive projects, working mostly with care-leavers and those who had been abused. He sits on the executive committee of the Society for Applied Philosophy for which he is Information Officer.

DENNIS ROHATYN is a native New Yorker. Educated at Queens College, City College of New York, and Fordham University, he has been Professor at the University of San Diego since 1977. He is the author of several books, including *Naturalism and Deontology, The Reluctant Naturalist, Two Dogmas of Philosophy,* and *Philosophy, History, Sophistry* (Rodopi: Value Inquiry Book Series, 1997). He is an Orwell scholar, a Leonardo aficionado, and a dog lover. These are not his first published poems, but they may be his last.

RON SCAPP is Director of the Graduate Program in Urban and Multicultural Education at the College of Saint Vincent in the Bronx, New York, where he also teaches education and philosophy. He is co-editor of *Eating Culture* and is currently at work on a book entitled *Teaching Values: Education, Politics, and Culture.*

DAVID E. SCHRADER teaches philosophy at Washington and Jefferson College in Washington, Pennsylvania, and is an Associate at the Center for Philosophy of Science at the University of Pittsburgh in Pennsylvania. He is the editor of *Ethics and the Practice of Law* (Prentice Hall, 1988) and author of *The Corporation as Anomaly* (Cambridge University Press, 1993). He has also published numerous journal articles in philosophy of religion and social philosophy and is past President of the Society for Philosophy of Religion.

ANTHONY J. STEINBOCK is Associate Professor of Philosophy at Southern Illinois University at Carbondale. He holds a Ph.D. in philosophy from the State University of New York at Stony Brook. He has been a research fellow at the Ruhr Universität Bochum, Germany, and at Ecole des Hautes Etudes en Sciences Sociales, Paris, France. His publications on phenomenology and social and political theory include: *Home and Beyond: Generative Phenomenology after Husserl* (1995); "Back to the Things Themselves," *Human Studies* (1997, Editor); "Phenomenology in Japan," *Continental Philosophy Review* (1998, Editor); and "The Philosophy of Michel Henry," *Continental Philosophy Review* (1998, Editor). Steinbock is also the translator and editor of the English critical edition of *Edmund Husserl: Analyses Concerning Passive and Active Synthesis* (forthcoming, Kluwer Academic Publishers). His current project is a mono-graph, provisionally titled *Vertical Presence and Idolatry: On Aesthetic, Moral, and Religious Experience.*

ANITA M. SUPERSON is Assistant Professor of Philosophy at the University of Kentucky in Lexington. Her areas of interest are ethics and feminism. Some of her papers have been published in *The Southern Journal of Philosophy, The Journal of Social Philosophy, Dialogue: Canadian Philosophical Review, The Journal of Value Inquiry*, and *Social Theory and Practice*.

INDEX

1940 Nationality Act, 229
1948 United Nations Universal
    Declaration of Human Rights,
    222, 229

abode, 41-43, 45, 47, 50, 52
absolute spirit, 48-50
abuse, 2, 147
    child, 8, 10, 94-96, 109, 113, 145,
        190
    sexual, 94, 96, 99
    substance (*see* substance abusers)
    verbal, 9
action, 217, 220, 221, 223, 225, 230
    political, 220, 221, 225, 227, 230
Adams, John, 221
adoptees, 10, 105-118
    foreign, 107, 108, 111, 116-118
adoption-isolation, 113
Aesthetics of Excess, 235
Affirmative Action, 83
African-American community, 81
After Virtue, 86
Aid to Families with Dependent
    Children, 146
AIDS, 142, 179
akinesia, 194
alienation, 3, 35, 37, 38, 41, 50, 51,
    61
    existential, 44-46
    Marxist, 44
aloneness, 224
Altimari, Judge, 154, 159
Ancient Greece, 41, 47, 48, 99
anxiety, 3, 41, 42
Aquinas, Saint Thomas, 81
Arendt, Hannah, 11, 51, 217-230
areté, 47, 48
Aristotelianism, 82, 84, 87. *See also*
    Neo-Aristotelianism
Aristotle, 47, 63-65, 67, 70, 72, 74-
    76, 81-85, 87, 88, 234
asylums, 19
autarchy, 47

autonomy, 11, 63-67, 69-76, 156,
    189-197, 200, 202, 205, 206,
    208, 209, 211, 233
    conventional, 10, 192, 196, 197
    libertarian, 188, 191, 192, 197
    natural, 189, 190, 197

baby boomers, 8
Bakke. See *Regents of the University
    of California v. Bakke*
Balkan War, 31, 34, 35. *See also*
    Yugoslavia
Ballachey, Egerton L., 105
basic needs, 188, 191
basic rights, 61, 72, 188, 189, 199
begging, 30, 145, 148, 153-162
    ban on, 10, 153-161
    as communication, 155-157
    communicative value of, 154-156
    constitutional issues, 153, 154,
        155, 157, 161
    Democratic Governance Value of,
        155, 156
    Enlightenment Value of, 155, 156
    moral value of, 155, 156
    political value of, 155
being, 41, 43, 44, 45, 48. *See also*
    Being-as-history; Non-being;
    There-being
Being and Nothingness, 45
Being and Time, 2, 41
Being-as-history, 43, 44, 52
Bellah, Robert, 171
belonging, humanitarian, 37
Bill of Rights, 67-69
Blackstone, Sir William, 65, 66
Blau, Joel, 175, 176, 182
Board of Elections and Ethics, 147
Bolshevism, 227
Bombay, 171, 176-179, 182
Bork, Judge Robert, 68
bottomless pit syndrome, 109, 110
Bowery, the, 8
Bradley, F. H. (Francis Herbert), 197
Brennan, Justice, 165
Brief Über den Humanismus, 43

bums, 19, 20
bureaucracy, 226
Burke, Edmund, 228
Bykofsky, Stuart, 143, 144

Calcutta, 33
capitalism, 148, 149, 225
Cartesian memory, 42
Castoriadis, Cornelius, 234
catastrophes, 10, 172-175, 180
Categorical Imperative, 85
cause, final, 42
Centrepoint, 94, 95, 102
charity, 30, 31, 154-156, 159
    organized, 33, 34, 175, 179
Child Abduction Act (1984), 95, 96
children
    abused, 8, 94-96, 109, 113, 145, 190
    foster, 8, 10, 107, 109, 110
    homeless, 10, 93-97, 99, 101, 102, 143, 145, 224, 225
    rights of, 10, 93
    step-, 107, 109
    See also adoptees; runaways
Children Act of 1989, 102
children's homes, 106, 107
choice, 75
    homeless by, 146, 160
choices of the homeless, 141, 145-148
Christ, 48, 49
Christian Right, 237
Christianity, 48, 49, 218, 228
cities, 7, 8, 29, 79, 80, 85, 87, 88, 173, 181. *See also* Bombay; New York City
citizens, 162-164, 167
    obligation of the state to protect, 200, 209-210
    "standard," 162
citizenship, 10, 11, 63, 66, 67, 70-73, 84, 220, 226, 229
    Ancient Greek, 41, 47, 48, 84
    Jews and, 227, 228
civic personality, 63, 64, 71, 73, 76
civil rights, 144
Civil Rights Movement, 83

Civil War, American, 7
civilization, 34
Coates, Judge, 181, 182
Cohen, Adam, 154-156
Commentaries on the Laws of England, 65
common law. *See* English common law
communication, begging as, 155-157
communism, 212
communitarianism, 99
community and communities, 9, 10, 47, 79-89, 93, 96-102, 181, 182, 187, 189, 192-194, 197, 234
    demoralization and destabilization of, 144
    goals/ends of, 10, 79, 83, 86-88
    membership in (*see* membership; nonmembership)
    moral, 10, 63, 74-76
    social, 65
Community Mental Health Centers (CMHCs), 194
Community Mental Health Centers Act (1963), 142
confidentiality, 207, 208
consciousness, 43, 45-49
Constitution. *See* United States Constitution
constitutional issues, 153-167
constitutional protection, 154, 163, 166, 167
constitutional rights, 163
Copernicus, Nicolaus, 25
crime, homeless as victims of, 142, 148. *See also* violence, against the homeless
Critique of Dialectical Reason, 45, 50
Crutchfield, Richard S., 105

Daedalus, 25
dangerousness of the homeless, 142, 143, 149, 160. *See also* threat of the homeless
Dante Alighieri, 25
Dasein, 236
de-ontology, 41

death, 37, 38
deconstruction, 237, 238
deinstitutionalization, 10, 174, 192-194. *See also* mental illness
democracy, 10, 41, 51, 52, 83, 172, 179, 200, 209, 237
   authentic, 217
Department of Human Resources, 9
depersonalization, 59
Derrida, Jacques, 237, 238
Descartes, René. *See* Cartesian memory
destiny, 47, 48
destitute, the, 153, 155-157, 159-167
destitution, 154, 156, 166
detachment, 97, 98, 100
dignity, 156, 157, 162, 188, 189, 192, 206
   moral, 63
dispersion, 51
Donahue, Charles, Jr., 66
Douglas, Justice, 68, 69
Down and Out in America, 160
Dred Scott v. Sandford, 71, 73
Dreyfus Principle, 161
drugs, psychotropic, 194
Dubrovnik, 31. *See also* Balkan War; Yugoslavia
duties, rights and, 101
dwelling. *See* private dwelling; public dwelling, right to

Economic Bill of Rights (1944), 228
economics, 220, 225-228
Eighth Amendment, 195
eleutheros ("free"), 47
Elizabeth, Queen, 1
emancipation, 52
Employment Guarantee Scheme of Maharashtra, 178
English common law, 63-67, 70, 72
Epistemology of the Closet, 236
equal liberty, 189
equal rights, 179
equality, 83, 84, 86
   right to, 200, 205, 207-210
estrangement, 9, 41-44, 47, 50
Eternal Peace, 85

ethical life, 79
ethics
   communities and, 93, 96-101
   virtue, 10, 81, 82
ethnic cleansing, 3
excess, 236, 237
existence, 42, 47
   physical, 58
   prison/hell of, 41, 44-46
   See also human existence
existential alienation, 44-46
existential authenticity, 42, 43
existential condition of humanity, 41-43
existential experience, 55
existential harm, 60
existential homelessness, 51
existential rights, 57
existential situation, 1
existentialism, 41, 42, 50
expatriation, 229
   "state of," 42-44, 52

family and families, 10, 64, 65, 98, 101, 229
   adoptive, 105-107, 113
   biological, 105, 112, 114
   homeless, 8, 142, 145, 224
   of the homeless, 147
   privacy and, 70, 203-205, 224, 225, 229
   runaways and, 94, 95, 97, 102
   See also parents
fear of the homeless. *See* the homeless, dangerousness of *and* threat of
Feinberg, Joel, 144, 145
Feuerbach, Ludwig, 50
First Amendment, 153, 154, 156, 157
food, 146-148
foster children, 8, 10, 107, 109, 110
foster homes, 143
foster parents, 8, 94
Foucault, Michel, 1, 19
foundationalism, 233, 238
Fourteenth Amendment, 166, 196
   Equal Protection Clause, 161, 165
Fourth Amendment, 67-70

Franklin, Benjamin, 221, 228
free expression, 155-157
free speech, 156. *See also* free
    expression; speech
free-riders, 145
freedom, 10, 31, 47, 60, 189, 191,
    192, 195, 201, 221, 222, 225,
    227
  from interference, 163, 164
  necessity vs., 200
  See also liberty; necessity
Freire, Paulo, 4
French Revolution, 228
Freud, Sigmund, 3, 234
Frost, Robert, 187
Führer, 27
Fuller, Lon, 195
Future of an Illusion, The, 234

Garman, Patricia H., 194
gentrification, 8, 179, 180, 194
Gilman, Charlotte Perkins, 31
God, 22, 42, 49
Goffman, Erving, 203
Goldberg, Justice, 229
good life, the, 65
Good Life, the, 82, 88
Good, the, 83, 87, 88
goodness, 99
government, 11, 226, 227
governmental services, 33-34
Great Depression, 7
Greece, Ancient, 41, 47, 48, 99
Griswold v. Connecticut, 68-70
Gross, Hyman, 69, 70
guardians, legal, 94, 96, 97, 102
Gypsies, 227

handouts, 30, 31
happiness, public vs. private, 221-223
harassment
  begging as, 158, 159
  legislative, 153, 167
harmony, 41
  universal, 47, 48
Hart de Ruyter, Theodore, 110
hate, 46

health
  mental (*see* mental illness)
  poor, 142
health care, 146, 148, 161
Hegel, G. W. F. (Georg Wilhelm
    Friedrich) 41, 42, 45, 48-50
Heidegger, Martin, 2, 41-45, 50, 234,
    236
Heimatlosigkeit, 9, 52
hell
  existence as, 44-46
  "is other people," 41, 45
Hellenistic age, 41, 48
Hershkoff, Helen, 154-156
Hitler, Adolf, 228, 230
Hobbes, Thomas, 219
homanity, 29, 36
home(s), 1-3, 7, 23-26, 28, 29, 31, 32,
    34-38, 41, 43, 52, 63-70, 72,
    73, 75, 76, 105, 187, 193, 217-
    231, 233-236, 238
  autonomy and, 63-65, 67, 69, 70,
    72, 75, 76
  feeling/being at, 3, 41-43, 47, 48,
    50, 51
  morally required, 202-207
  obligation to provide, 10, 11, 187,
    207-212
  privacy and, 64, 69, 70, 199-212
  right to a, 51, 188, 193, 199, 207,
    228, 229
Home Improvement, 235, 236
homecoming, 43, 47, 52
homeland, 34-36, 43, 47, 48, 50, 51
homeless, the
  choices of, 141, 145-148
  dangerousness of, 142, 143, 149,
    160
  images/perceptions of, 55, 145,
    149, 233 (*see also*
    stereotypes)
  mentally ill (*see* mental illness)
  municipal treatment of, 141, 142
  offensiveness of, 144, 145, 148,
    149
  rights of, 10, 141, 149, 199
  threat of, 30-32, 36

violence against, 9, 18, 19, 142, 153
who are, 7, 8, 145
The Homeless: Opposing Viewpoints, 174
homelessness
    authentic, 33
    causes of, 141, 145, 149
    children and (*see* children, homeless; runaways)
    as choice, 146, 160
    discourse of, 2, 3
    existential, 51
    history of, 1, 7, 8
    the human condition, 41-43, 48, 51
    involuntary, 33, 38
    as moral plight, 1, 2
    metaphysical, 33, 36, 38
    ontological, 2, 3
    physical, 106, 113
    prevention of, 209
    protection from, 200, 207-211
    psychic, 105-115
    reasons for, 32
    as social disease, 199, 207
    types of, 33
    as universal destiny, 44
    voluntary, 33, 38, 199
homemakers, humans as, 31
Homer, 235
homosexual relations, privacy and, 204-206, 208, 209
hostels, 96, 97
household, 64, 65, 67, 70, 74, 75, 217, 220, 225, 234, 235
household management, 65, 225, 234
householders, 227
householding, 226
housing, 147, 162
    in Bombay, 177-179
    low-income, 145, 181, 182
    public, 147, 164, 182
    skid-row, 8
    subsidized, 15, 145, 146
human condition, homelessness as, 41-43, 48, 51
Human Condition, The, 51, 217, 225

human existence, goal of, 87
human nature, 84
human rights, 195, 222, 228, 229
    universal, 99, 100
human situation, 58
human value, 59
Humanismusbrief, 43
humanity (humankind), 34, 36-38, 42, 44-51
    existential condition of, 9, 41-43
    homelessness as the condition of, 41-43, 48, 51
humanity (quality of), 29, 75, 76
Husserl, Edmund, 2, 45
Hutus, 33

Ideal Observer, 98
identity, 1, 51, 55, 59, 60, 99-101, 106, 109, 111, 114, 115
    group, 166
ignorance, veil of, 98
in-betweenness, 10, 107, 115
indeterminacy, 3
India. *See* Bombay
individuality, 11, 200, 202-205
individuals
    abstract, 100
    community and, 99-101
    social embeddedness of, 98-101
inner person, 100
intellectualization, 32
intentionality, 59
intersubjectivity, 3, 45, 46, 50, 51
intimacy, 200, 203
Ishmael, 27
isolation, 109, 113

James, William, 222
Jefferson, Thomas, 221
Jews, 227-230
justice, 55
    distributive, 81
    theory of, 211
    virtue of, 81

Kamp, Leo N. J., 110
Kant, Immanuel, 74-76, 85

Kantianism, 85, 86
Keilson, Hans, 110, 111
Kennedy, John F., 27, 142 , 194
Kessler, Brad, 180, 181
Kolodny, Emmy, 111
Kosovo, 34. *See also* Balkan War;
    Yugoslavia
Krech, David, 105
Kreimer, Richard, 144, 195, 196

labor, 217-221, 223, 225-227, 230
lack, 2. See also *rareté*
Ladd, John, 172, 180, 181
Lane, Charles, 19
law
    natural, 99, 100
    property and, 65-67, 219
    punitive, 1
    statutory, 65
    See also English common law
laziness, 55, 145, 149, 160
legal guardians, 94, 96, 97, 102
legislative harassment, 10, 153, 167
Leo, John, 144
liberal state, 209, 210
liberalism, 11, 99, 199, 200, 202, 212
    political, 209, 210
liberality, virtue of, 81, 88, 89
liberation from necessity, 221, 225,
    226
libertarianism, 10, 188-195
liberty, 45-48, 73, 75
    American, 233
    equal, 189
    political, 205, 209
    See also freedom
libraries, public, 9, 141, 144, 153,
    162, 195, 196
Life of the Mind, The, 51
limitation, 46
Locke, John, 218
loneliness, 113, 212
Lotringer, Sylvere, 237
love, 22, 23
loyalty, 111, 114
Luban, David, 68, 69

MacIntyre, Alasdair, 81, 82, 86
madmen, 19
madness, 1. *See also* mental illness
Marcuse, Herbert, 50
Marshall, John, Chief Justice, 167
Marx, Karl, 50, 219, 220
Marxism, 212
Marxist alienation, 44
Meiklejohn, Alexander, 155, 156
Melden, A. I., 193
membership, 10, 79-81, 84-89. *See
    also* nonmembership
memories, 59, 60
mental illness, 8, 10, 55, 56, 142,
    145, 149, 160, 161, 176, 187-
    197, 211. See also deinstitu-
    tionalization
mentally ill, the. *See* mental illness
*Metaphysical Elements of Justice,
    The*, 75
Mill, John Stuart, 74-76, 163, 222
Minogue, Kenneth, 66, 67
minority groups, 81
mistreatment. *See* abuse
Mohr, Richard, 161
moira, 48. *See also* destiny
money, 88
    lack of, 80, 147, 149
    requests for, 30, 31
    See also begging; poverty
Monteyne, Riet, 107
moral arguments, 56
moral community, 10, 63, 74-76
moral dignity, 63
moral judgments, 98
moral obligation, 9-11
    to protect rights of others, 55
moral offense argument, 144-146,
    148
moral personality, 63, 64, 73-76
moral philosophy, 98
moral plight, homelessness as, 1
moral responsibility, 63, 180
morality, 55, 56, 74-76
municipal treatment of the homeless,
    141, 142
Municipal Code 85.02, 141

National Children's Home, 94, 95
National Coalition for the Homeless, 142
National Institute of Mental Health, 176
natural law, 99, 100
natural rights, 228
nature, 217-220, 223, 224, 230
Nausée, La, 45
Nazism, 217, 227, 228
nearness, 43, 52
necessity
    biological, 224, 230
    economic, 225, 226
    freedom vs., 200
    liberation from, 221, 225, 226
    mastery of, 219
negation, 46
neglect, 106, 108, 109, 111, 113
negotiations, communal, 98-101
neighborhood, 79, 87
Neo-Aristotelianism, 79, 81-89
Netherlands, 10, 105-109, 116-118
New York City, 8, 79, 80, 82, 86-88, 155, 162, 196
New York Transit Authority, 153-155, 157-160
Newsweek, 143
Nicomachean Ethics, 65, 79, 82, 88
Nietzsche, Friedrich, 41-43, 47, 235
nightshelters. *See* shelters
nihilism, 41, 47
Non-being, 52
non-persons, 63, 73, 76
nonmembership, 79, 80, 83, 85, 87, 88. *See also* membership
Nordic Conference on the Right to Privacy, 201
nuisances. *See* public nuisances

O'Brien standard, 155-158, 161
O'Brien. See *United States v. O'Brien*
objectivity, 45, 46
obligation, 30
    to protect rights of others, 55
    to provide a home, 10, 11, 187, 207-212

    of state to protect citizens, 200, 209-211
obligations, 9
    moral, 9-11
    social, 9, 30, 208
occupancy, rights of, 177
Odysseus, 26
Oedipus, 34
offensiveness of the homeless, 144, 145
    moral, 144, 145, 148, 149
    physical, 144, 149
On Liberty, 75
On Revolution, 222
ontological homelessness, 2, 3
ontology, 41, 42, 55, 56
    Platonic-Christian, 42
Origins of Totalitarianism, The, 51, 227
orphanages, 143
other(s), 1, 45, 46, 48, 49, 51, 59, 61
    self and, 45, 59, 61
    See also hell, "is other people"
other persons. *See* other(s)
otherness, 47, 51
outsiders, 233
ownership, 7
    private, 219, 220
    property, 233
    public, 220

panhandling, 88, 148, 153, 155, 195. *See also* begging
Parent, W. A., 69
parents, 94, 96, 97, 102
    adoptive, 94, 105, 106, 109, 110, 113-115
    biological, 106, 107, 110, 112, 114, 115
    foster, 94
    natural (*see* parents, biological)
    See also family
parks, public, 141, 153, 158
Parmenides, 28
Peffer, Rodney, 163
Periclean Age, 41, 47
Perrow, Charles, 172-174, 179

personality, 9
   civic, 63, 64, 71, 73, 76
   moral, 63, 64, 73-76
personhood, 9, 56, 57, 59-61
   diminished, 56, 57, 60, 61
persons, 55, 59-61
   value of, 58, 61
   See also non-persons; other(s)
Phenomenology of Spirit, 45, 49
philosophy
   contribution of, 97, 98
   moral, 98
   Western, 43-45
place, 9, 57-61
   metaphysical, 59
   as particularization of space, 58
   primordial, 59
placelessness, 59-61
places, public, 141, 142, 145, 149,
   153, 159, 162, 164
placing, act of, 58, 59
Plato, 235, 236
Plutarch, 48
police, 95, 96, 102
polis, 41, 47, 48, 51, 84, 85, 220,
   221, 228
political action, 220, 221, 225, 227,
   230
political liberalism, 209, 210
political liberty, 205, 209
politics, 41, 51, 52, 220-222, 225-230
Politics, 65, 79, 83, 84, 234
poor, the. *See* poverty
post-traumatic stress disorder, 114,
   115
poverty, 8, 51, 55, 80, 146, 147, 177-
   179
pragmatic arguments, 56
pragmatism, 56
"pre-emptive strike" arguments, 55,
   56
press, freedom of the, 205
Primal Wound, The, 105
prisons, 1, 19
privacy, 11, 64, 68-70, 74, 75, 162,
   199-212, 223-225, 229, 230
   home and, 64, 69, 70, 199-212
   legal right to, 202

   moral right to, 202
   right to, 68, 69, 199-212
   types of, 202
private, the, 65, 70, 74, 75
private dwelling, 162
private happiness, 221-223
private institutions, 146
private ownership, 219, 220
private property, 72, 206, 207, 219
private/public distinction, 223-226,
   230
private/public/social distinction, 217,
   223, 225, 230
private space(s), 223, 225, 228
private world, 31, 70
privileges, 55, 57, 67, 71
property, 64-67, 72, 73, 75, 76
   ownership of, 233
   personal, 65
   private, 72, 206, 207, 219
   public, 72
   real, 64-67
property rights, 66, 67
protection
   constitutional, 154, 163, 166, 167
   from homelessness, 200, 207-211
   from nature, 218-220, 223-225,
     230
   from publicity, 219, 223-225, 230
   of rights, 55, 56
public dwelling, right to, 10, 141-149,
   161
public education, 161
public happiness, 221-223
public housing, 147, 164
public libraries, 141, 144, 153, 162,
   195, 196
public nuisance laws, 153
public nuisances, 160, 162, 164, 196
public ownership, 220
public parks, 141, 153, 158
public places, 141, 142, 145, 149,
   153, 159, 162, 164
public property, 72
public safety, 158
public sensibilities, morally
   problematic, 160, 161

public space(s), 80, 153, 157, 158,
    160-166, 220, 223-225, 228
publicity, 80, 85
punishment, 1, 195

race, 167
racism, 143
Raphael, D. D., 190
rareté (lack), 50, 51
Rawls, John, 98
Reagan, Ronald, 145, 146, 148, 160,
    237
real property, 64-67
reason, 42, 49, 50
refuges, for children, 96, 97, 102
*Regents of the University of
    California v. Bakke*, 165, 166
relationships, meaningful, 99, 101
religious institutions, 34, 146
rent control, 174, 177
Republic, The, 236
Rescue Mission, 146
resources, lack of, 80
responsibility, 10, 55, 202, 208, 226
    American, 55, 233
    communal, 93, 94, 96, 101, 115
    conceptions of, 180
    fiscal, 180
    moral, 63, 180
    positive, 172, 180, 182
    social, 115, 208, 209
    as a virtue, 180
Richard II, King, 1
Richards, David, 156
right to a home, 51, 188, 193, 199,
    207, 228, 229
right to communicate, 156
right to eat, 148
right to equality, 200, 205, 207-210
right to political liberty, 209
right to privacy, 68, 69, 199-212
right to public dwelling, 141-149, 161
right to self-defense, 200, 207-210,
    212
right to shelter, 146, 149
right to a voice, 101, 102
rightlessness, 228, 229

rights, 9, 55-57, 61, 63, 70-72, 74, 79,
    99-101, 188-193, 195-197, 199,
    207, 208, 210, 228-230
    of adoptees, 115
    basic, 61, 72, 157, 163, 164, 166,
        188, 189, 199
    of children, 10, 93
    civil, 144
    collective, 189, 192
    Colonial "settlement," 7
    constitutional, 163
    duties and, 101
    equal, 179
    existential, 57
    to freedom from interference, 163,
        164
    of homeless, 10, 141, 149, 199
    to housing, 182
    human, 195, 222, 228, 229
    of individuals, 99, 100
    legal, 84
    natural, 228
    of occupancy, 177
    of parents, 96, 97
    property, 66, 67
    protection of, 55, 56
    subsistence, 166, 188
    universal human, 99, 100
    voting, 147, 148
    welfare, 161, 163, 190-192, 195,
        197
    See also Bill of Rights
rights claims, 187
Rights of Man, 228
Rilke, Rainer Maria, 42
Rogers, Will, 31
Roosevelt, Franklin Delano, 228
Rossi, Peter, 160, 187
Rough Sleepers Initiative, 94
Ruffin, Judge Thomas, 71, 74
runaways, 10, 93-97, 101, 102, 145,
    179

salvation, 42, 49
Salvation Army, 146
sanctuary, home as, 63
Sartre, Jean-Paul, 41, 42, 44-47, 50,
    51

schizophrenia, 195
Scott, Dred, 71
Second Treatise of Civil Government, 218
secrecy, 230
  privacy vs., 200, 201
Sedgwick, Eve Kosofsky, 236
self, 10, 69, 75, 202, 203, 204, 206
  autonomous, 206, 211
  other(s) and, 45, 59, 61
self-consciousness, 48, 49
self-defense, right to, 200, 207-210, 212
self-definition, 61
self-determination, 48, 75
self-expression, 233
self-image, 59, 60
self-respect, 156
sexual relations, privacy and, 204. *See also* homosexual relations, privacy and
shame, 202, 206
shelter, 29, 37, 38, 61, 146, 153, 160, 162, 176, 188, 218, 224
  right to, 146, 149
shelters, 1, 3, 8, 9, 15-19, 95, 96, 146-148, 195, 211
Shue, Henry, 188
Sidewalk Stories, 19
silence, 19, 20
  class of, 19
Singer, Peter, 55
single-room-occupancy units (SROs), 8, 145, 162
skid-row housing, 8
"slave," 45, 46
slavery, 220
  Aristotle and, 83-85
  American, 71-74
Slote, Michael, 81, 82
social, the, 217, 223, 225, 226. *See also* private/public/social distinction
social community, 65
social construction, 60
social disease, homelessness as, 199, 207
social dissonance, 61

social embeddedness of individuals, 98-101
social engineering, 10, 171-175, 179, 182
social interactions, 100
social obligations, 9, 30, 208
social reform, 33
social responsibility, 115, 208, 209
social services, 33, 96, 102
social utility, 56
social workers, 94, 95, 102, 105, 115
socialism, 212, 225, 226
Socrates, 236, 237
solipsism, 45
solitude, personal, 43
space, 57-60. *See also* private space(s); public space(s)
speech, 153-157
Spheres of Justice, 79
spirit, 41, 42, 48, 49
  absolute, 48-50
state, the, 64-68, 70, 71, 73
  democratic (*see* democracy)
  liberal, 209, 210
  modern, 66, 67, 70, 71, 73
  obligation to protect citizens, 200, 209-211
State v. Mann, 71, 72
statelessness, 41, 52, 228, 229
statutory law, 65
stepchildren, 107, 109
Sterba, James, 163
stereotypes, 160, 161. *See also* homeless, the, images/perceptions of
Stoic philosophers, 99
streets
  life on the, 148
  world of the, 20
subjectivity, 45-47
subsidized housing, 15, 145, 146
subsistence, 161-167
subsistence benefits, 164
subsistence interests, 156, 157, 161-165, 167
subsistence rights, 166, 188
substance abusers, 8, 9, 55, 56
subways, 141, 148, 153, 158-160
Superson, Anita, 161, 162

Supplemental Security Income, 146
Supreme Court. *See* United States
    Supreme Court
suspect class, 161, 165, 166
Swanson, Judith, 65, 70, 74, 75

Taney, Chief Justice, 71, 73, 74
taxes, argument from, 143, 144
teloi. See community and
    communities, goals/ends of
territory, physical, 200, 204, 211, 212
There-being, 42, 43, 52
Third Amendment, 67-70
This Old House, 235, 236
threat of the homeless, 30-32, 36. *See*
    also dangerousness of the
    homeless
thrown-ness, 42, 43, 52
Torrey, E. Fuller, 194
Transcendence of the Ego, The, 45
transiency, 7
Transient Centers, 7, 8
Trop v. Dulles, 229
Tucker, D. F. B., 156
Tutsis, 33
tyché, 48

uncanniness. *See Unheimlichkeit*
Ungaretti, Giuseppe, 44, 47
Unheimliche, 3
Unheimlichkeit, 3, 24
United States Constitution, 10, 64,
    67-72, 75, 146, 167. *See also*
    First Amendment; Third
    Amendment; Fourth
    Amendment; Eighth
    Amendment; Fourteenth
    Amendment
United States Court of Appeals for
    the Second Circuit, 154, 159
United States Supreme Court, 68, 70,
    148, 164-166
    expatriation and, 229
    privacy of home and, 206
United States v. O'Brien, 155, 158,
    159. *See also* O'Brien standard
universal, the, 48, 49

urban areas. *See* cities
utilitarian arguments, 56
utilitarianism, 85, 86
Utilitarianism, 222
utility, social, 56
utopia, 52

valor, 47. *See also areté*
value, of persons, 58-61
values, 59, 60
    of personhood, 56
Vecsey, George, 238
veil of ignorance, 98
Verrier, Nancy Newton, 105
victims
    of crime, homeless as, 142, 148
    of the system, 149
    See also violence, against the
    homeless
Vietnam veterans, 145, 162
violence, 55, 61, 233, 234
    against the homeless, 9, 18, 19,
    142, 153
Virilio, Paul, 237
virtue, 74, 75
    of liberality, 81, 88, 89
    responsibility as a, 180
virtue ethics, 10, 81, 82
Virtue Theory, 79, 81
virtues, 79, 81-84, 87, 88
voice, right to a, 101, 102
voluntary homelessness, 33, 38, 199
voting rights, 147, 148
vulnerability, 19, 153, 156, 166, 167

Walden, 25
Walzer, Michael, 79
war, 26, 51
    just, 210
Warren, Chief Justice, 229
wealth, 88
Weiss, Allen S., 235
welfare, 146, 148, 161, 174, 175, 179
welfare benefits, 164
welfare hotels, 147
welfare rights, 161, 163, 190-192,
    195, 197
Western philosophy, 43-45

Whelan, Frederick, 65
Will, George, 162
Wolfe, Thomas, 37
women, 81, 84, 143, 145, 178
work, 217-221, 223, 225-227, 230
working classes, 56
world, as home to humanity, 36-38
World Bank, 178
World War II, 8, 108, 111, 227-229

Young v. New York Transit Authority,
       154, 155, 157-159
youth homelessness. *See* children,
       homeless; runaways
Youth Aliyah, 229
Yugoslavia, 34, 35, 51. *See also*
       Balkan War

Zolo, Danilo, 173, 174
zoning regulations, 158, 167

VIBS

The **Value Inquiry Book Series** is co-sponsored by:

Titles Published

1. Noel Balzer, *The Human Being as a Logical Thinker*.

2. Archie J. Bahm, *Axiology: The Science of Values*.

3. H. P. P. (Hennie) Lötter, *Justice for an Unjust Society*.

4. H. G. Callaway, *Context for Meaning and Analysis: A Critical Study in the Philosophy of Language*.

5. Benjamin S. Llamzon, *A Humane Case for Moral Intuition*.

6. James R. Watson, *Between Auschwitz and Tradition: Postmodern Reflections on the Task of Thinking*. A volume in **Holocaust and Genocide Studies.**

7. Robert S. Hartman, *Freedom to Live: The Robert Hartman Story, edited by Arthur R. Ellis*. A volume in **Hartman Institute Axiology Studies.**

8. Archie J. Bahm, *Ethics: The Science of Oughtness*.

9. George David Miller, *An Idiosyncratic Ethics; Or, the Lauramachean Ethics*.

10. Joseph P. DeMarco, *A Coherence Theory in Ethics*.

11. Frank G. Forrest, *Valuemetrics^N: The Science of Personal and Professional Ethics*. A volume in **Hartman Institute Axiology Studies.**

12. William Gerber, *The Meaning of Life: Insights of the World's Great Thinkers*.

13. Richard T. Hull, Editor, *A Quarter Century of Value Inquiry: Presidential Addresses of the American Society for Value Inquiry*. A volume in **Histories and Addresses of Philosophical Societies.**

14. William Gerber, *Nuggets of Wisdom from Great Jewish Thinkers: From Biblical Times to the Present*.

15. Sidney Axinn, *The Logic of Hope: Extensions of Kant's View of Religion*.

16. Messay Kebede, *Meaning and Development*.

17. Amihud Gilead, *The Platonic Odyssey: A Philosophical-Literary Inquiry into the Phaedo.*

18. Necip Fikri Alican, *Mill's Principle of Utility: A Defense of John Stuart Mill's Notorious Proof.* A volume in **Universal Justice**.

19. Michael H. Mitias, Editor, *Philosophy and Architecture.*

20. Roger T. Simonds, *Rational Individualism: The Perennial Philosophy of Legal Interpretation.* A volume in **Natural Law Studies**.

21. William Pencak, *The Conflict of Law and Justice in the Icelandic Sagas.*

22. Samuel M. Natale and Brian M. Rothschild, Editors, *Values, Work, Education: The Meanings of Work.*

23. N. Georgopoulos and Michael Heim, Editors, *Being Human in the Ultimate: Studies in the Thought of John M. Anderson.*

24. Robert Wesson and Patricia A. Williams, Editors, *Evolution and Human Values.*

25. Wim J. van der Steen, *Facts, Values, and Methodology: A New Approach to Ethics.*

26. Avi Sagi and Daniel Statman, *Religion and Morality.*

27. Albert William Levi, *The High Road of Humanity: The Seven Ethical Ages of Western Man*, edited by Donald Phillip Verene and Molly Black Verene.

28. Samuel M. Natale and Brian M. Rothschild, Editors, *Work Values: Education, Organization, and Religious Concerns.*

29. Laurence F. Bove and Laura Duhan Kaplan, Editors, *From the Eye of the Storm: Regional Conflicts and the Philosophy of Peace.* A volume in **Philosophy of Peace.**

30. Robin Attfield, *Value, Obligation, and Meta-Ethics.*

31. William Gerber, *The Deepest Questions You Can Ask About God: As Answered by the World's Great Thinkers.*

32. Daniel Statman, *Moral Dilemmas.*

33. Rem B. Edwards, Editor, *Formal Axiology and Its Critics*. A volume in **Hartman Institute Axiology Studies.**

34. George David Miller and Conrad P. Pritscher, *On Education and Values: In Praise of Pariahs and Nomads*. A volume in **Philosophy of Education.**

35. Paul S. Penner, *Altruistic Behavior: An Inquiry into Motivation.*

36. Corbin Fowler, *Morality for Moderns.*

37. Giambattista Vico, *The Art of Rhetoric (Institutiones Oratoriae, 1711-1741)*, from the definitive Latin text and notes, Italian commentary and introduction by Giuliano Crifo, translated and edited by Giorgio A. Pinton and Arthur W. Shippee. A volume in **Values in Italian Philosophy.**

38. W. H. Werkmeister, *Martin Heidegger on the Way*, edited by Richard T. Hull. A volume in **Werkmeister Studies.**

39. Phillip Stambovsky, *Myth and the Limits of Reason.*

40. Samantha Brennan, Tracy Isaacs, and Michael Milde, Editors, *A Question of Values: New Canadian Perspectives in Ethics and Political Philosophy.*

41. Peter A. Redpath, *Cartesian Nightmare: An Introduction to Transcendental Sophistry*. A volume in **Studies in the History of Western Philosophy.**

42. Clark Butler, *History as the Story of Freedom: Philosophy in Intercultural Context*, with Responses by sixteen scholars.

43. Dennis Rohatyn, *Philosophy History Sophistry.*

44. Leon Shaskolsky Sheleff, *Social Cohesion and Legal Coercion: A Critique of Weber, Durkheim, and Marx*. Afterword by Virginia Black.

45. Alan Soble, Editor, *Sex, Love, and Friendship: Studies of the Society for the Philosophy of Sex and Love, 1977-1992*. A volume in **Histories and Addresses of Philosophical Societies.**

46. Peter A. Redpath, *Wisdom's Odyssey: From Philosophy to Transcendental Sophistry*. A volume in **Studies in the History of Western Philosophy.**

47. Albert A. Anderson, *Universal Justice: A Dialectical Approach*. A volume in **Universal Justice.**

48. Pio Colonnello, *The Philosophy of Jose Gaos.* Translated from Italian by Peter Cocozzella. Edited by Myra Moss. Introduction by Giovanni Gullace. A volume in **Values in Italian Philosophy.**

49. Laura Duhan Kaplan and Laurence F. Bove, Editors, Philosophical Perspectives on Power and Domination: Theories and Practices. A volume in **Philosophy of Peace.**

50. Gregory F. Mellema, *Collective Responsibility.*

51. Josef Seifert, *What Is Life? The Originality, Irreducibility, and Value of Life.* A volume in **Central-European Value Studies.**

52. William Gerber, *Anatomy of What We Value Most.*

53. Armando Molina, *Our Ways: Values and Character*, edited by Rem B. Edwards. A volume in **Hartman Institute Axiology Studies.**

54. Kathleen J. Wininger, *Nietzsche's Reclamation of Philosophy.* A volume in **Central-European Value Studies.**

55. Thomas Magnell, Editor, *Explorations of Value.*

56. HPP (Hennie) Lötter, Injustice, *Violence, and Peace: The Case of South Africa.* A volume in **Philosophy of Peace.**

57. Lennart Nordenfelt, *Talking About Health: A Philosophical Dialogue.* A volume in **Nordic Value Studies.**

58. Jon Mills and Janusz A. Polanowski, *The Ontology of Prejudice.* A volume in **Philosophy and Psychology.**

59. Leena Vilkka, *The Intrinsic Value of Nature.*

60. Palmer Talbutt, Jr., *Rough Dialectics: Sorokin's Philosophy of Value*, with Contributions by Lawrence T. Nichols and Pitirim A. Sorokin.

61. C. L. Sheng, *A Utilitarian General Theory of Value.*

62. George David Miller, *Negotiating Toward Truth: The Extinction of Teachers and Students.* Epilogue by Mark Roelof Eleveld. A volume in **Philosophy of Education.**

63. William Gerber, *Love, Poetry, and Immortality: Luminous Insights of the World's Great Thinkers.*

64. Dane R. Gordon, Editor, *Philosophy in Post-Communist Europe.* A volume in **Post-Communist European Thought.**

65. Dane R. Gordon and Józef Niżnik, Editors, Criticism and Defense of Rationality in Contemporary Philosophy. A volume in **Post-Communist European Thought.**

66. John R. Shook, *Pragmatism: An Annotated Bibliography, 1898-1940.* With Contributions by E. Paul Colella, Lesley Friedman, Frank X. Ryan, and Ignas K. Skrupskelis.

67. Lansana Keita, *The Human Project and the Temptations of Science.*

68. Michael M. Kazanjian, *Phenomenology and Education: Cosmology, Co-Being, and Core Curriculum.* A volume in **Philosophy of Education.**

69. James W. Vice, *The Reopening of the American Mind: On Skepticism and Constitutionalism.*

70. Sarah Bishop Merrill, *Defining Personhood: Toward the Ethics of Quality in Clinical Care.*

71. Dane R. Gordon, *Philosophy and Vision.*

72. Alan Milchman and Alan Rosenberg, Editors, *Postmodernism and the Holocaust.* A volume in **Holocaust and Genocide Studies.**

73. Peter A. Redpath, *Masquerade of the Dream Walkers: Prophetic Theology from the Cartesians to Hegel.* A volume in **Studies in the History of Western Philosophy.**

74. Malcolm D. Evans, *Whitehead and Philosophy of Education: The Seamless Coat of Learning.* A volume in **Philosophy of Education.**

75. Warren E. Steinkraus, *Taking Religious Claims Seriously: A Philosophy of Religion*, edited by Michael H. Mitias. A volume in **Universal Justice.**

76. Thomas Magnell, Editor, *Values and Education.*

77. Kenneth A. Bryson, *Persons and Immortality.* A volume in **Natural Law Studies.**

78. Steven V. Hicks, *International Law and the Possibility of a Just World Order: An Essay on Hegel's Universalism.* A volume in **Universal Justice**.

79. E.F. Kaelin, *Texts on Texts and Textuality: A Phenomenology of Literary Art*, edited by Ellen J. Burns.

80. Amihud Gilead, *Saving Possibilities: A Study in Philosophical Psychology*, A volume in **Philosophy and Psychology**.

81. André Mineau, *The Making of the Holocaust: Ideology and Ethics in the Systems Perspective.* A volume in **Holocaust and Genocide Studies**.

82. Howard P. Kainz, *Politically Incorrect Dialogues: Topics Not Discussed in Polite Circles.*

83. Veikko Launis, Juhani Pietarinen, and Juha Räikkä, Editors, *Genes and Morality: New Essays.* A volume in **Nordic Value Studies**.

84. Steven Schroeder, *The Metaphysics of Cooperation: A Study of F. D. Maurice.*

85. Caroline Joan ("Kay") S. Picart, *Thomas Mann and Friedrich Nietzsche: Eroticism, Death, Music, and Laughter.* A volume in **Central-European Value Studies**.

86. G. John M. Abbarno, Editor, **The Ethics of Homelessness: Philosophical Perspectives.**

www.ingramcontent.com/pod-product-compliance
Lightning Source LLC
Chambersburg PA
CBHW020341270326
41926CB00007B/277